W9-COW-924

WHAT MY PARENTS
DID RIGHT

INNERKIP
UNITED CHURCH

INNERKIP
UNITED CHURCH

What My Parents Did
RIGHT

Compiled and edited by
Gloria Gaither

LIVING BOOKS®
Tyndale House Publishers, Inc.
Wheaton, Illinois

Copyright © 1991 by Gloria Gaither
All rights reserved

Cover design courtesy of Star Song Publishing Group

Living Books is a registered trademark of Tyndale House Publishers, Inc.

The "NIV" and "New International Version" trademarks are registered in the United States Patent and Trademark Office by International Bible Society. Use of either trademark requires permission of International Bible Society.

First Living Books edition 1994

Unless otherwise noted, Scripture quotations are from the *Holy Bible,* King James Version.

Scripture quotations marked NIV are from the *Holy Bible,* New International Version ®. Copyright © 1973, 1978, 1984 by International Bible Society. Used by permission of Zondervan Publishing House. All rights reserved.

Scripture quotations marked NRSV are from the New Revised Standard Version of the Bible, copyrighted 1989 by the Division of Christian Education of the National Council of the Churches of Christ in the United States of America, and are used by permission. All rights reserved.

Scripture quotations marked NASB are taken from the *New American Standard Bible,* © 1960, 1962, 1963, 1968, 1971, 1972, 1973, 1975, 1977 by The Lockman Foundation. Used by permission.

Scripture quotations marked RSV are from the *Holy Bible,* Revised Standard Version, copyright © 1946, 1952, 1971 by the Division of Christian Education of the National Council of the Churches of Christ in the United States of America, and are used by permission. All rights reserved.

Verses marked TLB are taken from *The Living Bible,* copyright © 1971. Used by permission of Tyndale House Publishers, Inc., Wheaton, Illinois 60189. All rights reserved.

The Strong-Willed Child. Copyright © 1978 by Dr. James C. Dobson. Used by permission of Tyndale House Publishers, Inc. All rights reserved.

Straight Talk to Men and Their Wives (revised edition). Copyright © 1980, 1991 by Dr. James C. Dobson. Used by permission of Word, Inc. All rights reserved.

Dr. Dobson: Turning Hearts toward Home. Copyright © 1989 by Rolf Zettersten. Used by permission of Word, Inc. All rights reserved.

Grace Encountered. Copyright © 1988 by Walter Wangerin, Jr. Used by permission.

"Nobody's Home." Lyrics by Ray Boltz and Steve Miliken. Copyright © 1989 by Shepherd Boy Music and © 1989 by Son Worshippers Music. Used by special permission of Diadem Music.

Library of Congress Catalog Card Number 94-60212
ISBN 0-8423-8136-8

Printed in the United States of America

00 99 98 97 96 95 94
8   7   6   5   4   3   2   1

Contents

This book is dedicated . . .
To faithful parents who have been persistent
and consistent through the good times and the
hard times. May your children rise up and
call you "blessed."
To weary parents who are in the thick of it
right now. May you be given wisdom,
perseverance, great joy—and a sense of humor!
To young couples and new parents who are
intimidated by the immensity of the task and
frightened by today's prophets of doom. May
you have courage, insight, and a strong
commitment to parenting, the most worthy of
earth's vocations.

"*And a little child will lead them*"
(Isaiah 11:6, NIV).

Prologue

◆───────────────────────────────◆

We hear a great deal these days about family dysfunction. Abuse, alcoholism, drug addiction, and neglect have indeed taken their toll. Much material is now being written and published to help individuals recover from the damage done to them by dysfunctional family systems. Counseling centers have opened their doors and support groups their arms to the many who are struggling with scars from the past. It is good that such help is available.

The avalanche of self-help publications and recovery workshops has, however, left many parents wondering if they are doing anything right. With television talk-show hosts declaring that "every home is dysfunctional in some way" and guest after guest sharing horror stories about their early home life, many young couples are too paralyzed by fear of failure to even think about becoming parents. People who are dealing with the daily perplexities of the early adolescent and teenage years are overwhelmed by the demands of the family and are almost tempted to give up.

In spite of the cacophony of voices condemning the American family, I had a feeling that most men and women who are functioning in society and impacting the world for good did not come from debilitating dysfunctional backgrounds. I also had a hunch that most were not raised by parents who were authorities on child psychology or well trained in the sociology of primary relationships. Neither could I accept that all families are "dysfunctional in some way." Instead I believed that all families have their particular set of challenges to work through, and doing so in the unique climate of personality blend called "family" is what home is all about.

Acting on these hunches, I contacted a cross section of people from many walks of life, well-known men and women who are making a difference in their chosen fields. I knew few specifics about most of these people's family backgrounds. I did not know what, if anything, these families would have in common. I did not know what could be deduced from the stories these leaders would relate.

The personal accounts presented here have confirmed the fact that no family is immune to problems and hard times. Yet, as I have compiled these pieces, I have laughed at and cried over, reverenced and celebrated the wonder of family. And I've been encouraged—as I hope you will be—to "keep on keeping on" in this God-given job of parenting with its ever-so-daily tasks and its eternal consequences.

Gloria Gaither
June 1991

Gloria Gaither

What My Parents Did Right

For twenty-five years, I have had the joy of seeing and hearing words I've written being sung, read, quoted, translated, memorized, and excerpted. But when I was a little girl, probably the last thing I ever dreamed of becoming was a lyricist and singer. As a preacher's kid growing up in Michigan, I only knew that I wanted to be somehow involved in full-time Christian work, but there weren't many careers available to women in the church. One could marry a minister, become a missionary overseas, or teach.

I enrolled in Anderson College and majored in French in preparation for being a missionary (I thought then I would go to Africa). I took a minor in education so I could teach, and then because I loved words and writing, I also majored in English. I didn't think God would mind. And what a sense of humor he must have!

In my early efforts at obedience, I had prepared for a mission I could never have foreseen. I thought I would put writing on the back burner in order to be a missionary, but God gradually gave Bill and me a passion for words and music. We have worked with persons from every walk of life, and our songs have been translated into many languages—including French! And it was French, too, that led me to Bill in the first place, but I'll let you read Bill's biography to see how that came about.

As a child I had always written poetry, speeches, and stories, but it never occurred to me to write lyrics. I had never thought of myself as a musician, but gradually I began helping Bill with the words. Our ideas for songs always came from our lives . . . something we were learning, some new insight, maybe an incident involving our kids. Our songs grew out of our love for God and for life.

And my love for God came early in life. Through their day-to-day activities and with their very being, my mother and father taught me about God and about serving him. That's just one of the many things my parents did right, as I share with you here.

It was not until college that I became aware that most of my peers were rebelling against their upbringing. In fact, that seemed to be what one did when he or she reached their sophomore year. I listened without much comment when some other preachers' kids revealed the resentment they felt toward their pastor fathers who had had time for everyone's children except their own. I heard stories about growing up in a fishbowl and trying to measure up to parishioners' unreasonable demands. I saw up close the anger and frustration of not being able to fight back because the "villain" who stole their father's time seemed to be the church or even God himself.

During those college years, it began to dawn on me that my love for my home, my respect for the church, and my commitment to God were not the automatic results of growing up in a parsonage. I found myself asking, "What did my parents do right?" I had to conclude that *home* doesn't just happen. Somebody had done something on purpose, and part of the beauty of what had been done was that my parents never seemed to be "put out" by the effort. *Homing* had seemed, well, regular.

Robert Frost once wrote that "home is something you somehow haven't had to deserve." It is a place, he said, where "when you go there, they have to take you in." Having now been both someone's child and someone's parent, I have had to conclude that home is a great deal more than that.

When it became apparent that Bill and I would be raising our children in the public eye, we again—this time even more earnestly—began to ask, "What *did* our parents do right?" When we discussed this together, Bill always said that the most important thing his parents did was to always "be there." The way he said these two words suggested a great deal more than physical presence on a somewhat regular basis. He seemed to be saying that his parents were there for him in other ways, too: that they were there for emotional stability, for financial and spiritual undergirding, and for intellectual encouragement. "Being there" also had a hint of an all-knowing surveillance and suggested consistent discipline that did not laugh at mischief one day and punish it the next.

My parents were always there, too. In fact, I felt sure my mother had eyes in the back of her head, and I knew better than to even try to con her. Yet she also had eyes for catching us when we were up to something good and for ferreting out some hidden talent or latent ability in us. When no one else could see it, when others saw only an awkward, clumsy kid, Mother saw beyond the unpredictable growth spurts and adolescent acne to some great rainbow of promise circumventing the obvious.

Right next to "being there" in importance to my life was the fact that my parents taught by *being*. But then all parents—good or bad—teach by *being*. You know the old adage: "What you are speaks so loudly I can't hear what you're saying." The clearest biblical instruction for parents is found in Deuteronomy. Here in God's Word is the bottom-line lesson parents are to teach their children: "The LORD our God is one LORD: And thou shalt love the LORD thy God with all thine heart, and with all thy soul, and with all thy might" (6:4-5, KJV).

The instruction continues: "And these words, which I command thee this day, shall be in thine heart: And thou shalt teach them diligently unto thy children, and shalt talk of them when thou sittest in thine house, and when thou walkest by the way, and when thou liest down, and when thou risest up. And thou shalt bind them for a sign upon thine hand, and they shall be as frontlets between thine eyes. And thou shalt write them upon the posts of thy house, and on thy gates" (Deut. 6:6-9, KJV). This is a lot of teaching! How could any parent teach so long, so tirelessly? The answer, I believe, is in *being*. If the commandment to love God is indeed written on a parent's heart—if we as parents truly love the Lord—we will be teaching our children by how we live, by how we are.

The only way a parent can ever hope to teach the sovereignty and lordship of God—the only way a parent can teach children to love God with all their passion and commitment, with all their being and intellect, with all their energy and stamina—is for that truth to come from what the parent truly is in his or her own heart. Only then can lessons about God come up at the table, at bedtime, on walks, in the busyness of the day, and the first thing at dawn. Only when parents truly love God can his lordship express itself in what they do with their hands, in how they see things, and in the atmosphere of the home from the minute a child comes through the doorposts of the house.

And my parents taught me by being. They surrounded me with the gospel and nestled me in their love for it. I often happened in on my father as he sat alone with the Bible in his hands, tears streaming down his cheeks at the beauty of some revelation. Also, in our home, prayer was a natural response to problems and crises as well as good news and celebrations. Our home was filled with great thinkers, teachers, missionaries, evangelists, and theologians. Mother made sure my sister and I sat by these great men and women at the table and were involved in their deep conversations. Our home was also filled with waifs, orphans, strays, and runaways. I often gave up my bed to the homeless, my plate to the hungry, and my clothes to a child who needed them more. Mother and Daddy didn't just talk about servanthood; they lived it.

My parents were verbal about their relationship with God, with each other, with us children, and with others. "I love you" was heard daily, not only when we were having family hugs but also when we were having family worship.

My parents gave me an appreciation for nature and the connectedness of all things. I was taught a reverence for life and an awe for the fact that something—plant as well as animal—gave up its life for every bit of food we enjoyed. From this I learned that we should live in gratitude and practice responsible conservation. I was taught the names of things—trees, wildflowers, algae, animals, constellations, human beings—and I learned that naming was important to identity and value. I was given the gift of solitude in which to listen to the woods, the lakes, the stars, my own conscience, and the voice of God.

My parents also gave me a sense of humor and, believe me, survival in the parsonage often depended on our ability to laugh. Daddy, for example, doubled over with laughter when we told him he had declared in his sermon that "Judas is a carrot," and we all got a hearty chuckle from the prayer meeting in which a dear old saint testified that "my head hurt and I asked the Lord to take it away—and he did!" A great sense of humor helped my parents not only tolerate but actually enjoy having hundreds of young people use our home as an activities center, couples use our living room as a marriage chapel, children use our sidewalks as a roller skating rink, and the infirm use our front bedroom as a nursing home.

While teaching us to not take ourselves too seriously, my parents took *us* very seriously as human beings and as fellow Christians. In our home, we could ask any question without being belittled and question any answer without being condemned. But we could not say, "I can't." Failure was allowed, but we were always expected to try. I don't remember my parents ever talking down to us, but instead they included us in family decisions and important discussions. Other preachers sent their children out to play when it was time to pray about the concerns of the church, but my parents called us in from play to pray with them about some tragedy or need that had been phoned into the parsonage. Daddy would say, "The Word promises that when two or three agree together touching any one thing, it shall be done, so let's agree together now about this need." Often he would call on one of us to voice the prayer as we joined hands.

I don't remember my parents ever telling us to try to impress or conform to someone in the church or to do or not to do something because we were the preacher's kids. Instead, they often told us to "mind God no matter what happens," and they made it clear that if we were obedient in our commitment to God, they would stand by us even when others didn't understand us or agree. When peers in high school or college were making destructive choices, one of my greatest deterrents from wrong and encouragements toward right was my parents' trust. They believed in me and in my good judgment, and that trust was a treasure so precious that I didn't want to risk losing it.

Now that I have grown children of my own, I am thankful that my parents remained childlike and that we were all becomers in process. To this day, my mother and sister are two of my dearest friends, and there are days—especially when Bill and I have written a new song about some grand theological concept—when my first impulse is to run and share it with Daddy. Somehow in God's eternal present tense, I know that Daddy is hearing the song waft its way through time and space to vibrate down the corridors of heaven. His eyes twinkle, and I hear him say, with a pleased grin, "That's good, Shug. The Lord is pleased and so am I."

Lessons on Love

◆─────────────────────────────────────◆

*I*t's always inspiring to talk with Kay Arthur. Her love for
God's Word is contagious, and her knowledge of the
Scriptures has produced a vital and exciting ministry that
reaches around the world.

Kay serves as executive vice president and principal
teacher for Precept Ministries, which she cofounded with her
husband, Jack. The goal of the ministry is to establish God's
people in God's Word. Based on the conviction that people
will be changed into God's likeness through the knowledge of
his Word, Precept teaches the inductive method of Bible study
and thereby gives believers the opportunity to grapple with the
truths of Scripture for themselves. Precept classes are currently
underway in forty-three states, and the study has been used
in more than sixty foreign countries.

Besides writing the Bible studies for Precept Upon Precept
and In & Out, Kay teaches on the ministry's fifteen-minute,
daily radio program and on its television program, both of
which are titled "How Can I Live?" Kay has also written
eleven books.

Kay has known both tragedy and triumph in her life, and
experiences of both kinds lend genuineness and compassion
to her ministry. Here Kay shares from some of the pain of the

past, but there is also a message of hope as she writes about how her parents broke the pattern of dysfunction. In fact, Kay's mother and father demonstrated Christian principles that helped Kay when she later became a believer.

I got out of the car, my arms loaded down with books. As I closed the car door with my backside, I looked down at the ground. The fragile new grass growing along the dirt path awakened childhood memories. It had been a hard day, and I was hurting. I wasn't eager to go inside. There was no one in the house I could share my hurt with, no adult I could talk to. My two precious sons were there, but they were not to be my confidants. I was their mother. I was their parent—a single parent. My husband was dead.

The grass reminded me of Grandpa's cabin at the lake. For an instant it had looked like the grass on the path leading down to the rickety old dock, and I remembered the time I fell into the water and some-how came up under the dock, choking and scared. Daddy took me in his arms and held me while I cried, brushing back the wet hair that had escaped my pig-tails and now covered my eyes. When my sobbing stopped, he convinced me to get back into the water.

I loved my daddy's arms and welcomed any oppor-tunity to be in them. When I'd skin my knees—which was frequently for this tomboy—I'd run to Daddy. Or in the evenings, sometime between doing the dishes and my homework, I'd often curl up in his lap, lean my head on his chest, and feel so secure.

The grass and my present hurt reminded me of all that. How I wished I were a little girl again. I wished I had someone to hold me right now, to tell me that everything would be all right and reassure me that I'd survive.

As I turned to walk into the house, I suddenly saw in my mind's eye a little girl in pigtails flying down a vast marble corridor. Oil paintings bigger than life hung on the walls. As she ran, I could almost hear her little shoes on the marble floor. Tears flooded her eyes and overflowed, leaving white streaks on her dirty face. Blood trickled down her skinned leg, making a path in the dirt and gravel embedded in her knee and shin. She was calling for her daddy and sobbing as she ran.

It was a long corridor. At the end, two huge gold doors glistened in the sunlight that filtered through beveled cathedral windows. On either side of the imposing doors stood two magnificently dressed guards holding huge spears and blocking the entrance into the room beyond.

Undaunted, the little girl ran straight toward the doors, still crying, "Abba!" She never broke her stride for, as she neared the doors, the guards flung them open and heralded her arrival: "The daughter of the King! The daughter of the King!"

Court was in session. The cherubim and seraphim cried, "Holy, holy, holy!," and the elders sat on their thrones, dressed in white, wearing crowns of gold, and talking with the King of kings. But none of this slowed down his daughter!

Oblivious to everything going on about her, she ran past the seven burning lamps of fire and up the steps leading to the throne, and she catapulted herself into the King's arms. She was home and wrapped in the arms of his everlasting love. He reached up and, with one finger, gently wiped away her tears. Then he smoothed the sticky hair on her face back into her braids, tenderly held her leg, and said, "Now, now, tell your Father all about it."

I walked into my house, went to my bedroom, and got on my knees.

Never once have I had a hard time telling my heavenly Father all about it. Never once have I feared he would push me away. My daddy never did and neither did my mother, so why would God?

Although I didn't come to know the Lord Jesus Christ until I was twenty-nine years old and very confused, I've never doubted God's love. I've also never doubted my parents' love for me—even though I messed up my relationship with them before I was saved, and even afterwards! And although I knew they were not always pleased with my behavior or my response to them, I've always known that they loved me unconditionally and that they believed in me.

I remember when, as I entered womanhood, Mom and Dad sat me down and told me that, no matter what happened and no matter what I did, I could always come home. And because of what those words meant to me, I said the same thing to my sons.

I remember a childhood filled with affection—lots of kisses, lots of hugs, lots of spoken "I love you's." I never wanted for physical affection, and because of what that affection meant to me, I gave the same thing to my sons.

I grew up in a home where love was openly talked about and warmly expressed. I can still picture myself in my attic bedroom, sitting on my bed and fuming at my parents. They had been mean to me and totally unreasonable—at least that was my evaluation of the situation. They hadn't understood that I was a teenager now and should be allowed certain freedoms. With eyes closed, lips taut, and hot tears streaming down my face, I leaned back against the wall and planned how I would get even with them for hurting me. What would be the worst thing I could do to punish them, to show them how much they had hurt me? It didn't take me long to figure it out—I would never kiss them again. That would do it! They'd see then!

That's how important physical expressions of love were in my home. And those physical expressions of love were indicative of the singularly greatest thing my parents did right: They loved me unconditionally while expecting me to live according to their rules, not mine. I also learned from my parents' example and by their training not to focus in on myself and wallow in pity parties.

Both my parents came from broken homes and had difficult childhoods, yet they never dwelt on how "dysfunctional" their families were. They were both survivors, but not survivors at someone else's expense. They never gave up, walked away, or blamed their parents for some of the great hardships and even cruelties they endured at their parents' hands. I saw in my mother and father love's ability to forgive.

I found out about their childhoods in digestible pieces. They never dumped on me or my brother and sister. They never blamed, accused, or held the actions of the past against their parents. Although Daddy's stepmother lied about his behavior as a young boy until his father beat him, I watched my dad and mom care for her in her old age, even taking her into their home.

I saw my sweet momma love my real grandfather even though he had abandoned her and my grandma and failed to provide for their needs as he should have. I never saw Mother treat Grandpa Miller in any way but lovingly, even though he was far from lovable. I learned how love behaves and forgives because I saw it demonstrated by my mother. I saw what a woman can do and be if she wants to and if she is not willing to let her past determine her future.

I watch her now as, at seventy-nine, she takes care of my ninety-nine-year-old grandmother who, in her blindness, deafness, and feebleness, needs almost total care. And when I'm in their home, I still hear what I've heard all my life: "I love you, Mother." She says it a minimum of five times a day—every time she gets Grandma up, tucks her in, or prepares her meals. And I hear love's response as Grandma says, "And I love you, too, Leah." I still see love, and I see the determination to survive, not to focus on what might have been, what could have been, or what I wish were different now. Instead, love's focus is on what needs to be done now and on doing it the best you can.

My mother taught me these lessons more clearly than my shorter-tempered daddy did. Yet, as I watched him, I gained hope, for I was more like him than like my mother in temperament. Before he died at age sixty-eight (an early age in our family), I saw in him this same persistent kind of love. My mother has continued to teach me this lesson even after her husband—the one person she loved dearer than life—was taken away from her.

My parents taught me to love; they taught me to press on, forgetting what was behind; and they demonstrated forgiveness. I wonder if they knew then that they were demonstrating principles of life my heavenly Father would teach me in his Word?

My transition from their arms to God's arms was easier because of what Mother and Daddy did right as parents. No matter the hurts, the pain, the skinned knees—I know enough to get up, go to my Father, and listen as he says, "Press on. Don't faint. Run with endurance the race that is set before you. I love you with an everlasting love."

William K. Brehm

A Song in Our Hearts

S ome of you will recognize the name William K. Brehm from his days in the Department of Defense. He was nominated by President Johnson to serve as assistant secretary of the army in 1968, a position he held through December 1970. After a two-and-a-half-year sabbatical from government, Bill was appointed by President Nixon to be an assistant secretary of defense. He served in that capacity until January 1977.

Returning to industry in 1977, Bill was appointed executive vice president and a director of Computer Network Corporation. At the same time, he served as a consultant for the Department of Defense, specializing in defense management and organization.

In October 1980, Bill became chairman of SRA International, a new company. He still holds that position. He also serves on the board of trustees of Fuller Theological Seminary in Pasadena, California, and is a director of Herman Miller, Incorporated of Zeeland, Michigan.

Besides his accomplishments in business and government, Bill is a published composer and lyricist who has written more *than seventy compositions for piano and voice. He also enjoys nature photography and trail climbing, especially in the High Sierras of California.*

Bill and his wife, Dee, have two married children, Eric and Lisa, and three grandchildren. You won't be surprised that the key to this man's success is the sense of security his parents gave him as he was growing up.

How do parents give a child a sense of security? For me, security came from simple things. Let me explain.

My folks were farm kids born late in the nineteenth century. That meant that their formal education lost out to the imperatives of farm work; that Dad would serve in the army in World War I; and that their new marriage and Dad's entrepreneurial adventure in the city would be buoyed up by the optimism of the twenties.

After their marriage, Dad started working in an automobile factory, but the yearning to be in business for himself led him to buy an old Mack truck. Soon he bought his second, and started a transportation business. He purchased waste products—ashes, specifically—from a plant that produced electricity and sold them to a plant that made cinder blocks. His profit came from both reselling the material and moving it across the city. Then came the thirties.

The depression and I arrived at about the same time. By then, my parents were in their mid-thirties. Dad's budding business was soon put aside in favor of a regular paycheck on the assembly line, courtesy of Mr. Ford of Dearborn, Michigan, near our home. I've been told that Dad was kept on that job through the worst part of the depression because he—under five feet eight inches and weighing in at about 160 pounds—worked harder than just about anyone else. In addition to his regular tasks on the line, he would, for example, occasionally speed production by lifting a Ford V-8 engine block from one conveyor belt and putting it on another, shortening the normal trip the block had to make.

Dad's pay was about twenty-five dollars per week, and that didn't go far even in those days when a kid could enjoy a matinee double feature and a candy bar for a dime! My folks were unable to make their house payments for three years. Although they managed to keep the interest paid, Mom was terrified at the end of each month that the bank would foreclose. It never did. In fact, the bank may have been just as nervous as my parents were—it probably had no desire to add our house on Indiana Avenue to its long list of empty properties.

During this time, the two Mack trucks were, literally, put out to pasture. Both the dump truck and the big flatbed with its solid tires were parked in the vacant lot next door. Struggle as I might, I couldn't quite manage to climb onto the platform of that flatbed. But I had friends—older and bigger friends—who not only could boost me up, but who also decided that we should use that flatbed for a stage. They organized neighborhood skits, musicals, and plays—especially musicals. We all had parts.

I was shy, but I liked being a part of the show. I guess I got two boosts from the older kids: a physical lift onto the platform and an emotional lift in self-esteem. So Dad's trucks, even when idle, were important in my life.

Now I know those were very hard times—I was too young to appreciate how tight things really were—but I never felt deprived or insecure. And why not insecure? Better question—why did I feel secure?

We were not openly affectionate in our family. We weren't free with the verbal *I love you's*. But the love was really there—in simple things.

When I was little, my mother always escorted me up to bed. Each night I sang the good night prayer that she had taught me. I learned the Lord's Prayer from her, too, and said that every night. I can still see her sitting on the edge of the bed in the dark. It was quite clear: She cared.

Then, three hours later, I might—just might—be back down in the living room in the dark, sitting on my dad's lap as he and I listened to "Harold True and the News in Revue" on WWJ. Dad didn't seem to mind my being there, and I know I didn't! That image— that memory—still seems warm to the touch.

Throughout my childhood, other simple things gave me a special sense of security and warmed and enriched my life. Dad, for instance, smiled a lot, even in the bleak 1930s, and he smiled not just with his mouth but with his eyes. And he whistled. And he could smile and whistle at the same time! He usually whistled his own melodies, except for "Yankee Doodle Dandy." That march captured his fancy and mine. I can even remember Dad singing it, especially on weekends. I can see him sitting on the side of his bed singing that funny little lyric. I say funny because it always made me laugh and because it didn't make any sense to me—and it still doesn't: "He stuck a feather in his cap and called it macaroni"?

Dad would whistle when he did chores around the house. And he often whistled when he and Mom did the bookkeeping—which couldn't have been a picnic in those days. What I learned was that when Dad whistled, he was OK, and that meant that everything was OK. And that meant I was OK.

Mom had her music, too. One she liked was "The Parade of the Wooden Soldiers." I'd sing it with "datta-da-da-da," and then, pretending we were wooden soldiers, we'd march around the living room, veer into the dining room, go through the hall, and then swing back into the living room. Mom also taught me "'Til We Meet Again," and I always felt close to her when she sang that part with me.

When Mom's friends came to visit, she would encourage me to sing for them. With a bit of coaxing and the promise of a piece of cheese, I usually agreed. But I also got to hide behind the door while I sang. You see, Mom gave me the freedom to be shy.

Mom, a romantic, had her dreams, and subtly she conveyed them to me through music and someone else's lyrics and melodies. When I was four, she had her piano shipped from the farm where she was born to our house so that my brother and I could study. I remember looking forward to my first lesson and being excited about the arrival of Mrs. Rowe, the teacher who made house calls. A lot of affection flowed through that piano, and I think it represented one of Mom's dreams. Perhaps her boys would learn to play the songs she loved.

My brother, Ervin, six years older than I, has a natural flair for music. He took piano lessons for a year and then changed to the guitar. That is another warm memory—listening to him play and sing country songs. He joined up with a musical friend or two to entertain civic groups. Occasionally he took his kid brother along to play a number on the piano for contrast—a number like "The Parade of the Wooden Soldiers."

Ours wasn't a family with a built-in string quartet. We weren't like the Lane sisters in the movies, performing under the watchful discipline of patriarch Claude Rains. But the music we had and the way it was part of my parents' lives and dreams made it a source of my security.

Our music didn't cost much, and it didn't take a lot of my parents' time. But I think it was part of the "I love you" in our family life, and maybe it was the most important part for me.

When Dad whistled and sang about macaroni, when Mom marched with me like a wooden soldier, when we sang "'Til We Meet Again," when Ervin sang country—well, things were OK. And that meant I was OK.

A Foundation
for Faith

◆————————————————————————————◆

As the following story illustrates, Jill Briscoe is a down-to-
earth and refreshingly honest person who has a deep
love for God and her family.

Jill was born in Liverpool, England. Educated at
Homerton College, Cambridge, she taught in the British
school system after she completed her studies. She married
Stuart Briscoe in 1958, and they are the parents of David,
Judy, and Peter and the grandparents of five.

Together, Jill and Stuart ministered with Capernwray Missionary Fellowship in England where Jill served as youth director.
She was also the superintendent of a nursery school there.

In 1970, Stuart was called to pastor Elmbrook Church in
Waukesha, Wisconsin. Jill is lay director of Women's Ministries at Elmbrook and a director of Telling the Truth media
ministries. Jill and Judy work as a mother/daughter team
and have an active speaking and writing ministry. The
author of more than twenty books, including children's books
and adult Bible study guides, Jill has spoken in many
countries around the world. She serves on the board of
directors for World Relief and Christianity Today.

I know you'll enjoy this glimpse into Jill's childhood and an account of how her parents, with their "simple yet private faith in Christ," modeled the values and priorities that enabled their daughter to become a vibrant Christian.

We were playing a game of cards with our school-aged children. One of them looked at the hand I had dealt him, threw a tantrum, and walked away from the game. I made that little person come back, pick up his hand, and play it out. He needed to learn about winning with whatever hand he'd been dealt—that's an important lesson for life. Some people are dealt a pretty lousy hand. Their parents are a mess and their lives are damaged. Other folks are dealt a pretty good hand, and still others are dealt a wonderful one. I am writing to testify to the wonderful "hand" I was dealt by my parents.

My parents had a simple, private faith in Christ. They believed in his salvation, and they put Christian principles into operation in our family as best they knew how. We didn't go to church, but we were taught that God does not live in a church-shaped box to be visited like a sick relative on Sunday. Our parents showed us a present-tense God who would hear our prayers, treat us kindly, and hold us accountable to them and to him at the end of the day. They gave us what they knew, and for me, it was enough to lay a foundation for faith and make it easy for me to accept Christ when I was presented with the gospel.

What did my parents do right? First, my sister and I never had any doubts about the fact that they loved us. Our parents—especially my mother—told us all the time. They didn't buy us off, but rather they emphasized that the best things in life (like love) are free. And our parents always gave us time.

Second, family was our parents' top priority. Now that I'm a believer, I know that this is not quite right. God is God and we put anyone or anything—however good—before him at our peril. But if putting family first was wrong, it was a good wrong—and I have to say that because family was my folks' top priority, we were the glad recipients of the blessings of that choice.

Among those blessings were our vacations. When I was growing up, vacations were family time. (It was unthinkable for them to plan time together away from us until we were into our late teenage and college years.) My father was a fly fisherman, but he didn't leave us at home and go off on weekends with his buddies. He took us all along. I remember trying to keep up with my father in his thigh-high wading boots, striding along ahead of me, as we followed the river trout for miles upstream in the incredibly beautiful English Lake District, southern Ireland, and Scotland. As a nonchurch family, Sunday was also a time for family, and we planned and prepared for it with eager anticipation. Sunday was spent at home with music, reading, tennis in the backyard in the summer, and games by the blazing coal fire in the winter.

A third thing our parents did right was teach us to obey and respect authority. How I thank God for that! It made it easier for me to be obedient once I found the Lord. When I received a letter of complaint from a teacher to take home to my folks (and I'm afraid I did on several occasions!), I felt a real sense of dread as I walked the mile and a half home. I knew my parents would nearly always take the side of authority. After all, teachers were to be respected, listened to, and obeyed. I was told they were to be believed, addressed correctly and politely, and apologized to if necessary. I look back on this part of my heritage with deep gratitude, for when Christ became my Schoolmaster, I easily transferred my learned submission and reverent obedience to him.

Another blessing from my family was their emphasis on commitment. Once you committed to something, you followed through—no ifs, ands, or buts! My sister, Shirley, and I used to say we would have to be dying to be allowed to stay home from school! If we signed up for an extracurricular activity or joined a club, we attended until the end! It mattered not if we were bored or disappointed. Once we had said we would do something, we did it, because following through on a commitment is right. As a result, even today I generally finish things I start, and people tell me they can rely on me to complete an assignment if I take it on.

Like our other commitments, the promises we made were extremely important, and we expected to be held accountable to those promises and vows. My sister and I knew that Mom and Dad enjoyed being married, would stay married, and hoped we'd do the same. Differences they had were kept between them and worked out in the context of the promises they made to each other and to God on their wedding day. There was no option out! As someone has said, when the doors on a marriage are shut and bolted and a fire breaks out, all your time and energy goes into putting out the flames. I have no doubt in my mind that my own marriage bears those same prints of commitment partly as a result of such modeling.

My parents also instilled in us a sense of responsibility concerning our family name. We were taught that our behavior could affect our good reputation, so it was important to live honorably even when we were out of our parents' sight. What we did and how we did it would reflect on them, and my love for them curbed my wild ways during my teenage years. Since I became a disciple of Jesus, living a life that honors his name has been easy for me. It's not hard to know why.

I also appreciate the way my parents allowed us to be our own persons and discover our own gifts. Looking back, I realize now that my father had hoped I'd be a boy, take over the family business, and fulfill his dreams. I never knew his disappointment in this regard until he was gone. He hid his feelings and set about being the best father a girl could have. Perhaps the fact that my sister wanted to go into the business helped, but at first he resisted her desire to learn mechanical skills and train for a man's job in a man's world at a time when women didn't do that sort of thing. But after sharing his concern for her, he did draw Shirley into the firm, gave her his blessing, and allowed her to blossom and grow. At the same time, he encouraged me to pursue my dream of being a teacher.

Finally, my parents let us go. How hard it was for them I'll never know. Now that I am a grandparent, I look back at my struggles to release my own children. How hard to set their sails and push them off from the jetty and into the sunset! But, with the Lord's help, I've learned that to grab or clutch kills the very thing I'm trying to keep intact—some very precious adult relationships. The dilemma is how to hold them lightly, not tightly. When I was at major crossroads as a parent, my parents' example helped me.

One day I traveled to Liverpool to tell my widowed mother that we were moving to the United States. Tears rolled down my cheeks when I saw her shock. When I heard her say, "How could you leave me?" I felt torn between the people I loved best—my mother and my husband. Then came an expression of the generous, giving, and sacrificial love so typical of her—"I'm sorry, Jill. How selfish of me. Of course you must go. Your place is at Stuart's side." We clung to each other, knowing she would never come to see us (she had an inordinate fear of flying), yet learning together once again the importance of release and sacrifice in love. When my time came to let go of our children, I was able to do so largely because my mother had taught me that you don't let go of a relationship—only your dependence on it. She had done it well, and for this and all the other things she and Dad did, I give thanks to God.

There are no perfect parents, and mine would have been the first to admit their shortcomings. But I have in my mind a lasting picture of my beloved mother kneeling at the side of her bed, a nightly ritual. One time I asked her what she was doing. She looked at me and answered without hesitation, "I pray every night, Jill, that God will make me a good mother." I want you to know that he heard and answered that prayer.

Dr. Anthony Campolo

A Dreamer for the Kingdom

Perhaps best known for his ability to make his fellow Christians laugh and squirm at the same time, Tony Campolo is a gifted communicator with important messages for today's often-too-comfortable believers.

Chairman of the Department of Sociology and Youth Ministry at Eastern College, St. Davids, Pennsylvania, Tony is a dynamic speaker and compelling writer. Among his books are The Success Fantasy, The Power Delusion, Ideas for Social Action, A Reasonable Faith, and Partly Right.

The concerns closest to his heart are also reflected in his extracurricular involvements. He is founder and president of the Evangelical Association for the Promotion of Education, an organization involved in educational, medical, and economic programs in various Third World countries, including Haiti and the Dominican Republic. Here at home, he serves as president and executive director of Youth Guidance of Southeastern Pennsylvania, a program for urban youth. He is also an associate pastor of the Mt. Carmel Baptist Church in West Philadelphia.

Tony lives in St. Davids with his wife, Peggy. They have two grown children, Lisa and Bart.

I know you'll enjoy reading about Tony's special mom and her way of believing in him that helped him believe in himself. She also modeled missionary work as the most important task of a Christian, and, as Tony himself says, he is now living out his mother's dream.

◆━━━━━━━━━━━━━━━━━━━━◆

She was a dreamer who never stopped dreaming. She was convinced that her life could count for Christ.

Her father died when she was just nine years old. She was the oldest of six children and, at the age of nine, went to work cleaning stores in the jewelry district of Philadelphia. Her income was the primary means of support for her impoverished immigrant family. But she had a dream. Even as a little girl, she was committed to becoming a missionary, so she went to night school. It must have been a remarkable sight in South Philadelphia, this bright-eyed, dark-skinned, Italian girl sitting in class with adult Italian immigrants as she learned to read and write.

When she was just sixteen years of age, her mother arranged a marriage for her, and all hopes of completing school ended. A girlhood friend of hers, who later went on to become a prominent American leader and a woman of letters, told me that she wept at my mother's wedding because she was convinced that this was the end of my mother's dreams. But that woman was wrong.

My mother kept on dreaming. She never got to the mission field, and she never completed her education. But she had children, and she was convinced that her dreams would be realized in her offspring. As I grew up, she told me that I was her "Samuel" and that, like that character in the Bible, I had been presented to the Lord for service. Nothing in my life motivated me to give my life to missions more than her constant reminder that she had raised me for this calling.

As I came of age, three things were prominent in her nurturing care. First, she was always there. Second, she believed in me and helped me to believe in myself. Third, she modeled for me what missionaries are supposed to be.

Living as we did in a congested and bustling city, my mother arranged with a teenage girl who lived next door to walk me home at the end of the day. For this arduous responsibility, the girl was paid five cents a day, or a grand total of a quarter a week. In second grade, I became irritated that our poor family was giving this neighbor girl so much money, and I offered a deal to my mom. "Look," I said, "I'll walk myself to school, and if you give me a nickel a week, I will be extra careful. You can keep the other twenty cents, and we'll all be better off." I pleaded and begged, and eventually my mother gave in to my proposal. For the next two years I walked to and from school all by myself. It was an eight-block walk with many streets to cross, but I crossed them all with great care. I didn't talk to any strangers. I always kept on the appointed path. I always did as I promised, and I did it alone—or at least I thought I did.

Years later when we were enjoying a family party, I bragged about my characteristic independence and, in a grandiose fashion, reminded my family of how I had been able to take care of myself even as a small boy. I recalled the arrangements for going to and from school that I had worked out with Mom. It was then that my mother laughed and told me the whole story. "Did you really think you were alone?" she asked. "Every morning when you left for school, I left with you. I walked behind you all the way. When you got out of school at 3:30 in the afternoon, I was there. I always kept myself hidden, but I was there and I followed you all the way home. I just wanted to be there for you in case you needed me."

Mom *was* always there for me, and Mom always believed in me. She believed that I could do well in school even though our family had nothing in the way of an academic background. My father was an Italian immigrant who spoke only broken English, and our home was devoid of books. But my mother made me believe that I could do well in school. English was my worst subject, and grammar was something beyond my comprehension. But Mom always let me know that it was what I said, and not so much how well I said it, that was important. She herself was proof of that. She could hold any crowd spellbound with her stories. There might be grammatical errors and mispronunciations, but her words were laced with humor, and her homespun stories always drove home profound messages. I admired the way she could hold people's attention with what she said, and I decided that I wanted to be like her.

My mother also had a way of minimizing my failures and accentuating my accomplishments. Over and over again she told me how proud she was of anything I did that had any value. I don't ever remember her saying, "You could have done better." Instead, she always made me feel that I had done more than had been expected of me. I would hear her tell her friends, "That boy of mine is really something. He doesn't have the advantages of most kids in this neighborhood, but look how well he's doing in school. Who would have guessed that my boy would be so successful?"

Every day as I left the house, the last thing she would say to me was "Remember! You can go over the top for Jesus!" We joked about that, but the last conversation I had with her before she died ended with those exact words. My mother made me feel special. She made me feel that I could do great things. She convinced me that, with Jesus, any limitations in my background could be overcome.

Years later, as a sociologist, I learned the famous concept of "Cooley's Looking-Glass Self." According to Charles Cooley, one of the founders of American sociology, what you think of yourself is for the most part determined by what you think the most important person in your life thinks of you. When I was a child, the most important person in my life was my mother, and there was never any doubt as to what she thought of me. In her eyes, I was the greatest child who ever lived, and that faith in me was one of her greatest gifts.

Lastly, my mother modeled the lifestyle of missionary service in ways that continue to amaze me, even years after her death. She taught me that where you are is not the important thing, but what you do where you are is of great significance. When she was a girl, she heard a missionary from Africa describe the need for the gospel on that continent, and she dreamed of going there to preach the Word of God and extend the love of Christ. She never went to Africa, and she spent her entire life in the Philadelphia area, but she made the place she lived her missionary field. She met people easily and could never be intimidated by anyone. She cared about everyone she talked to, and she expressed that concern by telling them about Jesus.

After my father died, she took to selling gift items door-to-door. She was a natural, and I doubt if she ever left a home without telling those who were there about her Jesus. She had a way of doing it that made even those who rejected Christ her friends. She didn't condemn people or threaten them with hell fire and brimstone. Instead, she simply told people how Jesus helped her day by day; how he gave her joy and made her life so very, very good. A man once told me that he did not believe in God, but he believed that my mother believed in God and that what my mother believed gave her something that he wished he had.

My mother constantly wrote notes and letters. I could never figure out where she got all the postage stamps. It seemed like she spent more on mail than her income could possibly allow. When people were sick, they got notes of encouragement from Mom. She sent notes of congratulations to every kid she knew who graduated from high school, and only God knows how many five-dollar bills she slipped into envelopes and sent anonymously to people she knew had special financial needs. She was a poor woman, but giving away the little she had gave her more fun than anything else.

When Mom died, we tried to explain to the funeral director that he should expect a crowd and bring in the police to direct traffic. He didn't listen to us, and an hour before the funeral service began, the church sanctuary was packed and hundreds stood outside the building. Amazed, he asked me, "Who was your mother? I never read anything about her. I never heard of her before this funeral." I told him that my mother was a prominent missionary who had touched the lives of thousands—and that was no overstatement.

Mom never took a course in parenting. She never heard those neo-Freudian theories about child rearing. I am sure that the "experts" in the field of child psychology could find many flaws in her practices. All I know is that she was always there. And she believed in me. And she modeled for me that missionary work is the best thing anyone can do. That's not a bad legacy for the daughter of Italian immigrants who had to drop out of school when she was nine years old. I hope that somehow she knows her dream lives on.

Playing to His Strengths

T his isn't the first time Bart Campolo has written about his dad. In fact, he and father Tony coauthored the best-selling Things We Wish We Had Said, *another glimpse into the special father-son relationship they share.*

Besides their writing skills, Bart and Tony share a heart for missions. Bart is currently executive director of Kingdomworks, an inner-city mission organization that develops children's and youth programs in partnership with urban churches. A popular speaker at conferences, youth gatherings, and college campuses across the country, Bart recruits students and adults to serve as volunteer staff for Kingdomworks' summer and year-round missions projects.

Bart grew up in St. Davids, Pennsylvania, and attended Haverford College before graduating from Brown University in 1985 with a degree in religious studies. He was married in 1987 and with his wife, Marty, is the proud parent of one-year-old daughter, Miranda. The Campolos live in Philadelphia. Here Bart encourages us to "play to our strengths" as we parent our children.

My father is very talented. He is bright, articulate, and charming. As a communicator of truth, he has few—if any—peers. He is a master in the truest sense of the word. These are facts.

My father is also very limited. He cannot cook, fix a car, or run a computer. He is easily frustrated. He is a disaster at social events. And, despite all of his accomplishments, he is insecure. After the applause is over, he wonders if people really like him. These, too, are facts.

My father, then, is simply a human being with strengths and weaknesses, abilities and inabilities, gifts and flaws just like everyone else. What makes him so magnificent to me is that he has not been paralyzed by what he cannot do or overcome by what he does not have.

Instead, my father has focused all of his energy on maximizing what he does have and realizing the potential of what he can do. He has played to his strengths, and he has won out by doing so. Tony Campolo is not good at everything, but he is undeniably great at being Tony Campolo.

It is no surprise that most of the things I remember about growing up with my dad have to do with the things he said. Playing to his strengths as he parented meant that he spent a lot of time talking with me. Someone else might have shown his son the wonders of nature or given the gift of music or taught the beauty of a finely tuned engine. There are all sorts of strengths a parent can play to. My mother, for instance, spent my entire childhood showing me kindness above all else because that is what she knew best. My father, though, filled my life with stories and ideas, philosophies and quotations, and endless visions of greatness. And my father spoke the truth.

The truth, of course, comes in many shapes and sizes, and when I was in fifth grade, it came awfully hard. I was on the outside looking in at my little elementary school, an unpopular boy at the age when popularity is all-important. Looking back, I was probably just too verbal for my own good, a know-it-all without the sense to keep my mouth shut. Maybe that was why I was a misfit. Then again, eleven-year-olds don't really need a reason to single someone out as a misfit. So, together with Daniel Keough, the biggest kid in school, I was an outsider. My only consolation was that Daniel kept me from getting beaten up—most of the time.

I don't know if being left out of the popular crowd bothered Daniel, but it certainly bothered me. I watched the other kids from a distance, looking for clues as to what made a person acceptable. After all, I had the same sneakers, and I wore the same clothes. I was as good an athlete as they were—and better than most. There was nothing wrong with me, but apparently that did not matter.

One day I noticed a few kids snickering over the index cards they were passing back and forth. It took me a while, but eventually I discovered that these were "People Cards" and that each one was dedicated to one of the kids in our class. Like a homemade baseball card, each was marked with a kid's name and a crude cartoon drawing of his face. A brief paragraph underneath the caricature described that person in either glowingly positive or viciously negative terms, depending on that person's position in the school pecking order. Finally, there was an overall rating on a scale of one to ten.

As I think about it now, I easily remember the fear that those cards inspired in me as each of the popular kids developed his or her own collection. I wondered if they had a card on me and, if they did, what it said. There was no way to find out, of course, because People Cards were a private joke. Even though I never saw my card, I felt I knew what it must have said.

Strange as it may seem, what hurt me most about People Cards was not the hatefulness of the kids who created them, but the fact that I was unacceptable to them. Rather than seeing their cruelty, I believed what they were telling me about myself. Instead of being put off, I only became more desperate to gain their acceptance. So I began my own collection of People Cards.

I suppose I thought that if I showed my cards to a few of the popular kids and they liked them, they might decide to like me as well. So I worked hard to make them clever enough and mean enough to win favor among the elite. Ironically, that is exactly what happened.

My cards were a hit. Indeed, they were so much a hit that for a few short weeks I was accepted as a full-fledged member of the same group of kids who had taunted and bullied me all year long. I thought such popularity would be the greatest thing in the world, but when it finally happened to me, I was unsure of what to make of it. I was still insecure, and I was particularly uncomfortable with the way my newfound acceptance affected my friendship with Daniel Keough. It simply would not do for a new insider to have too much contact with a confirmed outsider, and instinctively we both knew that. I drifted away from him, and he let me go without saying very much, saving me from facing up to my betrayal.

Whether I admitted it or not, though, I had a very real sense of uneasiness about my newly won position and my new group of friends. For all their good looks, correct clothes, and prestige among the rest of the school, the popular kids were not all that nice, even to one another. Like it or not, though, I had become one of them, and there was no turning back. Then my father found my People Cards.

I remember that he was waiting for me on a Friday afternoon when I came home from school. That was unusual in itself, but I didn't realize what was going on until he asked me to come into the living room for a talk. "Bart," he began softly, "I wasn't rooting through your stuff at all, but you left some things on the steps today. When I was moving them, I found these." He pulled out the cards. "I wanted to ask you what they were."

I didn't know what to say to him. I had avoided the truth until then, but as soon as I saw those cards in his hands, I knew that I was all wrong. I explained myself halfheartedly, and he listened quietly. Even after I finished, he didn't yell at me or tell me what a rotten person I was. He simply told me how cruel he thought the cards were. He explained that it was wrong to judge people, especially by such shallow standards. He asked me what I thought Jesus would think of my cards. Then he told me that he was not really angry with me, but that he was terribly disappointed. Hearing that was worse than a beating.

By that time I was crying uncontrollably, but he went on talking. Finally, just before he left me alone in my misery, he said the most liberating words that a mixed-up fifth grader who suddenly hated himself could have ever heard.

"This really isn't like you at all," he said. "That's why this caught me so off guard, I guess." He looked me in the eye. "You are a nice person, Bart, or at least I've always thought that you were. This just isn't the kind of thing a nice person like you would do."

What perfect words they were for me! Somehow they managed to make me feel both horrible and wonderful at the same time, and most of all they gave me the hope that all was not lost. My father still loved me even though I had let him down. I wasn't doomed to a life of being cruel because, as he put it, that was not like me. Sitting alone and feeling very ashamed of myself, I realized something absolutely crucial. My actions had been terrible, but in my father's eyes I was still a nice person. Or at least I could be.

As important as that final affirmation was, though, what was more important was the time my dad took to explain to me exactly why what I was doing was so wrong. Deep down I had been uncomfortable with People Cards all along, but as a fifth grader I didn't have the ability to articulate exactly why they were so terrible. I needed an explanation to go along with my instincts, and that is exactly what he gave me. He gave me the words both for myself and for anyone who cared to ask, and those words gave me the courage to take a stand.

I don't think that every parent could do what my father was able to do. In spite of all the "how-to" books about parenting, people cannot create in themselves capacities that God has not placed within them. Fortunately, there are many ways to express love and to help children grow. I remember that conversation—and a hundred others like it—because my father expressed his love to me the best way he knew how.

Sometimes I wish my father had taken me camping, coached my Little League team, or led a family outing every Saturday. My guess is that he wishes he had done some of those things, too. But in another way I am grateful that he didn't try to be a father he wasn't cut out to be. He did what he was able to do, and he did it with every bit of his love. And that is the most anyone can ask of a parent.

Reverence for the Lord's Day

There's more to Truett Cathy than his spectacularly successful Chick-fil-A restaurant chain. Here is a man who serves God with the business and success with which he has been entrusted.

The Chick-fil-A story begins back in 1946 when Truett sold his car, added his brother Ben's savings to his own, and borrowed money from a bank to open The Dwarf Grill (later called The Dwarf House). By 1963, he felt he had the perfect recipe and cooking technique for chicken, and four years later he opened the first of more than 450 Chick-fil-A restaurants.

Truett has been as innovative in his support of education as he is in his approach to fast-food dining. In 1984 he began the WinShape Centre Foundation at Berry College in Rome, Georgia. Supported by Chick-fil-A, WinShape provides college students with scholarships of up to ten thousand dollars.

A husband, father, and grandfather, Truett has also made time for the past thirty years to teach a Sunday school class of thirteen-year-old boys. Truett and his wife, Jeannette, have welcomed many of these boys to their farm to ride dirt bikes *and enjoy their horses. The Cathys have also been surrogate parents and big brother and sister to many.*

Truett has shared his story and his philosophy in It's Easier to Succeed Than to Fail. *Here Truett talks about his parents and an important lesson they taught him about "reverence for the Lord's Day."*

◆━━━━━━━━━━━━━━━━━━━━━━━━━━━━━━◆

I grew up in Atlanta during the Roaring Twenties, and, unlike many kids today, I was fortunate enough to have been raised by both my mother and father. I must admit, however, I was much closer to my mother, a hard-working and saintly woman. After the stock market crash of the 1920s closed my father's real estate business, he established a rural insurance route, and my mother opened our home to boarders. Growing up in a boarding house introduced me to hard work and taught me the value of diligent labor.

I am grateful to my parents, especially my mother, for teaching me how to do the best I can whatever the task might be and for instilling in me the importance of Sunday, the Lord's Day, and how we should keep it holy. Working hard is important, but I saw growing up that honoring God—especially on his day—is the top priority. I carried this teaching into my own business, the Chick-fil-A chain.

We started in the food business in 1946 with a small restaurant we later called The Dwarf House. At that time my brother and I set the hours: We'd be open twenty-four hours a day, six days a week, and we would be closed on Sunday. This was an important decision and, in light of the pressures of a twenty-four-hour operation, a wise one. I also believe that by closing on Sunday we honored God and directed our attention to more important things. Sunday is a very important day for my family and me, as it is for most people. I know that the nearly twenty thousand Chick-fil-A employees appreciate having Sunday off to be with family and friends and to worship if they so choose.

Since establishing this policy in 1946, we haven't deviated from it despite the pressure to do so. The Chick-fil-A chicken sandwich, a product concept originated at The Dwarf House, is now featured in thirty-one states. It's in more than 450 shopping malls, in twenty-one free-standing units, and in four Chick-fil-A Dwarf Houses—and throughout the country we still have that firm commitment to being closed on Sundays.

Since most of our Chick-fil-A restaurants are in shopping malls, people who do not know us assume we're open on Sunday along with the other mall stores. I recently received this letter of apology (which I reprint with permission):

Dear Mr. Cathy:

This is a letter of repentance and apology, though we have never met nor had communications or dealings of any sort. It is occasioned by my rashness in concluding, and in stating several times to individuals and groups of Christians, that there is an inconsistency of witness and deed in

*your business relationship with Chick-fil-A and
your involvement with The Lord's Day Alliance.*

*I again made the observation last Sunday morn-
ing before a Bible class, and several members ad-
vised me quickly that I am in error, that your
restaurants are not open on Sundays as I had
believed. (Obviously, I am not one of your regular
customers.) I never enjoy being wrong, but in this
case I am in a very real sense delighted to know that
you have not, as so many of us professed Christians
have, compromised your convictions on this matter
for economic gain.*

*I thus ask your forgiveness, as I have asked the
Lord's, and encourage you in your walk of the
Christian way. May you and yours always enjoy
the greatest blessings of God's service.*
Let Christ be Lord!

Delmar R. Yoder
Atlanta, Georgia

In dealing with shopping-center leasing agents
across the country, we're asked about our policy of
closing on Sunday. The more experienced leasing
agents know this is not a debatable issue. In all Chick-
fil-A leases, we have permission to close on Sunday.
Some of the agents permit us to close on Sunday—but
only as long as all the restaurants in our chain are
closed. That is no problem for us.

I often say that if any business is justified in being

open on Sunday, it would be the food service industry. I don't condemn people who open on Sunday, and I often eat out after church. But being open on Sundays is just not for me. When I teach my eighth-grade Sunday school class lessons about reverence for the Lord's Day, I believe my teaching is more effective and believable because my business is closed on that day. It's important that I practice what I preach.

I heard a few years ago that one of our restaurants in North Carolina was open on Sundays. That couldn't be right! All our operators have a thorough understanding that closing on the Lord's Day is a strict policy for the chain. One of our staff people called the restaurant and asked, "Are you open on Sunday?" The reply was, "We're open on Sunday during the month of December."

This greatly disturbed me because I was sure the operator understood the rule. This particular operator was a part-time church music director. When he came aboard, he had told me he appreciated the fact that Chick-fil-A closed on Sunday and that he'd be able to continue his church music responsibilities.

I suggested to other staff members that we not take drastic action until the daily report sheets were mailed in at the end of the month. I wanted to see how he handled his sales report, thinking and even hoping that somehow he had misunderstood operating policy. When the sales reports came in, there were no sales reported for Sunday, but the sales were unusually high for Saturday and Monday. He had apparently divided the Sunday sales and included them in the sales for Saturday and Monday.

We called the operator and asked him about the Sunday sales. He admitted that during December he had remained open on Sunday because of pressure from the mall management and other tenants. He said he'd done it in a "spirit of cooperation." Also, we were having an incentive contest for sales increases in December, so he was anxious for the award as well as the added financial rewards from additional sales and profit. We had no other alternative except to terminate our agreement with him.

The Lord set aside one day a week as his day. Genesis 2:3 says, "And God blessed the seventh day, and sanctified it: because that in it he had rested from all his work which God created and made" (KJV)—and he did so for our benefit (Mark 2:27). Some people believe that equipment works more efficiently and with fewer breakdowns when it rests. I'm inclined to agree—especially when that "equipment" is a human being.

Thanks be unto God for setting aside one day as a special day, a day for our enjoyment and worship of him. Thanks be also unto my dear, sweet mother for building our family on a Christian foundation. Without her leadership and guidance, I would not be where I am today in my personal and business life.

Charles W. Colson

In the Image
of Christ

◆─────────────────────────────────────◆

T oo many people recognize problems, shrug their shoulders, and walk away. Not Charles Colson. In 1976,
Chuck founded Prison Fellowship, a ministry with a staff of
226 people and a network of some forty thousand volunteers
working in more than six hundred prisons across the country.
Through in-prison seminars, which offer inmates Bible study
and religious training, Prison Fellowship extends a message
of hope to those who are living within the dehumanizing and
lonely walls of a jail.

Such walls led Chuck to discover a personal relationship
with Christ. Resigning from his position as a White House
aide for President Nixon, Chuck pled guilty to disseminating
derogatory information to the press about Daniel Ellsberg,
and served seven months in prison. Released in 1975, Chuck
could not forget the human tragedies he had encountered
behind bars. It was then that he established Prison Fellowship, and today he serves as its chairman of the board.

A graduate of Brown University with a law degree from
George Washington University, Chuck is a highly regarded
author and respected spokesman for evangelical Christianity,

Christian social action, and criminal justice reform. Among his books are Born Again, Loving God, Kingdoms in Conflict, Against the Night, *and* The God of Stones and Spiders. *He also writes a monthly column for* Christianity Today.

Here, Chuck talks about how his "parents served as a precursor of Christ" and the lessons he learned from them that proved important to him as an adult.

In 1973 I found myself in the middle of the biggest political upheaval in American history. As the Watergate storm thundered around me, week after week I was subpoenaed by grand juries, summoned before congressional committees, interrogated by special prosecutors and the FBI, and all the while pilloried daily in the national press.

The real crucible came on the day I was hauled before a grand jury in the District Court Building in Washington, D.C. I was a lawyer, sworn to uphold the law—yet here I was, guarded by federal marshals as I made my way down the long, drab corridor into the jury room. As I was ushered in, I saw twenty-five of my peers seated in the jury box, most of them looking terribly bored, some asleep, one or two even reading newspapers. At the front of the room was a graying— and, I thought, leering—prosecutor.

The questions were tough. Most had nothing to do with the Watergate case but rather were designed to embarrass and entrap me. As an attorney, I knew exactly what my adversary, the special prosecutor, was doing. My first instinct was to evade, maybe even shade the truth a bit, and throw him off the track.

But even as I felt that lawyer's instinct for survival, another voice sounded even stronger in my mind: *"There is nothing more important than telling the truth. Always tell the truth. It's the right thing to do."* It was my father's voice.

My mind flashed back to the earliest days I could remember. My dad and I didn't have a lot of time together—he worked all day and went to law school at night during those tough days of the depression. But on Sunday afternoons, my dad would take a break from his crowded schedule and sit with me on the back steps of our modest frame house just outside of Boston.

Though rugged and athletic, Dad was a gentle man who always spoke softly. I would listen, enraptured, as he described his law school classes or told me of his own boyhood experiences. Then he would invariably ask me—always in a loving, never in a demanding way—questions about school or my friends. And if he sensed I might be struggling with something, he made it clear that I could come to him anytime to discuss anything. "Just one thing," he would always add. "There is nothing more important than telling the truth. Always tell the truth."

Those words and my dad's faithful example over the years stayed with me through adulthood and the White House–magnitude struggles I never could have imagined as a child. And so that day in the courthouse, I took a few deep breaths, sat up straight in my chair, and gave truthful answers. I did the same thing the forty-four other times I was called to testify under oath during Watergate—and, as it turned out, I was the only major Watergate figure not charged with perjury.

That didn't keep me out of jail, however. As I've since realized, God had his own plans for me and my time in prison. But even as I went in, I realized that at least I would be able to serve my time, pay my debt for what I had done, and do so with a clear conscience.

My father died while I was in prison—and that was one of the toughest losses of my life. But I think he experienced the same peace I did. As I was being sentenced, his question was, "Have you told the truth?"

I told him I had. He looked at me with a confident smile. "Then you'll be all right." And he was right.

My father shared other character-shaping words during my childhood. "Whatever you put your mind to," he used to tell me, "you can do. And whatever you do in life—it doesn't matter if it's cleaning toilets—do it well. Do it with excellence." I'm sure my dad referred to cleaning toilets just to make his point. But his words turned out to be prophetic—twice.

The first time was during my service as a "spit-and-polish" marine lieutenant. Every Saturday morning the battalion commander, a gruff battle-scarred colonel, would inspect our platoon. Forty men stood ramrod stiff, each at the end of his bunk with rifle at the ready. On this particular day, the colonel finished his inspection and then faced me. "Lieutenant," he growled, "the head is dirty."

"Yes, sir," I replied. "I'll have it cleaned."

"No, you won't," he snapped. "Clean it yourself."

I was humiliated. *Officers don't clean toilets,* I thought. Then I remembered my dad's words. I put on my fatigue uniform and swabbed the decks until they shone.

The colonel knew what he was doing. From that point on, the men in my platoon worked feverishly: They didn't want to let down their lieutenant again. We never failed another inspection.

The second time I fulfilled my dad's toilet prophecy was while I was in prison. My Watergate sentence was a one- to three-year term. On the first night of that sentence, I experienced the peculiar horror of prison's dehumanizing effects.

I stood naked in a bare-walled receiving room while a guard searched me and my meager belongings. Then I was tossed a pair of underpants with five numbers stenciled on them: I realized I was the sixth person to wear them.

A few days later, I was handed a mop and bucket and told to clean the filthy latrine of our prison dorm, a facility shared by forty men.

Only months earlier I had occupied the office next to the President of the United States. I had a limousine and a chauffeur at my disposal, government jets standing by to fly me anywhere from Andrews Air Force Base, and generals saluting as I passed by.

Now I was cleaning prison toilets, and no one was saluting. But strangely, there was no shame, no sense of despair. At a time when my dad was physically far away, his lesson was very near: Whatever you do, do it with excellence.

And now, even more importantly, I was sustained by

faith in the One who had given up the honors of heaven to come to earth to die for me, the One who called me to serve "the least of these" as he had. I had a sense of purpose and peace and did my best, guided by my dad's words spoken so long before and by the presence of my heavenly Father who was with me even in the prison latrine.

Simple lessons: Tell the truth. Do what you do with excellence. These principles served as a foundation in my early development and a guide for the tough challenges that came with adulthood.

My parents were nominal Christians, occasional churchgoers who believed in God. (After my conversion, I had the opportunity to talk with both of my parents about the saving grace of Jesus Christ. Although they never told me explicitly, I like to think they chose to follow him before they died.) But, as I grew up, there were no nighttime prayers or talk about Jesus around our house. The family Bible was a large, dusty volume used primarily to record births and deaths.

Even so, my godly heritage was strong. What my dad taught me in those two lessons, among countless others, was—whether he knew it or not—at the very heart of Christian living: the belief in absolute right and wrong and a commitment to the work ethic (we do what we do with excellence because it brings glory to God). These truths were simply his way of life, and his life became the model for mine. As I wrote in the dedication of *Born Again,* he was the one "whose ideals for my life I have tried, not always successfully, to fulfill."

He was, in fact, a model in more ways than either

he or I could possibly have imagined. When Dad earned his law degree at age thirty-nine, he began practicing part-time while continuing his full-time job. The first case he took was to gain clemency for a man who had been sentenced to life in prison for a crime many believed he had not committed. My dad was a staunch political conservative with a passion for the law. At the same time, he had a tender heart, and injustice deeply offended him. And so, with limited resources, he gave vast amounts of time to right what he perceived to be a wrong in this case. I remember well the joyous night in our home when the governor announced that he would release the prisoner and return him to his family. My dad looked down at me that night, his eyes sparkling as he recalled the well-known quote: "Better that a hundred guilty men go free than one innocent man remain in prison."

It was not until after my dad's death that I discovered perhaps the greatest irony of all. Among his papers, I found records of his very active involvement with the United Prison Association, a prison reform group. My dad had helped inmates, visited the state penitentiary, offered instruction to the prisoners, and encouraged a debating society inside the prison. I guess he must have talked about these things when I was younger, but my memory is hazy. I had little interest in such subjects at the time—and little did I dream that one day I might be picking up where my dad had left off!

No one could have hoped for more loving parents. My mother, daughter of English immigrants, and my father, son of a Swedish musician, sacrificed everything in those lean depression years to give me opportunities they had not had. My dad worked sixty hours a week to keep our family afloat, yet there were times my mother cut corners on the grocery budget simply to buy me a toy.

In a very real way my parents served as a precursor of the Christ who in later years revealed himself to me. In 1973, when I cried out to the Father in heaven and tears streamed down my face, I could immediately understand his unconditional love. I'd seen a glimpse of it in my earthly father and mother.

For that gift, I am eternally grateful.

Dr. Lawrence J. Crabb, Jr.

Relationship: Nothing Matters More

A prominent Christian psychologist Larry Crabb shares his expertise with graduate students in the classroom as well as with the public through his writing and various ministry activities.

Larry earned his master's and doctoral degrees in clinical psychology at the University of Illinois. After first serving as an assistant professor in psychology there, he moved to Florida Atlantic University where he taught for three years before setting up a private practice in Boca Raton, Florida.

Larry later served as chairman and professor in the graduate department of biblical counseling at Grace Theological Seminary. He now holds that position at Colorado Christian University. Larry is also director and founder of the Institute of Biblical Counseling.

You may also have read some of Larry's writings—his books Inside Out, The Marriage Builder, Understanding People, *and* Encouragement: The Key to Caring, *or his articles in, among other magazines,* Moody *and* Christianity Today. *Larry and his wife, Rachael, have two adult sons, Keplen and Kenton.*

As you read about Larry's childhood, you'll understand something about how he developed his heart for God and for ministry. You'll also see how some of the lessons he learned growing up helped define what's important to him today.

Most adults have at least a few clear memories—some good, some bad—from their childhoods. I've noticed that people tend to report that the pain they experienced in relationship with their parents is more vivid than the pleasure. For whatever reason, many folks believe that hurt has touched them more deeply than joy.

As a result, the fear of pain and a stubborn commitment to avoid more of it take root in their souls and crowd out any realistic hope that relationships can be enjoyed. And life becomes empty, a futile pursuit of satisfaction in a lonely world full of people determined not to be hurt.

My story is different. And the difference accounts for the overwhelming sense of gratitude I feel toward my parents for what they did right. Certainly there were disappointments—our family was made up of four imperfect persons. But the good that I knew in my growing up years taught me lessons that are central in my thinking today.

One of my most vivid memories goes back to my teenage years. The event was simple, not the kind one would expect to make a lasting impression. But somehow the impression went deep, deeper than many Bible lessons have gone, perhaps because it fleshed out in a single moment a central biblical message.

It was Sunday morning and, as we did every Sunday morning, our family was driving to church. My brother, Bill, four and a half years my senior, was riding in the front passenger seat, Mother and Dad were in the back, and I was driving. I must have been sixteen or seventeen years old.

We were going down Ridge Avenue, an old, well-patched artery into Philadelphia, on our way to Roxboro Gospel Chapel. Just before we reached the intersection with Henry Avenue, I glanced in the rearview mirror and saw my parents: Dad had his arm around Mother as she nestled comfortably against his shoulder.

Now this was nothing unusual. To this day my parents like touching each other. They know nothing of that unholy separateness that is obvious in couples whose togetherness is more habit than desire. But their touching has never been overdone. Something of a British reserve moderated their show of affection, but their affection was (and is) there.

On that Sunday morning more than thirty years ago, I looked into that mirror and thought, *They really like each other—and that's neat!* A man and woman in their mid- to late-forties, married nearly twenty-five years, were hugging like a couple of teenagers in the back seat of a car. A lesson I had already begun to grasp became clearer in those few seconds: Nothing matters more than relationship. It really is the center of life and the source of life's deepest joys.

I learned that lesson and many others from my parents. But values that are naturally lived by people we watch become more a part of our soul than those values we are specifically taught. And my parents consistently and unself-consciously modeled that relationship is the center of life.

That lesson included more than the value of affection. I also learned that you're not an imposition to people who love you. As a kid, I struggled with two embarrassing problems. Neither difficulty was fashionable among my peers, so my self-esteem was not terribly strong. One of my problems was stuttering, so every week for months Mother drove me all the way from the suburbs of Philadelphia where we lived to the Temple University Speech Clinic in Center City. My other problem was acne, so Mother regularly aimed the car in a different direction toward the dermatologist who picked, burned, and medicated my face to help me feel better about myself.

I can't recall Mother ever complaining about the considerable time she spent carting me to speech therapists and skin doctors. Because she never complained, I never felt like an imposition. I learned from her something about the importance of sacrificial giving in a relationship.

Perhaps more than anything else, my parents taught me that relationship can be taken for granted in a good sense—it can be trusted—if it is built on commitment. Dad has often said to me that he and Mother have not been immune to real conflict but that divorce was simply unthinkable.

Some of my parents' rough times were financial.

Dad never had the opportunity for advanced education. His father died when he was a boy of five. Working to stay fed took priority over getting an education, and he worked hard all his life. Although he provided well for us, the pressure was unrelenting. Sometimes it got to him.

I remember one evening (I must have been eleven or twelve) when he left our house in a mood of obvious discouragement. As I watched him drive off, I panicked. I recall feeling scared to death that he wouldn't return. I asked Mother, "Where did he go? Is he all right?" With a matter-of-factness that instantly calmed me, she replied, "Oh, he's fine. He'll be back soon." There was never a thought in either of their minds that he wouldn't return. Discouragement and tension were never stronger than their commitment to God and to each other. Of course he'd come back. He knew that nothing matters more than relationship and that the joy of relationship depends foundationally on commitment.

Besides modeling lessons about relationship, another thing my parents did right was to believe in me. In fact, when I asked my folks what they thought they had done right, Mother quickly replied, "Well, we figured you were sensible enough to make good decisions."

As I grew up, I never felt overwhelmed with advice. I felt respected, even when I did dumb things. Once, when I was perhaps seventeen, I became enraged with our youth leader over what I regarded as his narrowly legalistic attitude in a certain matter. Our debate turned into a heated yelling match that ended when I hurled a hymnbook across the room in his direction, stomped out the door, and drove home. I knew I was wrong.

When I walked into our house, Dad was on the phone with the man I had assaulted, listening to a tirade against me. I wondered what Dad would do. I heard him end the phone conversation with something like, "Sounds as if he didn't handle things very well, but I'm glad he has spunk enough to have real convictions." He hung up, turned to me, and calmly asked what had happened. He listened as I presented a terribly biased account of the incident, and then he commented on the importance of handling convictions responsibly. That was it. He went on with his evening, and I felt respected. I also resolved to express my convictions in a more godly fashion.

My illustrations could continue for many more pages, but perhaps I've made the point. What did my parents do right as I was growing up? They believed then—and even more so now—that Christianity is a relationship initiated by a holy God who had every reason to turn away from his creatures in disgust but instead came up with a plan to develop good relationships with them, a plan that cost him the life of his only Son.

My parents believe that relationship with Christ frees people to relate well to others and that the center of everything is relationship. They taught me that nothing matters more than relationship, first with God and then with others, especially family.

Their style of relating is their own, reflecting the uniqueness and sometimes the deficiencies of their background and makeup. The details of how they related to me aside, by their affection for each other, their willingness to look after me without complaint, their confidence in me, and a host of other things, they communicated that life is defined by the quality of relationship we enjoy with God and offer to others.

Now I am a man in his mid- to late-forties, I've been married nearly twenty-five years, and I like touching my wife more than ever. I've let down my wife and our two sons in a thousand ways, but I love them, I respect them, I believe in them, and I'm committed to them. Our family has known rough times just as my parents have. I understand now that discouragement and conflict can overwhelm you to the point where relief seems more desirable than anything else. But beneath the occasionally unbearable turmoil is a well-learned lesson: Nothing matters more than relationship. Honoring commitments within relationship provides a joy that can come in no other way.

For teaching me this lesson, I am inexpressibly grateful to my parents.

Love in Large Quantities

A glance at John Dellenback's vita shows him to be a man who takes seriously Jesus' call to be a servant. John has used his Yale University undergraduate education and his University of Michigan law degree background to serve his fellow human beings in a variety of ways. While practicing law in Oregon from 1951-1989, John was an active servant in church, government, and various civic organizations.

As a member of both Westminster Presbyterian Church in Medford, Oregon, and the National Presbyterian Church in Washington, D.C., John has served as deacon, trustee, elder, moderator of the Oregon synod, and member of the Permanent Judicial Commission of the General Assembly. He was chairman of the National Prayer Breakfast in Washington, D.C., in 1975 and treasurer of the Greater Washington Billy Graham Crusade in 1986.

John's years of government service include tenure as director of the Peace Corps (1975–77) and several terms as a member of the United States House of Representatives (1967–75) and the Oregon House of Representatives (1961–67).

The holder of twelve honorary doctorates, John has also

served on the board of directors of World Vision U.S., World Vision International, Bread for the World, the Cancer Society, United Crusade, Kiwanis Club, the YMCA, and the Medford (Oregon) Chamber of Commerce.

Here John shares five values his mother instilled in him as he was growing up, values that shaped him into a faithful servant of God.

I fall within that unfortunate group of children who lost a parent at an early age and grew up in a single-parent family. To some degree, such children feel that loss throughout their life; they have missed out on an important element in their childhood. But high on my list of blessings is the fact that the parent I had really loved my siblings and me; her top priority in life was to see her children grow into productive and responsible people.

The memories I have of my father include some wonderful fun times when we played together, and several meaningful experiences still remain sharp in my memory. He had married when he was well along in years, and my parents' marriage had been a happy one. My father loved my mother and us children, and he worked hard to provide for us. He lived an honorable and productive life as a practicing attorney and was highly regarded by his friends and associates. When he died suddenly of a heart attack, he left a modest estate to help support my mother and four sons (aged eleven, nine, and seven and my mother's nineteen-year-old son from a previous marriage). I was the middle of the young threesome.

My mother had an earnest and sincere Christian faith to help her after my father's death. She also had two sisters and a group of supportive friends. The estate my father left her, coupled with financial assistance from one of her sisters, meant that she did not have to work outside the home. Of all that my mother gave me, I am deeply in her debt for at least five fundamental things.

The first is my faith in Jesus Christ as my Lord and my Savior, my Teacher and my Model. My mother attended church regularly, and she expected her sons to do the same. She wasn't a theologian and only infrequently—and then never very deeply—did she lead us into a discussion of biblical teachings. But for me she exemplified how one's belief in God should directly and clearly impact how one lives. Her faith extended beyond fundamental doctrine to a course of conduct. That pairing of belief and practice—strengthened through the years by prayer, study, role models, friends, personal experience, and a great marriage partner—has become the rock upon which the Lord has built my career and my life.

Second, my mother instilled in me that family relationships are important and that family members help each other. Instead of being a group of individuals, each concerned primarily for himself, we were a family. That meant we did things together, cared about each other's welfare, and were aware of how we could help each other. And this conviction that she preached called for action.

My mother's wise words, however, certainly didn't result in four young boys not having the customary brotherly fights over one thing or another. But it did mean that I entered adulthood with a deep affection for each of my brothers, an awareness of what their particular needs might be, and a deep-seated conviction that, as best I could, I would help each of them along the way. The importance of the family has also meant that for a good many years we brothers—and our wives—have faithfully traveled from Georgia, Indiana, Washington, D.C., and Oregon to an old family cottage in Michigan to spend some time together.

Third, it was a given that we boys would graduate from high school. Beyond that, our mother was invaluable in helping each of us go as far with formal education as we wanted. She hadn't determined that we should go a specific direction or a certain distance. Instead, she let us know that she would support each of us, whatever we chose to do. She also let us know how pleased she was when we did well.

When we three younger boys were in grammar school, Mother made it a point on one day each year to invite to lunch the principal and all the teachers in the school who had at any time had us in class. Mom graciously let each teacher know that she knew about her and appreciated her. At the time, none of us boys really liked the idea of being singled out so clearly in any teacher's mind, but I don't recall there ever being a time when I needed help from a teacher and didn't get it!

The four of us boys walked different educational paths. My journey took me through an undergraduate degree at Yale and a law degree at the University of Michigan Law School. Quite frankly, I think Mom was as amazed as I was by my academic success, but she didn't indicate that to me at the time. She simply contributed to my confidence by believing that I could do well. Her support never wavered during college or law school.

Fourth, Mom always expected that we each would pitch in when tasks needed to be done at home. Mom, for instance, did the cooking, my younger brother set and cleared the table, my older brother washed the dishes, and I dried them. So many meals followed that pattern that even today when we are guests at someone's home, I'm much more at ease helping clear the table or wash the dishes than I am sitting at the table while others do all the work. And still today I don't pile dirty dishes on top of one another. We boys never did that because then we had to wash the top and bottom of each dish instead of only the top!

Finally, I'm grateful to Mom for letting all of us know that we were loved even when we were disciplined. I grew up knowing that Mom loved us and would continue to indefinitely. Love is certainly a great encourager, a great bond, a great healer—and my mother taught me that no home and no life should be without love in large quantities.

I've been showered with a great many blessings throughout my life. They include faith, family, friends, health, and challenging opportunities to serve. I know that in creating the home in which I was raised, my mother didn't do a perfect job due largely to the less-than-perfect situation she had to work in and the less-than-perfect material she had to work with. But I also know that she did a great deal that was right, and I am and shall remain eternally grateful to her and for her.

Rich in All the Ways That Matter

*S*tarting an air service and flying school before the airfield is complete takes a lot of confidence in one's idea and in oneself. And confidence in himself is just part of what has led to the success of Richard DeVos, president and cofounder of Amway Corporation.

Besides founding and operating the flying school for four years, Richard and his longtime friend and business partner, Jay Van Andel, also formed the Ja-Ri Corporation, an import business, and in 1959 the internationally known Amway Corporation. Today, Amway is one of the world's largest direct merchandising companies, and its president is a popular motivational speaker around the globe.

As he explains here, Richard learned salesmanship—and much more—from his father. While teaching him to believe in himself, Richard's father also modeled his faith in the "limitless power of individuals who trusted first in God and, through him, in themselves."

These gifts of self-confidence and faith in God have contributed to the growth of the Amway Corporation and have earned Richard honorary doctoral degrees and numerous *awards like the National Management Association's American Enterprise Award, the Religious Heritage of America Business Leader of the Year Award, Calvin College's Distinguished Alumni Award, the Americanism Educational League's Free Enterprise Award, Industry Week's Excellence in Management Award, and recognition as the University of Missouri's American Entrepreneur of the Year.*

Richard has also served in a diverse number of organizations ranging from the Salvation Army, the United Way, and the Cystic Fibrosis Foundation to the President's Council on Physical Fitness and the Presidential Commission on AIDS to the Republican National Committee.

On Friday, November 16, 1990, I was honored with the Outstanding Service Award from the Layman's National Bible Association at the Plaza Hotel in New York. I received this award in recognition of my chairmanship of the Fiftieth Annual National Bible Week. But someone was missing from this elegant affair—and that someone was me.

Since my heart bypass surgery seven years before, I had observed a strict regimen of diet, exercise, and some modification of my hectic lifestyle. Nevertheless, it was time for my annual checkup, and this had led to the need for further checking. So there I was sitting in Butterworth Hospital in Grand Rapids rather than enjoying lunch with such old and dear friends as Norman Vincent and Ruth Peale in Manhattan.

Health problems like mine make one introspective. I believe that God looks over each one of us and that he has our ultimate good in his hands, but very real human concerns about one's health make us stop and reassess where we are and where we're headed.

Since this chapter was on my mind during that time of introspection, one of my most vivid thoughts and wishes was that my dad could have been alive to see this award bestowed. I thought of Proverbs 23:24-25: "The father of the righteous will greatly rejoice, and he who begets a wise son will be glad in him. Let your father and your mother be glad, and let her rejoice who gave birth to you" (NASB). I wished that my father as well as my mother could have rejoiced with me.

I've had the good fortune of becoming highly successful in the eyes of the world. God gave me the gift of communication, and with Amway in more than forty countries, I've had the chance to speak from platforms all over the world. Almost always someone asks, "What influences have shaped your life?" or "What underlies your philosophy about freedom and free enterprise?" Those questions help me reach back into my mental book of memories and realize the powerful influence my grandparents as well as my parents have had on my life.

My grandfather came from the Netherlands, and he was my first model of selling and entrepreneurship. Early every weekday he went to the vegetable market and bought fresh produce. Then he loaded it in his old truck and went from street to street selling his fruits and vegetables. The neighborhood depended on him. He met their needs, and he did so with dedication and enthusiasm.

Grandmother, who also immigrated to the United States, maintained a home rich with love. A feeling of warmth enveloped each of us like the aroma of baking bread as we sat around her dinner table—and that was more often than we might have wished. During the depression, my parents had to give up their home. My mother and father and I moved into the third floor of my grandparents' home. Of course it was difficult for all of us, but those years remain in my memory as fresh as the sound of Model A Fords or as pungent as the smell of fresh carrots. Those years taught me what family was all about—faith, caring, and sharing whatever my grandparents had. They were good parents and grandparents, and they did many things right.

My father was my next model of salesmanship, and it has always saddened me that he didn't live long enough to see Amway become a major world force for spreading the free-enterprise example because Dad was its model. He never asked for anything from anyone except the opportunity for a sale. He was an electrician and later a salesman for a major U.S. company.

Recently, I was told by one of my staff that the chief executive of a major Grand Rapids manufacturer remembers Dad coming to call on him. At that time, Harry Bloem was a young bookkeeper for the Bissell Carpet Sweeper Company. We had gone to high school together, so he knew my dad. He said Dad always came in the door immaculately dressed, but it wasn't just his apparel that stood out. It was his personality. Customers liked him—and they liked what he stood for. Dad was the soul of integrity. He also believed in the limitless power of individuals who trusted first in God and, through him, in themselves. That made Dad an optimist.

But Dad also stood for something else. As I was growing up, like all kids I sometimes wanted to take the easy way out. When I was asked to do something difficult, I often replied, "I can't." That wasn't acceptable to Dad. He taught me by word and by example that those who say "I can't" often mean "I won't try." That's how I learned to believe in myself. I overcame each little obstacle by repeating to myself, "I can if I try." And if it didn't work out the first time, I thought it through and tried it another way.

But there was one thing that Dad, with all his faith and positive thinking, wasn't able to change. As he entered his mid years, the company that employed him decided to end the relationship because he had complained to his boss's boss about his boss. That was a bitter lesson, but it reinforced what Dad constantly preached—that one way to succeed is to be in business for oneself. One could fail, but failure is merely a learning experience. The other side of that coin is success.

The idea of being an entrepreneur was exciting to Dad. No doubt that's why I was willing to join forces after World War II with Jay Van Andel, a friend from high-school days and my partner today. Both of us were from tough Dutch stock, and we were willing to take a "flyer"—and that's what we did! We started an air service and flying school when neither of us was a licensed pilot, and our instructor had to teach pontoon landings on the Grand River because our airfield wasn't complete. But we overcame those minor obstacles because we believed in ourselves.

I haven't revealed much about my mother, perhaps because I'm fortunate to have her still living. She lost Dad to a series of heart attacks in 1961 and 1962, just three years after we started Amway. When Dad died, Mother's Christian faith and survival instinct saw her through. (Looking back at our lives, I see Mother as the heart of the family and Dad as its head, and I guess my wife Helen and I used that model when we married.) Mother, in her self-sufficient and optimistic way, went to work at the telephone company. She enjoyed it so much that she continued to work well past her sixty-fifth birthday, even though Amway was thriving and I was more than willing to help her financially.

I will always be grateful for having been brought up in a home with both a mother and a father, a place of love and caring where God was honored, church was attended, and prayers were extended.

We were poor by today's standards, but we were rich in all the ways that matter.

What Makes Parents Godly

A talented musician, writer, and producer, Dez Dickerson is known to many as the former guitarist with Prince and the Revolution. From 1978 to 1983, Dez cowrote and recorded music with Prince as well as performed with him in his concerts, music videos, and television appearances. He is best known to Prince fans for his guitar and vocal work on 1999, an album that went gold, platinum, and then double platinum.

In 1983, Dez left Prince to pursue a solo career. He did a cameo in the movie Purple Rain and toured the country as the opening act for rock singer Billy Idol through most of 1984.

Between 1985 and 1986, Dez spent, in his words, "a turbulent time getting to know the Lord I had given my life to and leaving behind the selfish ambition that had fueled my success." On December 29, 1986, Dez received the baptism of the Holy Spirit and a renewed peace and direction in his life.

Recently, Dez has been working in both the contemporary Christian and gospel music markets as a writer and producer. In addition to writing songs for Reunion Records' artists

Renee Garcia and Greg & Rebecca Sparks, Dez produced and wrote the music for Vigilante Hope, *a recent album by Reunion artist Michael Peace. Dez also produced Peace's latest,* Loud and Clear, *a live rap album recorded in concert in New York. He is currently vice president of A. & R. at Star Song Communications in Nashville, Tennessee, where he lives with his wife, Becki, and his son, Jordan.*

In this thoughtful look back at his growing-up years, Dez is an articulate spokesman for the value of respect for parents, accountability within the family, discipline, and the unconditional love that means security, self-confidence, and encouragement for a child.

When we look back on our childhood, I think we all have a tendency to remember selectively. Most of us recall mainly the good things about our upbringing. I sometimes wonder if the Lord ordained this in order to turn our hearts toward our parents as we grow older and so deepen our appreciation for all they've done for us.

My pastor once told me that no matter what our opinion is of the job our parents did in raising us, we need to understand that they did the best they knew how. It's easy to emphasize the mistakes, the unpleasant incidents, and the times of strife, but I believe that we can just as easily count those things that have proved to be positive and beneficial. My parents would be quick to admit that they made some mistakes, but what they gave me and instilled in me far overshadows those things.

The black family in America faces challenges beyond the questions of social and economic equality. While these are indeed weighty issues, it is important to understand that the system that introduced black people into this country—slavery—was designed to systematically destroy the family. Not only were families torn apart and sold like furniture, but more significantly, black males were emasculated and made to feel powerless and subhuman. As a result, instead of the rich heritage of the work ethic, the rags-to-riches success stories, and the American dream that have been foundational to various immigrant groups that have come to these shores, blacks have a legacy of hopelessness, disappointment, and disenfranchisement. Even today we see that the family—the structure God intended to be the primary means by which we learn how to relate, share, love, cooperate, and achieve success in life—is crippled for many African-Americans.

I've taken the time to establish these facts only to underscore the tremendous odds my parents overcame to raise a family. Having grown up in the pre–civil rights era South, they moved north to Minnesota with hopes for a brighter future and greater opportunity. My mother, having lost her mother when she was four years old, was raised by a series of different relatives and spent most of her childhood in abject poverty. My father's family fared a little better, with my grandfather working backbreaking twelve- to fourteen-hour days lifting heavy tobacco bales for a mere two to three dollars a week. I believe parents universally desire to see their children experience opportunity and prosperity beyond what they themselves have seen, and my parents were no different.

It has been said that the hand that rocks the cradle rules the world. When I was a little boy, my father was working two jobs, and I really only saw him at dinner and on weekends. Though his impact on my life was undeniable (like most boys, I thought my dad was superhuman), it was my mother who influenced those crucial years the most.

Early on, my mother instilled in me a respect for parental authority. In no way did she spare the rod of reproof, and now (though it was definitely not so then) I greatly appreciate the character that results. Right and wrong were not abstract concepts in our home. Neither was spanking some remote possibility we kids could manipulate our way out of. The Word of God teaches us that if we train up children in the way that they should go, when they are older, they will not depart from it (Prov. 22:6). My life bears testimony to this biblical truth. In my young adult years, I tried my hardest to rebel against everyone and everything I could, only to find that the truth dwelt in me so richly that I could no longer deny its power.

To this day, I find myself stunned and repulsed when I witness a child being disrespectful to his parents, and I'm even more grieved when the parents fail to respond with proper parental authority. It is vitally important for Christian parents to avoid being infected with the spirit of the age regarding parenting. Humanistic concepts of so-called values clarification (where children decide for themselves what is right and wrong) and moral relativism have made their way into the church. The contention of the secular "experts" that spanking damages a child has many well-meaning Christian parents obeying psychologists rather than God's Word. If my mother had chosen Dr. Spock over the Word, I don't think I'd be serving God today.

Equally important as respect for authority and accountability was my mother's clear message of unconditional love. I knew that she loved us and would do anything for us, and she showed it by the way she lived every day. Looking back, I can see now how she poured her life into me (and later my younger sister and brother), always giving her best. Nothing was too small (she always took time to soothe a bump, scrape, or bad dream or answer one of a thousand off-the-wall questions) or too big (like making sure birthdays, Christmas, and other special occasions were extra special). In later years, she would tell me that she lived for her children during our growing up years.

Discipline and unconditional love gave me a great sense of security as a young child. I knew I could depend on my mother for anything, and that commitment helped me develop a great deal of self-confidence. My mother spent many hours of quality time with me during my preschool years, teaching me to write (not print, but in cursive!) my name, tie my shoes, and do basic arithmetic and even a little reading. In those days the major educational thrust of kindergarten was tying one's shoes and buttoning one's coat. By the time I reached school age, my mother had given me such a wide variety of educational opportunities that kindergarten almost seemed retrograde.

I recognize now, as an adult, that the time my mother took to invest herself in me equipped me from an early age to believe I was capable of achieving anything. Death and life are truly in the power of the tongue, and my mother spoke life into me during my formative years. I received great encouragement to develop the gifts God had placed within me, whether they were academic, artistic, athletic, or intellectual. My mother always made certain that—regardless of what she may have had to sacrifice in terms of convenience, time, or finances—there were no opportunities for growth, instruction, education, or experience that my siblings or I would miss out on.

During my high-school years when I began to pursue a career in music, my parents were extremely supportive. Their support went beyond merely paying for equipment and lessons. They also encouraged me in my choice. Many of my colleagues were berated, ridiculed, and even shunned by their parents for making such a "foolish" career choice. My parents, by contrast, endured years of the sounds of less-than-accomplished playing emanating from my room. They also eagerly provided rehearsal space in the basement for the succession of fledgling rock bands I played with (from the age of fourteen)—and we rehearsed at an extremely high volume! Like most parents, they had planned to sacrifice financially in order to help pay for my college education. When I chose to forgo college in favor of pursuing a career in music, they loved me enough to encourage me to do what I believed with all my heart I was meant to do.

I don't intend to paint a "Cosby" or "Ozzie and Harriet" picture of my upbringing. We were real people who faced real problems, obstacles, and tribulation. Though he has now been free of it for nearly twelve years, my father was in bondage to alcohol until I was in my early twenties. Alcoholism did not manifest itself in meanness or violence; neither was my father an everyday falling-down drunk. My father's affliction was predictably unpredictable. He would be fine for weeks or months at a time, but then he would suddenly binge for several days. As I grew older, it seemed I could depend on him less and less. Although he was a wonderful dad when he was sober, he was totally self-seeking and irresponsible when he was on a binge. Our family took on the characteristics of his malady, being the picture of domestic harmony and tranquility one day and utterly chaotic the next.

I share this darker side of my upbringing for only one reason. So many in the body of Christ are hindered in their life and walk by the enemy's attempt to use their past to oppress them. Dear friends, Jesus Christ is the Healer, and the Holy Spirit is the Comforter. It is the washing of the Word that makes us both clean and whole, and that same Word renews our mind day by day when we give ourselves, our values, our attitudes, and our perspective over to it. God has provided us with a blueprint for vital, healthy, and successful living, and anyone who is born again has access to the power source that enables us to follow his plan. For those who have received Christ, all things are made new, and we are marvelous, new creations. A newborn babe is not hindered by his past because he has none—and neither do we.

The most damaging and traumatic of childhood experiences need not prevent the believer from being an excellent and godly parent. The Lord himself is our model, and he desires to be that perfect parental example that you may not have had. I had a flawed paternal example of responsibility while I was growing up, but the Holy Spirit, loving and wise pastors, and the Word have shown me what it means to be faithful, to have my *yes* mean yes and my *no* mean no. God is no respecter of persons; he does not play favorites among his own. What he has done for me, he can and will do for you.

Likewise, Satan tries to use the specter of an ungodly upbringing to hold us in bondage to failure, insecurity, and self-doubt in our lives and Christian walk. Both my parents were raised in the church, and we were, in turn, raised in the church. However, it was only when I received Christ in December of 1980 that I came to understand that my experience until then had been merely religious in nature. Had I died knowing the Apostles' Creed and the Ten Commandments but not knowing Jesus, I'd have ended up in the same hell any heathen or pagan ends up in. Some of my friends whose lives are in the worst, most miserably backslidden state were raised in "Christian" homes. Conversely, some of the most vital, world-shaking Christians I know were brought up in completely godless homes. If you had godly parents, rejoice and be quick to follow their example. If you did not, rejoice in the Lord for he is your model. And remember that having Christian parents in and of itself is no guarantee that you will be a godly parent yourself. Living by God's Word is what makes parents godly.

A Lifetime of Friendship

---

*H*ow could I do a book on parenting without asking today's leading Christian expert on the family to contribute? It's a privilege to have Dr. James Dobson share this intimate portrait of his father with us.

Dr. Dobson is founder and president of Focus on the Family, host of a widely listened to daily radio program by the same name, and a well-known writer even outside Christian circles. His first book for parents and teachers, Dare to Discipline, *has now sold more than one million copies. His subsequent eleven books—among them,* What Wives Wish Their Husbands Knew about Women, Straight Talk to Men and Their Wives, The Strong-Willed Child, *and* Parenting Isn't for Cowards—*are also best-sellers. More than sixty million people have seen Dr. Dobson's first film series,* Focus on the Family, *and thirty million have viewed* "Turn Your Heart toward Home" *since its 1986 release.*

Dr. Dobson's expertise on family matters has not escaped the attention of our nation's leaders. Since the Carter administration, he has been honored with appointments to various government commissions and with commendation for his work. He was regularly invited to the White House to consult with President Reagan and his staff on family matters, and more recently he was asked to consult with President Bush on family related matters.

Dr. Dobson is married, the father of two grown children, and a voice of guidance and hope for many parents across our country.

The very happiest days of my growing-up years occurred when I was between ten and thirteen years of age. My dad and I would rise very early before the sun came up on a wintry morning. We'd put on our hunting clothes and heavy boots and drive twenty miles. After parking the car and climbing over a fence, we entered a wooded area where we would slip down to the creek bed and follow the winding stream several miles back into the forest.

Then my dad would hide me under a fallen tree that made a little room with its branches. He would find a similar shelter for himself around a bend in the creek. My dad and I were then ready to watch as the breathtaking panorama of the morning unfolded and spoke so eloquently of the God who made all things.

Most important was what occurred out there in the forest between my dad and me. The intense love and affection generated on those mornings set the tone for a lifetime of friendship. There was a closeness and a oneness that made me want to be like that man . . .

that made me choose his values as my values, his dreams as my dreams, his God as my God.

James C. Dobson, Sr. was a man of many intense loves. His greatest passion was his love for Jesus Christ. His every thought and deed were influenced by his desire to serve his Lord. And I can truthfully say that we were never together without my being drawn closer to God by simply being in my dad's presence.

This man and his Lord had a very unusual relationship. It often involved sessions of prayer and communion that lasted from four to six hours and focused especially on his ministry and on those whom he loved. During the early years of his ministry, he was known in Sulphur Springs, Texas, as "the man with no leather on the toes of his shoes." It was true. He wore out the toes before the soles because he spent so much time on his knees in prayer. At twenty-four years of age, he felt totally inadequate to lead his flock unless he spent many hours every day in communion with God. The Lord must have been listening because he blessed my father's ministry abundantly throughout the next forty-two years.

And one of those blessings has been his special partnership with me in my ministry to families. Let me explain. Two years before he died, he shared an experience that occurred while he had been praying and reading the Bible. He seemed almost embarrassed to reveal the details, but I coaxed him to tell me the story. It involved an overwhelming impression, almost a divine decree, that he and I were going to cooperate on a very important project. The months rolled by, and I filed the matter under the broad heading "Things I don't understand about the Lord."

Then came my father's initial heart attack. When we got the news, two friends rushed me to the airport. On the way, God had reminded me of his revelation to my dad: "You are going to write a book for husbands and fathers based on the life of your dad. The inspiration will be derived from his values, his dedication, his walk with me. This is the joint venture of which I spoke two years ago."

When I arrived at the hospital, I learned that my dad was doing remarkably better, and we had the chance to talk about the Lord's reminder to me as I had gone to the airport. I explained to my dad that his part of the project was already completed: It involved sixty-six years of integrity and devotion and love. Throughout my childhood, I had watched him at home where it was impossible for him to hide his true character. Never once did I see him compromise with evil or abandon the faith by which he lived. His character had been like a beacon for me, illuminating my way. The result of our partnership was a book entitled *Straight Talk to Men and Their Wives,* which has now sold more than a million copies.

My dad was a wise man, but very few people fully comprehended the depth of his love of learning. He had an insatiable desire to know, alternating regularly between biology, physics, astronomy, ecology, theology, politics, medicine, and the arts. Yes, my dad loved everything God made.

He especially loved furry little canines called toy terriers, and our Penny was a brilliant representative of that breed. We adopted him into the family when I was thirteen, and the two of us grew up together. He and my dad had a special understanding of one another. They were like two old friends who could communicate deep feelings without uttering a word.

But, alas, Penny grew old and decrepit. At seventeen, he was afflicted with a terminal case of cancer and was obviously experiencing severe pain. Hour after hour he would walk the fence and moan. My dad knew the time had come to put his little friend to sleep, but he couldn't bring himself to do it. "How can I kill my dog?" he would ask.

But it was more cruel to let Penny suffer, so Dad made an appointment with the veterinarian to discuss the matter. The doctor recognized how painful this event was for my father. He shared a similar situation with reference to his own dog, and these two grown men sat and wept together.

The decision was made to end Penny's life, and the day was chosen. Throughout the afternoon, a man and a dog sat together under the vine-covered arbor in their backyard. Neither spoke. (Penny communicated his thoughts with his ears and eyes and tail.) I suspect they both cried. Then they said good-bye for the final time.

My father grieved for Penny for several years. His ability to experience deep emotions made him much more vulnerable to the vicissitudes of life, but his sensitivity was worth the price he paid for it.

And nowhere was that special sensitivity more obvious than in my father's relationship with my mother. My dad loved my mother with great intensity and was deeply committed to her. Before they were married, he spelled out to her his conviction that "the marriage vows are inviolable, and by entering into them, I am binding myself absolutely and for life. The idea of estrangement from you through divorce for any reason at all (although God allows one—infidelity) will never at any time be allowed to enter into my thinking."

My mother was a godly woman, deeply devoted to her husband and wise when it came to raising her kids. I remember her test of my independence when I was seventeen. My folks were going on a two-week car trip and leaving me behind with the family car and permission to invite my (male) friends to spend the fourteen nights at our home. I remember being surprised by this move and the obvious risk my parents were taking. I wondered if they were wise to give me that much latitude.

I behaved responsibly while my folks were gone, but I always wanted to know why my mother took that risk. After I was grown and married, I asked her. She smiled and replied, "Because I knew in approximately one year you would be leaving for college where you would have complete freedom with no one to tell you how to behave. And I wanted to expose you to that independence while you were still under my influence." My mother exemplified two important child-rearing principles: She knew how to hold me with an open hand, and she knew how to hold me close and then let me go.

I knew my mother dearly loved my father, and I saw the depths of her passion after she died. Her journal entry tells of the agony she felt even a year after my father had gone to be with the Lord: "It's been one year and three days since you died, and tonight I am frantic with longing for you. Oh, dear God! It's more than I can bear. The sobs make my heart skip beats. I cannot see the paper. My head throbs. The house is lonely and still. Visions of you have been as real as if you were here and had not left me. Today, I thank God for letting an angel watch over me. But how desperately I miss you!"

God was the author of my mother's love for my father, and he melted the two of them into "one flesh." When she quietly slipped into eternity, finally free of the ravages of Parkinson's disease, I had to smile. I pictured her having been swept into the loving arms of the Savior whom she had served faithfully since she was a girl. And I know my father was there, too, embracing her in one of the great reunions of all time. My two dear parents—two of God's faithful and devoted servants—are now forever with the Lord.

I grew up knowing that my folks loved each other and that they loved me. I've known my dad loved me from my earliest moments of awareness, and I've known it in my adult years. I will long remember and be indebted to his words of tough love back in 1969. I was running at an incredible speed, working myself to death just like every other man I knew. Although my activities were bringing me professional advancement and the trappings of financial success, my dad was not impressed. He had watched my hectic lifestyle and felt obligated to express his concern. He did so in a lengthy letter that included the following paragraph:

I have observed that the greatest delusion is to suppose that our children will be devout Christians simply because their parents have been or that any of them will enter into the Christian faith in any other way than through their parents' deep travail of prayer and faith. But this prayer demands time, time that cannot be given if it is all signed and conscripted and laid on the altar of career ambition. Failure for you at this point would make mere success in your occupation a very pale and washed-out affair indeed.

Those words, written without accusation or insult, hit me like the blow of a hammer. My father reminded me that my number one responsibility is to evangelize my own children, as he had me.

My father had a generous assortment of flaws, but I loved him perhaps as much as any son ever loved his dad. He was my lifelong friend, my role model, a true inspiration, and a great man—great because of his uncompromising dedication to the Christian faith. And if I can be half the father to Danae and Ryan that he was to me, they will be fortunate children indeed.

Danae Dobson

Memories of a
Great Childhood

C an you imagine growing up the daughter of a well-
known expert on children and the family? Danae Dobson seems to have weathered very well the unique childhood
experience of being the test case of Dr. James Dobson's biblical
child-raising principles.

A delightful and confident young woman, Danae knows
she has benefitted greatly from her parents' devotion to Christ
and their deep and committed love for her. She feels that her
childhood and teenage years—she went to a public high
school—were more normal than might be expected. But when
she first went off to Azusa Pacific University, Danae remembers being watched closely by Christian peers who recognized
the name Dobson.

As Danae shares here, her parents practiced what they
write and teach about: Jim and Shirley Dobson always had
time for her; they made Danae and her brother, Ryan, their
priority; and they offered loving and constant support for
their children. And, perhaps the greatest tribute to her parents, Danae looks forward to passing along to her own
children the love and faith that she received from them. In

fact, through her Woof series of ten children's books (300,000 are in print), Danae is already sharing her faith with the youngest members of God's family.

It was a warm Sunday afternoon several weeks prior to my fourth birthday, and our family had just finished eating the big noon meal. I was still wearing my frilly church dress with my shiny patent leather shoes and lace-trimmed white socks. It was a fine day to be sure, but there was trouble ahead. The dreaded time had come to shed all those pretty clothes and lie down for a much-hated nap. There had to be a better way to spend a sunny afternoon!

At that moment, to my complete delight, my father entered the room and said, "Let's go for a bike ride, kid!" Excited, I ran along beside him as he retrieved his yellow ten-speed from the garage. Then he showed me the new passenger seat he had bought the day before. He carefully bolted it to the bar that held the frame together and then sat me there between his arms. We were ready to roll!

Unfortunately, my dad had made a fundamental mistake. He had positioned the seat too far forward, placing my feet in reach of the front wheel. Neither of us recognized the danger, however. We flew down the driveway and banked precariously onto the street in front of our house. Within seconds we were tearing through the neighborhood with the wind blowing through our hair. Even now, all these years later, I remember the thrill of riding that huge bicycle with my father!

The excitement was short lived. Somehow, I managed to thrust my left foot into the spokes of the front wheel. The entire weight of the speeding bicycle was locked on my ankle, throwing me to the pavement and launching my dad over the handlebars. My tooth was knocked loose, my foot was bloodied and swollen, and my little white shoe was chewed to pieces. It was a terrifying experience.

Although I remember the pain of that accident today, another memory is more prominent in my mind. I can still recall my six-foot-two-inch father picking himself up off the street and running back to my side. He gathered me in his arms and ran to the house. The bicycle was left upside-down in the road where it had crashed. My father cried as he ran, and I heard him say, "I'm so sorry, babe. I'm so sorry I hurt you!" Over and over he said it. I really think he was in greater pain than I was.

Somehow, the tenderness of my father on that distressing afternoon has come to symbolize his love for me through the years. Those arms that cradled me after the accident have always been there to offer a hug in times of challenge and frustration. Certainly, most fathers love and care for their children, especially when they are hurting. But the relationship with my dad was different. I *knew* I was special to him—that he was pulling for me and praying for me during each of the small crises that came my way. It's what every little girl needs from a father.

My dad was very busy when I was a child, but I could always manage to get his attention. I can still see him sitting at his desk during my preschool years. He was in the final year of his doctoral studies at the University of Southern California, and the pressures were intense. Nevertheless, my brother and I took priority. I would climb on the chair behind him and spend an hour or two on his lap or even on his shoulders. He never seemed to mind. Every now and then he would stop to toss me in the air or play a game. These moments, even more than gifts and surprises, were the way he expressed genuine love to this wide-eyed child.

My mother was also dedicated to her family. She was a full-time homemaker who poured all her energy into the lives of the people she loved. A former second-grade teacher, she made an enjoyable lesson out of each event and every encounter.

Indeed, Shirley Dobson is a woman of many talents. Through the years, she had collected an array of festive activities and suggestions for each holiday. In 1978, she and Gloria Gaither coauthored a book of their ideas entitled *Let's Make a Memory*. Nearly one-half million people have bought this book and implemented its concepts into their own family experiences.

One example included in *Let's Make a Memory* came right out of our own family traditions. Each year at Christmastime we have a "candlelight ceremony." Everyone sits in a circle and holds an unlighted candle. One at a time, we share something from the previous year we're thankful to God for and something we're hoping for in the new year. After one individual has shared, he or she lights the next person's candle, and it continues until all the candles are lighted.

This has always been one of my favorite traditions,

representing the unity of our family and dependence upon the Lord. It gives all of us a sense of spiritual renewal and optimism for the coming year. My mother originated this ceremony, and it will certainly be passed down to the generations to come.

In an age when there are so many broken homes and abused and battered children, it is a profound blessing to have enjoyed a stable, happy home life. No, it didn't prevent me from experiencing pain and heartache at various times. But it did provide me with a secure foundation that made the challenges more manageable.

The world is filled with heartache, as we all know. Even children who escape life's more difficult traumas still have to deal with pain and suffering in some form. There are moments when everyone feels lonely and rejected. There are times when we all fall victim to the ridicule and scorn of others. It is in these situations that the security of a good family is critical.

I know a father who described the rejection his three-year-old daughter experienced. She had no one but older children to play with in the neighborhood, and often the bigger kids would ignore her or exclude her from their games. The little girl couldn't understand why they refused to play with her, and she tried mightily to gain their acceptance.

One day, after following the older children around all morning, she suddenly came tearing into the house.

"Mommy! Mommy!" she shouted. "Give me Popsicles—I want lots of Popsicles!"

Her mother was suspicious, but she granted the

child's request. The little girl went running out the door with six Popsicles in her hands.

The mother watched as her vulnerable daughter ran to where the older children were playing baseball. The little girl stood at the fence and held out her hands, hoping they would see the Popsicles and want to be her friend.

But no one noticed. Still, she stood holding out the Popsicles through the fence.

Finally, one of the kids saw her and shouted, "Hey, look! Popsicles!" The boys and girls ran to the fence and grabbed the frozen treats from her hands without even saying "thank you." Then they ran off to play again, leaving the child standing alone. Her Popsicles were gone and so were her "friends."

Her mother stood breathlessly at the window as the sad little three-year-old turned to walk back to the house. She had given everything she had to please the big kids, but still they rejected her.

Haven't we all been through moments like this— times when we gave the best we had to offer and still the world failed to notice? We tried to buy friendship but were left alone and bewildered in the end. Such is the experience of every child, especially during the isolation and self-doubt of adolescence. How desperately we need the loving support of a mother and father to assure us of our value when no one else will. That kind of support has been my heritage in the Dobson household.

Not too long ago, I dropped by my parents' house on a Friday night to pick up something. A week earlier I had broken up with a guy I had been dating for quite some time, and I was still struggling to regain my balance.

As my car turned into the driveway, I saw my mom and dad walking toward the street. They were going for a stroll around the neighborhood and asked if I wanted to join them. I reluctantly agreed.

As we walked, I began to share my feelings and the grief I was experiencing. They listened and talked to me for almost an hour. We must have circled the block five times! I will never forget how my dad prayed for me that night before I went home. It gave me comfort to know that, even though an important relationship had ended, my family was still there. I'm sure that's why I was able to land on my feet and cope so well.

My mother and father are not perfect parents. They would be the first to admit their shortcomings. But they have never wavered in two all-consuming commitments: their devotion to Jesus Christ and their love for my brother, Ryan, and me. That kind of devotion covers a multitude of imperfections in the relationship between parent and child.

Someday soon, perhaps, it will be my task to pass along that love and faith to my own children. There is no higher calling in life.

Passion and Wonder

This glimpse into Joni Eareckson Tada's childhood will reveal her to be the warm and genuine person known by many of you through her books, her radio program, her music, and her art.

Joni is founder and president of Joni and Friends and the Christian Fund for the Disabled. She serves on the National Council on Disability to which she was appointed by President Reagan in 1987. She is also vice president of the Christian Council on Persons with Disabilities, a national consortium of Christian ministries serving disabled persons.

In 1976, Joni broke her neck in a diving accident that left her paralyzed from the shoulders down. Her story is known by many people around the world who have read one or more of her twelve best-selling books, including her autobiography, Joni, *or have seen the full-length feature film of the same name.*

With heart-wrenching honesty, Joni wrote about the difficulty she had accepting God's sovereignty in her paralysis in A Step Further. *Her subsequent books include* Choices . . . Changes, All God's Children, Friendship Unlimited, Secret Strength, Glorious Intruder, *and, her newest,* A

Christmas Longing. *She has also written books for children and recorded four albums, including her most recent,* Let God Be God.

Here, you'll learn about Joni's mother and father, two very special people in her life. As she shares with you her passion and wonder for life—two gifts from her parents—I know you'll find yourself refreshed and encouraged.

What did my parents do right? Even thirty years ago, I would have said what I say now—Mom and Dad were at the top. Funny thing is, my parents were anything but conventional. We never had traditional family devotions; my mother was the chief disciplinarian, and my parents never made a big deal about us staying up late.

My three sisters and I agree that our folks did a great job, and we enjoy the fact that Mom and Dad instilled in us rather unusual childhood enthusiasms. When I was a five-year-old, for instance, my passion was not to watch "The Mickey Mouse Club," but to snuggle next to my dad on the back porch, watch the moon rise, and then name all the constellations in the summer sky. Although there was a drawback—we became "night" rather than "morning" people—we learned early what passion and wonder are all about.

And God, I learned from my parents, was a great part of that passion and wonder. Mom and Dad were wise enough to broaden my knowledge of God beyond going to Sunday school, saying grace at dinner, and memorizing a lot of Bible verses. They understood that every dimension of our lives is indeed spiritual. As a result, every family function was sacred. We learned to love God and grasp intangibles like insight, wisdom, and fairness as much from mastering table manners as from getting to church on time.

If I were to pick out a verse that best describes the way my parents raised us, it would be Deuteronomy 11:18-19—"Fix these words of mine in your hearts and minds. . . . Teach them to your children, talking about them when you sit at home and when you walk along the road, when you lie down and when you get up" (NIV). That passage underscores the fact that every family function can and should be sacred.

Color and excitement characterized many of our lessons about God. When we'd go camping on the beach, nighttime stories around the fire included not only the real-life escapades of my father hunting bear and trading with the Indians but the real-life adventures of Noah, David, and Moses. Dad would talk about the days when he sailed clipper ships and explored the upper Yukon, but he'd also talk about Moses, brave and trusting, exploring the wilderness of the desert beyond Egypt. Wherever he led us in his stories, we knew that the people he loved were real, were adventurers, and were in love with life.

It was one thing to learn about God's creation by listening to stories or reading the Bible, but that creation came to life on each family outing. While horseback riding through the woods with my family, I learned at an early age the difference between oaks, maples, poplars, and elms. Along the trail, Daddy would point out the tracks of different animals. We learned to respect and not disturb the anthills and spiderwebs, and we also learned to leave the most delicate blossom untouched for the next passerby to enjoy.

My mother carried the "every family function is sacred" theme into the home. She made certain that we handled our knives and forks properly and learned good table manners. We were taught the proper way to pass platters and knives. It was important to answer the phone politely and to greet guests cordially.

Neither was responsibility for weekly chores taken lightly. In fact, family work days taught us spiritual lessons. When I was still small, my mother would often take me to Grandmom's house on cleaning days. I would help her carry in the buckets, the mops, and the Spic 'n' Span, and then she would delegate one corner of the kitchen floor for me to scrub with my little sponge. That was something I could definitely handle.

Thankfully, she didn't expect me to scrub the entire kitchen—that would have been more than a little demoralizing. But I did just fine with my corner, and I noticed that, as I got older, the size of my corner grew. The time came when I was expected to clean the entire kitchen floor—plus the countertop and appliances. My mother so delegated the responsibility that I didn't resent the increased workload. Instead I welcomed it as a sign that I was an "adult."

Music and art were especially sacred in our family. It was not uncommon to sit around the dinner table after dessert and sing a few old hymns. Even weekend trips in the car were a treat as we invented beautiful harmonies to help the miles pass quickly. I shall never forget sitting in the backseat of my mother's old Buick, near tears, thinking, *This is so beautiful . . . and I'm helping to make it sound this way.* Sometimes I would simply stop singing just to listen. Somehow, we always knew that we were making music to the Lord.

Even piano lessons were no chore—my heart would break just to master the sweet sounds of a simple concerto. What pleased me most—even more than having my parents attend my piano recitals—was to watch, out of the corner of my eye, my dad slip into the living-room chair behind the piano stool and listen to me practice. That action told me he cared more than mere words ever could.

My life at school was not out of the realm of my parents' interest or involvement. They would come after school to watch me play field hockey, and they always had time to meet and talk with a new friend. They wanted to hear about my science project and read my English compositions. The fact that my mom still has my old drawings from elementary school art classes reinforces what I believed then—she and Dad thought I had real talent. Their appreciation of my music, writing, and art made me want to do better and please them more.

I have very early memories of my dad stirring up my interest in art. Often when he was busy at his easel mixing oils and painting on his canvas, I'd sit on the floor at his side with my crayons and coloring book and work just as hard as he was. He'd set his brushes aside, reach down, and lift me up onto his lap. He would then fix my hand on one of his brushes and enfold his larger, stronger hand around mine. Then he'd guide my hand and the brush, dipping it into the palette and mixing burnt umbers and raw siennas. We would stroke the wet, shiny paint on the canvas before us, and I'd watch with amazement. More passion and more wonder for God's world around me!

Painting with my father was sacred because, more than teaching his youngest daughter how to paint, he was teaching me a valuable lesson about God's compassion. Psalm 103:13 says, "As a father has compassion on his children, so the LORD has compassion on those who fear him" (NIV). As a child, I was learning that God cares in a personal, heartfelt way—just like my dad.

I was reminded of God's care each night as my parents put me to bed. They had hung a plaque over my bed. It was a silhouette of a little girl in a tiny rowboat out on the ocean. She was surrounded by a dark night sprinkled with stars. Under the scene were the words "Dear God, my little boat and I are on your open sea. Please guide us safely through the waves, my little boat and me." As I gazed at that plaque, it amazed me that the girl was apparently not afraid of being out on the open sea at night. I remember thinking, *Wow! That little girl really trusts God—but I wonder where her parents are? I'm glad mine are here.*

Looking back, my parents took obvious care in making my bedroom a safe and secure place. Daddy had painted angels on one part of the ceiling and had pasted star-studded wallpaper on the rest. When they turned out the lights, the stars would glow. As I went to sleep, I'd look up at the stars, smile at the angels, and know that I was as safe as the little girl on the plaque.

A camping trip to Ocean City, Maryland, horseback

rides through the state park that bordered our farm, helping Mom make tapioca pudding for a late-night dessert—these are warm and positive recollections of a caring family. And the Lord Jesus was in it all. We spoke of him at our dinner table, praised him on moonlit hikes, and sang of him around the fire on our camping trips. It was my parents' way—and, most importantly, God's way—of preparing my heart for the time when I would come into the kingdom. I accepted Christ at age fourteen.

My Christian experience from then on was the slow and sometimes painful discovery that the fear of the Lord is the beginning of wisdom as well as passion and wonder. My mom and dad had sketched the broad background, but now I was to be responsible for what God revealed to me concerning him. Prudence, wisdom, discretion, discernment of right and wrong—none of these things were going to come either easily or quickly, especially after I was injured at age seventeen.

The accident in which I became paralyzed put me in a stark, dreary, and often depressing institution for nearly two years. Warm and sunlit memories of my growing-up years then became a rich source of comfort and joy as I lay in that dull and colorless place. I'll never forget the time my family brought in environmental recordings of thunderstorms, birds in a forest, and the crashing of ocean waves. I closed my eyes and was at once transported to the crackling campfire at our sandy beach.

The unity of my family, their pulling together after my disabling injury, helped push me toward eventual acceptance. I had learned as a child to be responsible for my actions. I was now to learn as a teenager in a wheelchair to be responsible for my attitudes and choices. I was still that little girl on the plaque—the one in the tiny rowboat, alone out on the open sea— but it was time to find the shore. I put childish things behind me and was literally pushed into the Word of God out of my desperate need. In its pages I discovered, as it says in Proverbs, that "the name of the LORD is a strong tower; the righteous run to it and are safe" (18:10, NIV).

For many years, my parents had tilled and nurtured the soil of my soul, giving me a willing heart to eventually accept the seeds of God's Word. But one other important thing has remained through all the years, too—I have never lost the passion and wonder, the joy of seizing the moment. Of the many good lessons I learned and the many joys we shared, pulling out of me passion and wonder was probably the most "right" thing my parents did.

Simple Blessings

◆————————————————————————◆

After serving in the Navy, Carl Erskine lived out the dream of many an American boy and played twelve major league baseball seasons with the Dodgers—ten in Brooklyn, New York, and two in Los Angeles, California. During those years, he won 122 games and lost 78; among his wins are two World Series victories. Carl also pitched two no-hit, no-run games, one against the Cubs in 1952 and the other against the Giants in 1956. In 1953, he led the National League with twenty wins and six losses, and he held the World Series single-game strikeout record of fourteen against the Yankees in 1953. And that was just one of the five World Series he participated in, playing in a total of eleven games.

Carl retired from professional baseball in 1960, but that wasn't the end of his involvement with the sport. At Anderson University, his alma mater, Carl coached the baseball team to four championships during his twelve seasons there.

Carl was a licensed agent for Midwestern United Life from 1960 to 1975. He is currently president of First National Bank in Anderson, Indiana, a position he has held since 1982.

A charter member and life trustee of Fellowship of Chris-

tian Athletes, Carl is also a national representative for the Special Olympics and a trustee at Anderson University.

Carl appreciates his dad for much more than the baseball tips he shared. This look back into a loving family who knew how to be faithful with the little they had during the depression will remind you of the simple blessings of life.

The first memory I have of my childhood is when I was three years old. I was playing in our fenced-in yard when a woman walked to the fence from the sidewalk and said, "Hello, sonny. Do you know where Mr. Amos lives?" I had watched my dad and mother help people who stopped to ask for directions, so I pointed to the house next door and proudly said, "Yes, right over there." This scene says much about what my parents were like: They were helpful, caring people who had the ability to give simple things a touch of real value.

I was born just before the Great Depression, so I grew up during very difficult economic times. My dad worked for Delco Remy, a division of General Motors. My two older brothers, Lloyd and Donald, had a variety of jobs, and we lived a very modest lifestyle. I refuse to use the word *poor* because we weren't. Oh yes, we did rent our house, we walked everywhere we went, we ate one-dish meals, and we lived from one paycheck to the next—but our clothes were clean, and there was a feeling of pride in making what we had be more than enough.

My mother had a large, white bowl, and many of

our one-dish meals were served from that large bowl. Often when we had finished our meal, Mom would fill the bowl with what was left in the pan on the stove (dumplings, stew, or soup), spread a cloth over the bowl, and say, "Carl, take this down to the Case family." This family lived four houses away. The father was doing his best to raise his six children; their mother had died. Welfare was helping them, but so was our little extra. This simple, caring attitude gave me a sense of appreciation for what we had and kept me from feeling sorry about what we didn't have.

When I was a kid, my buddies and I would take aluminum or other scrap metal to Phillip's Junkyard, hoping to get a nickel or a dime. On Mother's Day when I was twelve, I took my dime and bought my mother a fern at the five-and-ten-cent store. Was she proud of that little plant! She cared for it, and it grew and grew. In time, it was huge, spilling over the sides of its large container. She had it for years, and she never let me forget how much she appreciated that little fern. Again, she had made something beautiful out of very little.

I remember how hard my parents worked and how they still seemed to always have time for family things. We popped popcorn almost every night and played games around the kitchen table. My dad loved baseball. He had a very accurate throwing arm and had been a good sandlot player. In the summer when he came home from work, my brothers and I would be waiting with our gloves and baseball to play catch with him. He loved to throw and taught me how to make an overhand delivery, something I used many years later in the big leagues.

What really excited me about my dad coming home from work, though, was the surprise he always had in his lunch bucket for me. He always managed to save me something from whatever my mother had packed in his lunch that morning—half a Twinkie, a piece of apple, or a bite of a candy bar. The best part was knowing that my dad was thinking about me even when he was away.

Dad wasn't always so gentle, though. I could get by with almost any kind of boyhood mischief, but there was no excuse for not telling the truth. When I didn't, I would get the razor strop—the one that hung in our bathroom where he shaved and where he would strop his straight razor to keep it sharp. I also always got that strop with my pants down—hide to hide! Dad would say, "Take it like a man 'cause if you cry, I'll give you another one." I didn't cry very much. Just one good stroke was enough!

As I grew up, Mom was always at home, and she could get more done, stretch a dollar farther, and stay happy better than anyone I know. She canned, wallpapered, crocheted, quilted, cooked, baked, and never seemed to run out of energy. All the while she would be singing, usually a good old church hymn like "Love Lifted Me" or "In the Garden." (Even now, sometimes when I'm pressured and tense, I think of my mother and recall the words she sang. I always feel better.)

Mom also did weekly laundry for Dr. Nesbit. When it was ironed and ready, she would carefully stack the sheets, shirts, and dresses in my wagon and cover the load with a piece of her own white sheet. Then I would deliver it to Dr. Nesbit's house several blocks away. When I got there, Mrs. Nesbit would fill my wagon with another load of dirty laundry for me to take back home. Years later I learned that my mother was paying for mastoid surgery I had to have when I was nine.

My mother lived life with a deep sense of gratitude. She taught me to look for the good in everything and to appreciate the small daily blessings of life. One of those blessings came on Monday. Mom always washed on Mondays. The old Maytag and the double tubs would be out in the kitchen, and when I ran home from school for lunch, the house would be all steamed up. I had to fix my own lunch, and it was always the same: a plain cheese sandwich and a Pepsi that I bought for a nickel on my way home. It was the only Pepsi I got for the week, and, boy, was it good! Today, whenever I drink a bottle of Pepsi, I savor it more than any other drink.

When my mother was in her nineties, I would take her to church even though she was frail and hardly knew anyone—including me. But she would ride along looking out of the car window and exclaim excitedly, "Oh, look at that beautiful tree and that wonderful green grass!" In church, she would know every hymn and sing every word. Mom never lost her gratitude for the simple things that life offered.

I now have a wonderful wife, Betty, a great family of my own, and an ongoing appreciation for the simple things. Much of that appreciation comes from lessons from our youngest son, Jimmy. Betty and I had three healthy, athletic, and wonderful children—Dan,

Gary, and Susan. When Jimmy was born and I saw him in the nursery, I had this sudden and devastating feeling that something was terribly wrong. We soon learned that Jimmy had Down's syndrome, a genetic disorder that causes both physical and mental handicaps. Not before or after has anything ever hit us so hard, and we were so unprepared.

Betty was the real strength at this point, and she said that Jimmy was going home with us to be a part of the family just like our other kids. I remember going home that day to the other kids (Dan, twelve; Gary, ten; and Susan, five), sitting them down on the sofa, and telling them about their new little brother and the special needs he would have. From that day on, all three of them were great about bringing their friends home and treating their kid brother very naturally.

Mrs. Gaunt, a woman in our church, stopped me in the aisle one Sunday and said, "Now, Carl, I want you to read the Bible to that boy. Don't you worry about whether he understands it or not. You just read it to him and pray with him." Well, Jimmy is very limited. His speech is poor, and he gives little indication that he understands what you say. We did read the Bible, though, and we prayed with Jim. Recently at Christmastime, about thirty-five family members gathered at our house for Christmas dinner. Like most families, we hadn't been together for a while and several birthdays needed to be recognized. Betty set a birthday cake on the table and lighted the candles. We sang "Happy Birthday" first to a niece, then to Grandma, an uncle, and so on. Each time, Jimmy would blow out the candles, and we would start again.

Finally, we had finished with all the birthdays and were leaving the table when we heard Jimmy start the song again. Thinking that he wanted to blow out the candles one more time, we all gathered back around the table and let Jimmy lead us: "'Appy burr-day to you, 'appy burr-day to you, 'appy burr-day, Baby Jesus, 'appy burr-day to you." Mrs. Gaunt was right. We parents don't need to try to keep score. We just need to do the right thing.

Today, times are so different, lifestyles are so varied, and pressures are so overwhelming that it seems impossible to be the kind of parents that I had in times past. But I don't believe that people have really changed that much. In fact, in today's fast-paced world, a little caring, a gesture of genuine interest, or an unselfish act really stands out and has great positive impact.

I like the prayer, "Lord, don't make life easier; make me stronger." That's a perfect prayer for parents. My parents didn't have life easy, but they showed me that strength can come from a genuine appreciation of the simple blessings in life. Christ promised that if we are faithful with little, we will gain much (Matt. 25:14-23).

Colleen Townsend Evans

Spring-Loaded
for Fun

❖————————————————————————❖

W hat an encouraging portrait of a single-parent family! You'll enjoy the sense of fun and appreciate the trust that characterized Colleen Evans's special relationship with her mother.

And because of all that her mother did right, Colleen went on to become a wife, a mother, a writer, and a woman actively serving in a variety of ministries. Her ministry as the wife of a Presbyterian pastor began in 1950 when she married Louis H. Evans, Jr. They spent the first years of their married life at San Francisco Theological Seminary in San Anselmo, California, and then two years at New College, University of Edinburgh, Scotland. Colleen and Lou then served at Bel Air Presbyterian Church in Los Angeles and La Jolla Presbyterian Church in La Jolla, California, the National Presbyterian Church in Washington, D.C., and now in part-time ministry at Menlo Park Presbyterian Church in Menlo Park, California. Colleen and Lou have four adult children—Dan, Tim, James, and Andie.

Colleen is the author of several books, among them A Deeper Joy, Love Is an Everyday Thing, Start Loving:

The Miracle of Forgiveness, Teaching Your Child to Pray, *and* Vine Life. *She and Lou have coauthored a book on marriage entitled* Bold Commitment.

Colleen is also a member of the board of Presbyterians for Renewal, board of directors of World Vision, U.S., and is personally involved in a church-related inner-city ministry to the poor. She was chair of the Greater Washington Billy Graham Crusade in April 1986.

◆————————————————————————◆

Her name was Stella. She was young and exceedingly attractive when her husband left her—and their baby—and never returned. It was rough going.

The depression was at its height. Jobs were scarce, and even if her husband had been gainfully employed—which at the time he was not—it is doubtful Stella would have sought alimony or even child support. She was that hurt, that proud, and that determined to make it on her own.

With only a few office skills and her high-school diploma in hand, she felt fortunate to land a job in an insurance office where she worked from eight to five, five days a week, plus a half day on Saturday—for twenty-five dollars a week. It was hardly a good schedule for a woman totally committed to being a loving and responsible single parent, but that's the way it was, and somehow she made it work. I know because Stella was my mother, and I will be forever grateful to the Lord for giving me such an incredible parent.

Those were difficult years for most Americans. Fam-

ilies learned to pull together, and that's what we did.
In order to manage financially, we moved in with my
mother's elderly and widowed father. He provided the
house, and she made the house a home. Every morning she left for work at seven, and she got home at six.
Her evenings were spent doing what most women did
during the day, and she did it all on a budget that
would challenge even the most frugal homemaker.
Looking back, I realize how difficult those early years
must have been for her and how hard she had to work
to provide a simple home for the three of us. We were
poor—by the world's standards—but I didn't know it.
She didn't dwell on the sacrifices she obviously was
making for me, so I didn't grow up feeling guilty.

My mother and I were such pals! It seemed to me
that we had more fun together than many of my
friends had with either or both of their parents. That
was one of the many things my mother did right. In
the midst of the daily struggle simply to survive and
the very real pain she experienced over her broken
marriage, she managed to *have* fun and *be* fun. She did
not allow the grim circumstances of her life to turn
her into a grim person.

Even as I write those words, I ask, "How did she do
it? What did she do that was 'fun'? Be specific, Colleen." And I realize that she didn't *do* anything, really.
She was too busy doing all she had to do. There was
no time or money for special events, parties, gifts, or
vacations. No, it was not what she did; it was who she
was. "Stella is so much fun," her friends would say—
and that was it. She was not at all a Pollyanna. She was
practical, realistic, and quick to speak her mind and

call a spade a spade. She carried a heavy load of responsibility that she took very seriously. But she was a woman anointed with mirth and gladness, spring-loaded for fun, ready in an instant to give a wink, pull a prank, dance a jig. And that was a real gift to me. In fact, rather than feeling deprived as the only child of a single parent, I felt I had an enriched childhood because Stella was so much fun!

There was another thing my mother did right. She trusted me. I was still young when my grandfather, whom I loved deeply, died. That meant my mother had to leave me from early morning until six at night while she was at work. I was old enough to get myself to school on time and home again, but there were many hours every day when I was on my own. My mother was a model of moral and ethical standards both in princi-ple and in practice—and she shared those convictions with me. She laid down guidelines and boundaries for me, but again it was not what she did in a structured way as much as who she was that really made the difference. Her attitude towards me was always one of trust. She had to trust me and she did.

Years later, when I was grown and had children of my own, she shared with me the struggle she had during those years when—against every instinct in her being—she left me alone day after day. Appar-ently she often spent her hour-long morning bus ride to the office holding back tears and praying. Al-though she was not particularly religious, she had a deeply spiritual dimension, and she would fervently ask God to keep me from harm of any kind. She prayed for God to nurture within me a character worthy of trust. Surely God's grace is available in powerful ways to all parents, but I believe it is especially so for single parents who have to trust God and their children in unique situations. But even with God's faithful love and care, it wasn't easy. With wavering voice, my normally unemotional mother confessed those to be the most agonizing years of her life. But her trust in God and in her child brought her through. And all through our life together trust was the core of our relationship.

When I was fourteen and a Hollywood film contract beckoned, my mother neither pushed nor held me back. She said, in essence, "It's your decision, honey. If it is what you want, Hollywood won't change you. I know you. I trust you." Years later when I came to faith in Christ, my life was radically redirected and everything began to change. Again, her response was one of trust: "I don't quite understand it all, dear. But I see how much it means to you, so it must be right." And still later when I left my career to go where I sensed God was leading, she made no attempt to talk me out of that decision either. While other people around me lamented the financial and professional "sacrifice" I would be making, my mother was unwavering in her confidence and support: "I only want what is right for you, for your happiness. If you think this is what God wants of you, do it. I am with you all the way." At each crossroads, my mother said, "I trust you."

Through the years, my mother's spiritual heart and simple belief in God became a true faith and trust in Jesus Christ. She joined and was active in a church, and you might even say she became a little "religious."

But consistent with her God-given personality, it was not so much what she said or did that made her so. It was who she was and how she lived.

My mother's willingness to trust me has been an incredible gift. God used my mother and that trust to give me a sense of security and the desire to give to our children the same depth of commitment and trust in them that my mother gave to me. But that isn't all. God also used my mother to teach me to have fun, not as a separate event, but as an integral part of all the work, the responsibility, and even the agonies of parenting.

As if to remind me and our whole family of that truth, my mother acted it out in a very memorable vignette. Louis and I and our four children had stopped by her house for a visit when we were on vacation. After we had enjoyed one of her incredible meals, she walked with us to the car. As we said our hasty good-byes and fastened our seat belts, she stood by the curb, lifted her tailored skirt above her knees, and did a fancy little jig. Our teenaged children, who absolutely adored their grandmother Mimi, roared with laughter. As we pulled away from the curb, my mother, still dancing her jig, called, "Hey, hey! Not bad for an old girl, eh?" That's the last memory my children have of her life on this earth. Not bad, Mom. Not bad at all.

James Evans

Love That
Takes Risks

◆━━━━━━━━━━━━━━━━━━━━━━━━━━━◆

*J*amie Evans knows the meaning of defeat—but it is not a posture he accepts in himself! "God wouldn't have given me problems without providing the resources to cope with them," he says. Like millions of Americans, Jamie suffers from dyslexia and hyperkinesia.

Jamie is the son of longtime friends and Praise Gathering speakers Dr. Louis Evans and Colleen Townsend Evans. Though his family provided a nurturing and loving support system and offered him excellent educational opportunities, Jamie still fought a lonely battle, struggling with many learning disabilities and the low self-esteem, anger, and emotional scarring that resulted. But then the Lord took over. What emerged was a person who has a heart tender towards the special needs of others.

A graduate of the College of Wooster in Ohio and Princeton Theological Seminary, Jamie is now serving in the Chaplain's Department at St. Albans School for Boys in Washington, D.C. He is also the author of An Uncommon Gift.

Jamie is married to Karen Kristine Evans—a graduate student in psychology. They were raised together in California.

As Jamie talks about his struggles growing up, we parents will be reminded that sometimes the best thing we can do—as hard as it can be—is to let our children fight their own battles.

In 1969 I was a fourth-grade teacher's nightmare. I was trouble personified. My three elder siblings had moved through La Jolla's public education with strong marks and many friends, but I was fast proving to be quite the exception. I was different, and neither my teachers nor I seemed to like the difference. I stuttered, was difficult to control, often fought with my peers, and my academic performance was dismal.

My parents worked hard to get some explanation from the school administration. Their inquiries brought merely the frustrating reply: "Be grateful you had three smart ones. The fourth lacks what they had in abundance." Now my parents are fighters, and to simply accept that their youngest was somehow flawed was not a possibility. For years they struggled to find the key to my problem. Tutors were called, after-school sessions with teachers were arranged, and school administrators were bombarded with requests for smaller classes and extra help.

Godly people, Louis and Colleen Evans prayed to find some help for their youngest. By fourth grade, I was showing definite signs of damage from the academic and social failure I was experiencing. My self-esteem was sinking fast, my behavior was turning surly, and, on occasion, dishonest. Teachers' warnings were coming faster, and my siblings were avoiding any and all contact with me. Those years were lonely. I saw groups of schoolmates walking home together, heading off to play as gangs of friends do. I was a gang of one.

I still remember watching a teacher correct my spelling test after grading an *A* student's. The difference was marked. Her red pen hesitated over my classmate's paper, never touching down except to indicate the perfect score. When she turned to mine, the red pen struck, jabbing here, crossing out there. The points to be subtracted were tallied, and I wasn't even near a passing grade. Her jaw tensed in frustration as she explained for the umpteenth time that *does* is not spelled *d-o-s-e*, it is spelled *d-o-e-s*. Couldn't I tell the difference? No, I couldn't. I saw no difference.

And there lay the answer. Dr. Carrie, a wonderful pediatrician, made the lifesaving diagnosis. After exhaustive tests, he declared me not stupid or lazy or slow but dyslexic and hyperkinetic. In other words, I had a defect from birth that affected neither my intelligence nor my ability, but placed me at a considerable disadvantage when it came to learning in a crowded public school.

As I mentioned, my parents are fighters. Give them a hurdle and they will seek to clear it. Yet for the dyslexic this is of little or no help. The answer to my problem rested not in their parenting skills or efforts at remediation. My help was to come from within. They could not carry the cross for me.

Dr. Carrie had made clear to them that I was facing years of special school with small classes and tutors. I had to be motivated by my own desire if I was going to make it through an educational system designed to frustrate and stymie the dyslexic. He stressed that my childhood would be quite different from the norm. Two hours of homework for the average child would take me five hours. Spelling would never come easily, and the self-esteem issues, which would surface at times, would need healing. Mine was not to be a typical childhood or adolescence.

Now parents yearn to shield their young from the traumas of life, and my mother in particular desired to do this for me. Yet when it came time for my reeducation to begin, my parents left most major decisions up to me. The tutors I was to work with, the school I was to attend, the hours I was to study—these and many other decisions were solely mine to make. My parents didn't hide the fact of long-term struggle and the nature of the task before me. I was in the proverbial deep end, treading water on my own. Had I sunk, they would have dived in, of course, but the act of keeping my head above water was for me alone to do. I felt the seriousness of this predicament. I mourned the carefree childhood I had lost, yet I passionately hoped to someday count myself as my peers' academic and social equal. I was the only person who could accomplish this.

I can only imagine the agony my folks must have felt as they watched me first stumble along in my reeducation. How often they must have wanted to take that cross off my shoulders. But to do so would have robbed me of the lessons I was to learn from my struggles and the maturity these were to bring. In saving me temporarily, my parents would have forever impoverished me.

I think Jesus knew the kind of awful burden my parents carried—wanting to help but not really being able to—when he faced his beloved rich young ruler. In Mark 10:17-22, the gospel writer goes to great lengths to demonstrate that this young man who asked Jesus what he needed to do to be saved was no ordinary follower. Here was a youth whom Jesus loved because of the young man's devotion to the law. But the young man faced his own cross: His possessions ruled his heart and set his priorities. Jesus, despite or perhaps because of his love for this remarkable youth, allowed him to walk away with a fallen face and heavy heart. Jesus would not lift the cross this man had to bear if he were ever to find spiritual health. I can understand the temptation Jesus must have suffered: "Surely this youth has done enough. Why not let it slide this time?" But, no. This lesson was for the youth alone to struggle with; he alone could choose. Jesus did not chase after him, but let him go. We don't know for sure what became of this young fellow. I can only hope that he chose to free himself from his strangling possessions and follow Jesus.

There was great risk in what Jesus did in letting go. So, too, with my parents, for they were called to allow me to grow up years before my time and to stumble against hurdles that most parents would avoid for their children's sake. Parental love must aim to guide and instruct, yet it must never suffocate or impede the necessary stretching process that builds character and spiritual depth. Parental love must value maturity more than security, and it needs to know when to relax one's grasp. This letting go process brings anxiety because our human love yearns to protect and hold our loved ones close. But such security is not ours to give.

This kind of risk-taking love is perhaps my father's strongest parenting gift. When we were children, he packed the whole clan of us up to hike into the High Sierras. There he had been shown an isolated mountain lake resting at the base of a massive mountain and rimmed with tall pines and glacial ice. We spent many summer weeks during our youth in this nine-thousand-foot paradise. There were no roads to the lake, only a ten-mile horse path up steep escarpments of granite. I knew it worried my mother greatly to be so isolated, so far from the protection of modern society with its ambulances and hospitals. Yet in my father's mind, the possible benefits unique to such a removed and uncivilized environment were worth the risks. He took the chance—and it's paid off. He's raised a clan of environmentally conscious children who have grown up to put that love for God's creation into action. My eldest brother has even dedicated much of his political life in Washington, D.C., to protecting Washington State's wilderness.

The Christian life is full of many balances and tensions. But the call to let Jesus Christ have his way in the hearts and lives of our children must stand above our hopes for our offspring's comfort and security. Life is a holy training ground where many hurdles and tumbles are disguised blessings if only we will let them be. I praise God that I was born "different" from my peers and that my parents had the faith in God's maturing process to let his trials do their work. As earthly parents, we are called to a vital recognition that, ultimately, it is God who does the deepest and most profound parenting of all.

Thank You

A nd he thought he was just showing up to teach high-school English! I was a junior in college filling in for a high-school French teacher who required emergency surgery, and I reported for duty the same day a teacher named Bill Gaither transferred from a junior high school teaching job in another town. For us, that was the first day of more than just a teaching tenure at Alexandria (Indiana) High School!

Bill and I were married in 1962, and we continued to teach English at Alexandria until a growing family—Suzanne, Amy, and Benjy—and an expanding music ministry forced us to give up the teaching we both loved. People were becoming more and more interested in the songs we were writing together, and requests for copies were trickling in from as far away as Florida—pretty amazing for a couple of Indiana kids! Weekend concerts were also growing and demanding more of our time. Using one hundred fifty dollars from savings, we printed our first song in sheet music form. We made our first recording in the hopes that "real singers" might hear our songs and sing them.

Since then, The Bill Gaither Trio has recorded some forty albums. Bill has been a publisher, inspiration, mentor, writer, and communicator, but most of all he is a teacher. Many *young artists have learned important lessons for life from him. Little did we know in those first days at Alexandria High School that God would use our music and our writing as he has these twenty-seven years.*

If I were to say, though, what Bill does, I would say he starts things that matter. He senses needs in the world and comes up with solutions. Whether it's an idea for a song that needs to be written, a retreat for young artists, a Praise Gathering for Believers, a New Year's Eve celebration for Christians called Jubilate, a summer Christian arts academy for young people, or a new tree in the backyard, Bill likes to start things that matter.

It's been fun sharing my life with this man . . . not always easy, but never boring. He has been a wonderful father to our children, and I know he learned much of his parenting skills from my beloved in-laws. I hope that, through Bill's letter to them on their fiftieth wedding anniversary, you gain a sense of the special lessons George and Lela Gaither have taught all of us about life.

◆────────────────────────────────────◆

This is a very special day for all of us. Human relationships at their best are very fragile, but you have shown us that it is possible for two imperfect human beings to live out a commitment to each other despite not-always-perfect circumstances. And you have done this without really making a big deal out of it. You've simply done it. We all get a little weary of those who talk about it all the time. It is good to see examples of those who simply do it.

In your quiet, unassuming way, you have shown us what real strength and commitment are all about. You have shown us the importance of being there when there's simply nothing else you can do. You have shown us the importance of dependability in this day when there seem to be few things you can really count on. It has made us proud to hear people say, "You can always count on George and Lela." You have also shown us that, in life, sometimes we win and sometimes we lose, but more important than winning or losing is how we react to both of these "imposters," as Kipling called them.

Thank you for showing us the importance of old-fashioned hard work and that, without it, nothing great is accomplished. You've also shown us that, even if the work sometimes gets dull and routine, we can create our own joy and excitement whatever the job.

Thanks for laughter. It's good to come from a family that knows how to laugh. It's helped us never take ourselves too seriously. We all still remember the last time Dad tried to kick me in the you-know-where, and he fell on his you-know-what because, by the time I was seventeen, he was too short to reach me. And who could forget the time when Mom had bought a new girdle—which, for all practical purposes, was probably a size or two too small—and the whole family ended up helping her into it? After the arduous task was accomplished, Dad said, "Now step back, kids. If that thing breaks loose, we're all in bad trouble!" We laughed about it then, and we still laugh today, but that incident helped teach us that our personal identity and worth are not tied up in whether we are tall or short, skinny or not-so-skinny, or in possession of a "Gaither nose." Instead, you taught us that our worth lies in the real, unique, special person that God intended us to be.

Also, thank you for the gift of music and for piano lessons; thanks for taping music programs for us when we weren't home (although we have since learned that it was illegal); and thanks for driving us all over the country when we were kids so we could sing in churches (even if we did sing "Every Day Will Be Sunday By and By" in the Seventh-Day Adventist church). We hope that what we've done with the music you gave us has made you proud and the world a better place.

And thank you for showing us how to grow old graciously, which is no small feat. Now that all three of us are in midlife, we hope that we can learn to face the next periods of life with the grace and dignity that you have. That is not an easy task because something in human nature is always asking for more.

Thank you for creating a real awareness of the value of life and how to appreciate it while we're living it. "This is not the rehearsal—it's the real thing" is more than just a saying with you. It's been a way of life. God has been so good to all of us, and we're all living in a bonus situation. You have taught us that a cool, summer evening in the swing under the red maple is a gift—a bonus; that raising your own food in your garden is a gift—a bonus; that walking three or four miles every day with your dog is a gift—a bonus; that getting hooked on pro football at the age of seventy and learning that a quarterback sneak is not a bad guy and a tight end is not what you think it is—this is a gift and a bonus; that enjoying a good meal at Captain D's is a gift—a bonus. We didn't deserve this rich life, but thank God, we live in a country where we have these blessings, and we're thankful for them. And maybe being thankful is what living together for fifty years is all about.

So we are all here today to salute you. As Dizzy Dean said, "If you done it, it ain't braggin'—and I done it." You both done it, and you deserve to be proud of it on this very special day. So walk proudly! We love you very much and want to thank you for simply being you and for always being here for us.

Love,
Billy Jim

The Lord's Presence

S teve's music is definitely music with a message. Each of his albums emphasizes a specific aspect of the Christian life.

His first album, Steve Green, *focused on repentance and revival.* He Holds the Keys *celebrated the deliverance and power available to believers because of Christ's death and resurrection. Believers are called to a life characterized by holiness and purity on* For God and God Alone *and by perseverance and obedience on* Find Us Faithful. On The Mission, *Steve calls his listeners to make loving the Lord their first priority and to let that love fuel their Christian service.*

In 1985 and 1987 Steve was named Male Vocalist of the Year by the Gospel Music Association (GMA). He received two more GMA Dove Awards for Inspirational Album of the Year for Find Us Faithful in 1988 and The Mission in 1990.

Steve became a Christian when he was eight years old. At the time he was living in Argentina with his missionary parents. There in South America he and his four siblings *learned to play musical instruments and often provided music for their father's Sunday services.*

In his piece "The Lord's Presence," Steve looks back on Christmas 1990, which he and his family—his wife, Marijean, and their children, Summer and Josiah—shared with the rest of the Green clan at a family reunion in Nashville. It was a time of celebrating his Christian heritage and the faith that he and his family share.

For the Green family, Christmas 1990 was surrounded by more than the usual anticipation and excitement of the Advent season. It was the first time in four years we would all be together. It's next to impossible to gather families from Venezuela, Texas, New Jersey, and Tennessee, but by God's grace it happened!

Mom and Dad, coming directly from Caracas, were the first to arrive in Nashville. The last time I had seen Dad was in a hospital in Phoenix right after his heart attack. While flying to Phoenix, I had reviewed the events of our lives and wondered about the possibility of life without this man who had so shaped my destiny. Miraculously, within a month he was back in South America overseeing the growth of two new churches.

One by one, the families arrived. After getting reacquainted and expressing disbelief at the growth of the children (why do we always do that?), we settled into a week of rehearsing childhood memories, catching up on the details lost by the miles, discussing important events, and having precious times of prayer filled with gratitude for the Lord's sustaining grace.

As we sat around the fireplace and talked, I was again impressed with how carefully my father guarded his speech. Always choosing appropriate words, he seasoned conversation with insight and wisdom. I remember that as children we had sometimes sensed people-problems among the missionaries, noticed injustices, and felt the tension of living in a foreign culture among people whose customs often flew in the face of our own; yet I don't remember ever hearing a hint of criticism or seeing a telltale sign of condescension from my parents. I'm not suggesting that they were perfect. Certainly they would remember failures in these areas, but as the years pass, I have increasingly appreciated their example of James 3:2: "We all stumble in many ways. If anyone is never at fault in what he says, he is a perfect man, able to keep his whole body in check" (NIV).

At our Christmas gathering, with two missionaries, a seminary professor, and a pastor in the family, there was always a good conversation after breakfast. One morning, the conversation centered around key verses that had shaped Dad's life. Quoting Philippians 2:14-15, he told us how much he desired to be "blameless and pure" in all that he did, and I remembered back to 1972, the year my oldest sister, Barbara, was married.

Shortly after the wedding, the rest of us headed back to Argentina for another term. Since mail service from the States was measured in weeks and months, we were thrilled when our copies of the wedding pictures finally arrived. Within a short time, they were framed and hung on the wall. A day or so later, though, my father took them off the wall, gathered us around, and told us what had happened in the customs office. (Those who have lived in a foreign country will understand the pain of trying to get packages through customs. Often there is a heavy duty to be paid, either at the whim of the official or because the shipper has sent a heavily taxable item.) The package had been marked "PHOTOS," but it contained other items not identified on the outside. Dad had been aware of the contents of the box and knew there was no problem with them, so in order to receive the package duty-free, he had let the customs official believe that it contained nothing more than pictures. You can imagine the impression it made on us to see him box up the photos and return to the post office to show the official and ask forgiveness for not telling the truth. When the pictures went up on the wall again, they were not just wedding pictures, but a vivid reminder of the value of a clear conscience.

After dinner on our last evening together, we watched a video called *America, You're Too Young to Die,* an urgent cry for spiritual revival as the only hope for saving America. Throughout the presentation, our hearts were moved as we considered the great spiritual need of our nation and then our own personal need for a renewed passion for Jesus Christ. At the end of the video, which had originally been a television special, there was an invitation to kneel and humbly call on the Lord. For a brief instant, I wondered what to do; it was one of those moments when my heart knew what must be done yet my mind argued to act sensibly.

Out of the corner of my eye, I saw my father slip from his chair and fall to his knees. As we all knelt, my first thought and prayer was, *Lord, forgive me for waiting to see if it was appropriate. Help me to swiftly obey the prompting of your Spirit.* The next moments were filled with the presence of the Lord as we prayed for God's will to be done in our nation and in our own lives.

Throughout the days after our time together, as I pieced together the recent experiences and the past events that had so deeply affected our family history, I began to recognize what a real gift my parents had given me. Psalm 34:8 says, "Taste and see that the LORD is good" (NIV). Even though my folks made choices that I might not make and though they were not perfect in the way they disciplined, I have stirring memories of the Lord's presence in our home. When Dad apologized to Mom and, with sincere humility, acknowledged a wrong done, I tasted the Lord's goodness and sensed God's presence. When from the heart Mom forgave an obvious injustice, or when, together, Mom and Dad chose to love or give or serve, we children experienced a mysterious joy in it. During my college years and beyond, I drifted away from the Lord and experimented with the tastes that the world has to offer. I can truly say that the world's tastes didn't satisfy. Still in my memory was the sweet savor of the goodness of the Lord, and once a person has tasted the goodness of the Lord, everything else tastes flat.

How grateful I am for parents who, through their daily routine of life in simple obedience to the Lord, allowed our home to be permeated with the sweet fragrance of the Spirit of God.

Believing in Me– and My Dreams

President and cofounder of Star Song Communications, *Darrell A. Harris is highly respected in Christian music circles and beyond. The artist roster he has developed at Star Song reflects the wide range of today's diverse Christian music. The broad appeal of the company's products—from the rock sound of White Heart to the adult contemporary orientation of Twila Paris and The Gaither Vocal Band—is the result of his influence and hard work.*

Darrell's success with Star Song Communications can be attributed to his knowledge and interest in music as well as his firsthand understanding of the music industry. He learned the dynamics of promotion, artist management, and record production when he served under two noted producers and managers, Bill Ham and Erv Woolsey. Later, Darrell was employed by Word, Inc., the nation's leading distributor of gospel music. There he worked closely with Billy Ray Hearn to create media interest in the newly formed Myrrh Records. He has also held positions with ABC Dunhill and Arista where he worked with the now-legendary Clive Davis.

In addition to the various executive roles he has assumed

over the years, Darrell is recognized throughout the music publishing business as a man whose integrity and professional ethics are unfailing. In fact Billboard *magazine has identified him as the "unofficial conscience of the industry."*

Darrell's work in the music industry seems a fulfillment of a long-held dream. Here, he talks about the beginning of that dream.

It was the summer of 1962, and Daddy wasn't in a good mood. In fact my sister, Cindy, and I had noticed it to the extent that we had asked Mom if we really had to take a summer vacation and spend all those hours in the car together. That kind of request was unusual enough in our almost-always-happy family that she talked to Daddy about it.

That summer we did make the five-hour-plus drive from Houston to Dallas to visit the newly opened Six Flags over Texas amusement park. It was hot, but we had a great time.

Now that I am a father, with wage-earning responsibilities and a family of my own, I have a better understanding of why Daddy wasn't his usual easygoing self that year. He was a machinist at Shell refinery, and his union had been out on strike for a number of months. I now wonder how he had it within himself to give me one of the greatest gifts I have ever received. . . .

That autumn we were asked at school to prepare our elective choices for the next four years, taking the first real steps of defining career direction. I had brought home the folder with all the information and options.

Perhaps we only spent an evening or two at the endeavor. But, I remember filling out those forms as if it took up the better part of a couple of weeks. Daddy seemed to really enjoy it, and so did I, because in our kitchen during those evenings, the gateways to a million possibilities seemed to open up before me.

"If you could be anything you want, what would it be?" he asked. His question seemed to imply that I could become president of the United States or king of the world if I so chose. But, having begun to play the clarinet in the school band, and being fascinated with the junior high band leader with his baton and knowledge of the world of composers and instruments, I answered, "A band director."

Daddy never batted an eye. If my answer brought him any displeasure, I never knew it. Without hesitation, he put *band* in one of the elective blanks for each year—all the way through high school.

After that, he asked what my second choice would be. Having just watched *The High and the Mighty* with John Wayne, I answered, "A commercial airline pilot." In retrospect it was probably the Dimitri Tiomkin score that had really interested me!

Later that autumn, Daddy died suddenly of a heart attack. And after he was gone, Mom continued to encourage me. She too seemed to approve of whatever my career inclinations were, simply because they were mine. She seemed to think I could do anything. And I was never chided for failing in any way . . . only for failing to try.

My mushrooming interest in music—indeed in all the arts—and something of a struggle with algebra and geometry let me know I probably would not be entering a "technical field." So, I have never flown a plane. A call to ministry helped guide these artistic interests toward the work I have known for the past fifteen years: leadership in a Christian communications company, and particular responsibility for overseeing product-development activities.

Thanks, Mom and Dad, for believing that these interests were OK just because they were in my heart and for believing I could achieve whatever I set my sights upon. I'm having a great time!

Who Won?

A five-time Grammy winner. A recipient of eight Gospel Music Association Dove Awards, including Songwriter of the Year and Male Vocalist of the Year—three times! The choice for a 1988 Stellar Award for excellence in the black gospel field. A gifted songwriter, a talented singer, and, to my joy, a regular guest at many Praise Gatherings.

The list of songs he's recorded goes on and on. Let me just mention a few of the award-winners: "More Than Wonderful" (1984) and "I've Just Seen Jesus" (1986) with Sandi Patti; "How Excellent Is Thy Name," for which he received a 1986 Grammy for Best Solo Gospel Performance; "I Miss My Time with You," which Larnelle wrote, held the number one spot on Christian radio charts for eight weeks in 1988; and "I Can Begin Again," named the Contemporary Gospel Single of the Year in 1989 by Cash Box magazine.

Larnelle's most recent project was the recording of his first live album, Larnelle Live . . . Psalms, Hymns, and Spiritual Songs. A standing-room-only crowd at Radio City Music Hall in New York City enjoyed a spellbinding performance as Larnelle shared his powerful vocals and uplifting lyrics for an inspirational concert experience with the Brooklyn Tabernacle Church.

Larnelle has been an important part of Praise Gathering for Believers in Indianapolis many times, and I could go on about Larnelle's awards and talents, but he prefers to talk about his family. He and Mitzy have been married nineteen years, and they have two children, Lonnie, sixteen, and Teresa, twelve.

Deeply committed to the Lord, refreshingly honest, and wonderfully talented, Larnelle offers much in the way of example and encouragement to many. Here, see how his father—who now makes time for Larnelle's son—made time for Larnelle in this special family moment.

It was a warm spring morning, and we were returning from the daily chore of slopping the pigs and feeding the other animals. It was the most unexpected question I'd ever heard from him. Walking up Randolph Hill, the only road that led back to our house, my dad asked, "Lonnie, want to race?"

Well, I considered myself pretty fast in those days. I also had a reputation for never turning down a challenge. But race my dad? *What if I beat him?* I thought to myself. *Boy, if I beat him, I might be slopping those pigs alone for the next ten years! Or, worse yet, what if he beats me? What would I say to my friends? Or what if this old guy suddenly keeled over after inhaling the cloud of dust—my trademark at takeoff? After all, he must be twenty-five years old! He could have a heart attack! Mom would never forgive me. In a few short minutes, I could be fatherless and Mom could be without a husband.*

I regained my composure and looked up at him

with a kind of smugness in my smile and thought, *Lonnie, this man has challenged you—and that's that!*

Then, before I knew what was happening, he interrupted my thoughts with his words. He shouted them quickly, almost as though he were trying to get an edge by catching me off guard. "Ready, set, go!" And we were off.

In the distance, I could see Mom as she stepped out of the back door of our house, her hands waving in the morning sun as though she were cheering for her favorite team. Oh, it was nip and tuck, neck and neck for the first few yards. But soon it was all over.

The next thing I remember is the three of us lying in the yard gasping for air and laughing so hard that tears ran down our faces. Dad's laughter was probably due to the fact that it had been some time since he had run thirty yards like that! Mom gathered the both of us up in her arms, laughing and enjoying the fun of being together. My laughter came from the discovery that my dad could run—he really could run!

When I had kids of my own, I realized another reason why this memory is special. It was a moment very typical of my parents. Dad and Mom, though busy always making ends meet and dealing with all that grown-ups have to be concerned with, often took time to be involved in my little world.

Oh, who won the race? It didn't matter.

Journeys

Stephen and his partner, Jerry Cohagan, have been performing comedy and drama with a Christian perspective since 1980. Believing that we can laugh while we learn and grow, Stephen and Jerry offer witty and warm messages and timely observations about the Christian journey. We have been pleased to have them touring with The Bill Gaither Trio and The Gaither Vocal Band since 1984.

Stephen attended Northwest Nazarene College in Nampa, Idaho, graduating with a degree in speech communication. Since then, he and Jerry have been involved in theater, television, and film across the United States and from the Caribbean to Canada. Both are contributing writers for several religious periodicals.

The Hicks and Cohagan team has also appeared in two award-winning film series, One Is a Whole Number and Teacher Training Insights: Youth. Their newest collections of sketches are available on audio cassette, "Help Wanted," and on the video cassettes "Serious Humor" and "Going Up."

You'll see here some of the family roots of Stephen's "serious *comedy" as he shares a serious side of himself and a lesson he learned—with the help of his parents—about self-pity and gratitude.*

My first solo journey was a surprisingly short trip. It began early one morning in the kitchen at the top of the stairs leading to the basement. Taken against my parents' advice, this journey ended abruptly seven steps later when my tricycle and I came face-to-face with two rose bushes waiting to be planted in the front yard.

The next day my parents had a pastor come to the house to dedicate me to the Lord. Ironically, it seems to me, Dr. Young said God was entrusting my parents with the responsibility for my safety and well-being. My parents never did discipline me for my toddler tour down the stairs, and I always suspected that they felt a little guilty about the timing of my dedication. I've wondered about that myself.

I don't mean to imply that my parents weren't responsible adults or that they lacked the will or ability to discipline me. Actually, Mom and Dad were willing to use a variety of means to encourage appropriate behavior. Their repertoire included a thump on the head for talking during church, Ivory soap for telling my sister to shut up (would you want to listen to her sing the "Hokey-Pokey" a million times?), and even granting me quality time all alone in my room for hiding lima beans under my napkin at supper.

Mom's trump card was the proverbial "I'm calling your dad." My father traveled sixty thousand miles a year representing our church's publishing house. The very thought of Mom racking up thousands of dollars in long-distance telephone calls usually subdued my rebellious spirit. I was much older before I realized that most of the time Mom didn't have a clue as to Dad's actual location. And what would Dad have done anyway? Threaten to spank me the minute he got home—in three weeks?

From the time of my first ill-fated excursion until now, my parents have reminded me that life itself can be a perilous journey—but that a life without risk isn't much of a life.

With their words and actions, my parents have taught me that, when God calls, don't look back to see who else is following. For Mom and Dad, that has meant sometimes doing the Lord's work for little or no pay, giving sacrificially to build the kingdom of God around the world, and continually offering themselves and the family to the Lord for service.

Today I understand that the path of life is lined with thorns and roses, rich with laughter and tears, and—if I choose to receive it—overflowing with the abundance of God's love and grace.

It seemed to me that the entire month of December had been nothing but snow, ice, bone-chilling wind, and endless gray skies. Kansas City had never looked so bleak. I stared out my apartment window one afternoon at the frozen tundra that passed for a yard. I felt the last drop of Christmas spirit in me evaporate. *Probably frozen in midair,* I figured, ruefully.

I would be spending Christmas alone in Kansas

City—my first Christmas away from the family. They couldn't afford to fly me to Seattle. It wouldn't have mattered anyway. I couldn't afford the gallon of gas to get to the airport.

Everything at home would go on without me. Mom would make fudge, my sisters would decorate their homes, my niece and nephew would wrap presents, and Dad would complain about the price of a Christmas tree. Carol singing, Russian tea cakes, secrets, surprises—all this was in Seattle, and I was not.

I was not happy. I was not happy at all.

The spirit of the season seemed to mock my circumstances. Was it my fault that Jerry (the other half of our struggling comedy team) and I had moved to Kansas City just before the holidays? Was it my fault that our writing and acting careers were nonexistent? Was it my fault that my parents had always made holidays such a special family time?

It was not fair. No one seemed to care at all that I was the victim of so much injustice—least of all my own family. How could they celebrate Christmas without me? How could they even try?

As Christmas drew closer, I never missed a chance to remind them of my dissatisfaction. Telephone calls that began with tidings of good cheer soon ended with a recitation of my misfortune. Christmas found me wallowing in self-pity as I unwrapped unappreciated gifts.

A letter from Seattle arrived shortly after Christmas. *Finally,* I thought, *Mom and Dad are going to own up to their callous insensitivity.* I tore open the envelope.

"Dear Stephen," it began. "What a bitter young man

we have raised. So full of selfishness and self-pity. How sad we are for you."

I stared at the page, my hands shaking. My parents had spoken the truth, the hard truth, and it was breaching the fortress of my self-centered kingdom.

"Can you imagine for one moment that we wouldn't do everything possible to have you home with us? You must know how bad we felt not being able to afford even half the cost of a plane ticket for you. Do you think your mother's tears of disappointment were only for herself?

"We had hoped the memories of all our Christmases together would remind you of the joyous truth of this season. The innocent little babe in a manger was a gift for all of us. The selfless sacrifice that child would make changed everything for you and me. We have every reason to celebrate his coming no matter what our circumstances.

"As always, your mother and I love you and pray for you daily. Merry Christmas, Son. Love, Dad."

The warm tears on my cheeks seemed to loosen the icy grip of bitterness that had held my heart. I was home once again. It had been a needlessly painful journey, but I had learned the truth. I basked in the warmth of my parents' love.

It was late. I lay in my bed, perfectly still, straining so hard to hear that the silence roared in my ears. There it was . . . underneath the constant whir of the attic fan . . . just beyond the symphony of cicadas outside my bedroom window . . . across the hall. The low murmured tones of my father's voice. He was home, and the last conversation of the day was taking place. The darkness seemed to quiet the house.

A pause.

I imagined him sitting beside my mother on the edge of the bed. "Our heavenly Father," he began. And I knew it would all be there: my grades, Cynthia's braces, Marilyn's school-girl crush, the bills, the Holmans, the church, the missionaries. All whispered in a bedside prayer that was offered nightly throughout fifty years of marriage.

Then: "I love you, baby. You're a sweetheart."

"I love you, too, hon."

In that moment, the light of a thousand stars flooded my room, the bogeyman vanished, and angels danced on my dresser. I knew God himself lived in our house! It was too much to bear.

"I love you, Mom! I love you, too, Dad!" I cried out in the darkness.

"We know," came a voice from across the hall. "We love you, too. Now go to sleep. Tomorrow is another day."

Smiling, I fell asleep and dreamed of journeys yet to come.

Dann Huff

They Chose Me

A talented guitarist, Dann Huff is known for his work in both Christian and secular music. He has lent his talents as a studio musician to projects with such diverse artists as— among others—Bob Seger, Michael Jackson, Madonna, Barbra Streisand, Whitesnake, Neil Diamond, Kenny Loggins, Amy Grant, Hank Williams, Jr., Reba McEntire, Whitney Houston, Rod Stewart, and Chaka Khan.

Dann calls Nashville home, and it was there that he first started playing demos when he was fifteen or sixteen, and as he describes it, he was hooked! The year after he graduated from high school, he traveled with The Gaither Trio, and it was there that a group of musicians came together that eventually returned to Nashville to form a new band. The musicians were Dann, David Huff, Billy Smiley, Mark Gersmehl, and Steve Green, and the band was White Heart.

Moving on from White Heart and west to California meant studio work with a variety of popular contemporary artists. For the past five years, though, Dann has been devoting much of his time and talent to his role as lead singer for the group Giant.

When asked what he likes to do in his free time, Dann is quick to respond, "Free time is for family—for my wonderful

*daughters, Ashlyne and Madelyne, and my wife, Sherri."
This love for family is deeply rooted: Dann was blessed with,
in his words, "incredible parents" and a childhood rich in
love and important lessons for life.*

I have incredible parents. I could talk for hours about
them—and I have. Through the years and even today,
discussions with people at dinner or in the course of
everyday business invariably turn to parents. Most of
the time people end up talking about things their
parents did wrong and how they are having to deal
with the consequent problems. But for me it is a
different story.

It's not that my parents are the most perfect people
in the world—but they're pretty close! I love my parents and respect them. Part of the beauty of our
relationship is that it's ongoing, continually growing,
evolving, and changing. In their parenting, the communication and the process matter. It's not that you
arrive at a certain point—you never arrive at a finish
line in a relationship. Instead, you constantly change
and grow, stretch and squirm. And that growing still
goes on today.

Thinking about my parents, I see some striking
parallels between my folks' adult life—especially my
father's—and my adult life. And, as a parent now
myself (my wife, Sherri, and I have two children,
Madelyne, one year old, and Ashlyne, six years old), I
also see some lessons my parents taught me that I
want to teach my daughters—and implicit in those

lessons are some tangible standards to which I hope to measure up.

First of all, I'm a musician, my father is a musician, and my mother is a musician. My dad had a budding career when, in his late twenties or early thirties, he made a career change and became an orchestrator. He found a great deal of joy in that. My mom was a very fine pianist, but from the time we were kids through most of our teenage years, she chose to be a homemaker and put her career second. Throughout those years, my mother was always right there for us—and I understand enough to know that just because you are home raising kids doesn't mean that your time is any less precious. (If anything, being at home is a much more time-consuming job, and the few moments you get by yourself are worth that much more!) Lately, my mom has been involved in helping cancer patients, AIDS patients, and transplant patients. She has a real love for people who are dying and a real talent for being with them. She has found true fulfillment there.

Through his music, my father enjoyed more and more success every year, and life moved very fast. Yet, in the midst of all that was happening to him, I can't remember a single time when I felt I had to take the backseat to anything. I never once felt that I took second place to all that was going on in my parents' lives. Now, as a busy musician who's also a father, I realize even more clearly the value of time and the sparseness of it in life. It's the most priceless commodity that we have, and the fact that my parents always gave us their time first continues to amaze me.

I remember very vividly my days as a Little League pitcher. Even though my father always had deadlines for his writing, he never missed a baseball game. I can still picture him with his big score pad sitting in the stands. The only thing that made him look different from the other fathers was the fact that, between pitches, his head would go down and he would continue his writing and arranging. While I received the signal from the catcher, Dad would jot down a few more notes. I still can't figure out how he could concentrate so deeply on his music. I have to have dead silence to write, but he managed to work on his music at my games. Whether they were attending a ball game or some other function of mine, my parents—my dad with his music and my mother with her ever-present knitting or crocheting—were always doing something, and yet, at the same time they were always with us and giving us their attention.

Often at night when deadlines were approaching, I went to bed with the sound of the piano in the background. Without fail, though, whenever one of my brothers or I had a problem or just needed to talk, Dad put down his pencil, and we got 100 percent of his attention. Whether it took fifteen minutes or an hour—and I remember many times when it was four or five in the morning when we stopped talking—Dad took the time.

I learned important lessons from those talks. I learned, for instance, that you have to keep talking no matter how much it hurts. My folks taught me that you have to keep that wound open and clean and that, to change metaphors, you have to keep chopping that wall down one brick at a time because you don't want it to get too high. When we did talk until four in the morning—and I would get an hour or two of sleep—my dad would pick up his pencil as I went off to bed, and he'd still be writing when I left for school. He never once complained about it. For both my parents, it was give, give, give, give—and my parents never became martyrs.

My father had his office at home, and I can't imagine writing with the house full of music like he had! I was playing guitar constantly, my brother Dave was playing the drums, and at the time my youngest brother, Ron, was also interested in music. Dad never asked us to sacrifice any of our practice time; he never told us to turn down the volume and be quiet so that he could write. Instead, he just turned on the TV by his desk to kind of drown out the noise. Anyone visiting our house would have thought we were a bunch of lunatics! How he managed to write and arrange in that setting baffles me to this day.

Ours was a house of open doors—both literally, as I just described, and figuratively. My parents' philosophy was that, as parents, you don't dictate the direction your children go. Instead, you just open doors and, with your nudging and applause, help make the childhood years an adventure. You open all the doors and let the kids close them as disinterest in one settles in and interest in another flourishes. That's how I got interested in music. My parents never pushed me, but I guess I had enough interest on my own to walk through the door they opened.

My parents constantly encouraged us to pursue

whatever we were interested in, but they never over-did it. They never tried to live through us, and they were also aware of the dangers of applauding too much. For instance, we excelled in sports, and my parents were at all our games. But they never seemed to be any more excited about sports or music than they were about anything else. Are you interested in working with people? What are you reading? Are you interested in working with animals? Everything was equal. They wanted to open doors for us.

Another thing I really appreciated about my folks was—and you hear this term all the time now—the "quality time" they spent with us. Well, I believe in quality time, and I suppose my folks did too, but they never let that outweigh the idea that plain ol' time is worth much more than you can measure. My parents gave a lot of time *and* a lot of quality time.

I guess I just don't buy this idea that if you give a child an hour here and an hour there, that will really do the trick. It's not just scheduled "quality time" that matters. How can you expect a child to live according to the hours you set and the times that are convenient for you? "I'm going to be gone this week, but the week I'm home, I have these hours for you. At this time we'll get emotional; these are the times you'll have needs I can help with; and this is when we'll have fun together." You can't do that! Life is spontaneous, and you can't force that kind of living within certain hours. And that means parents make sacrifices. I know my parents didn't think about it that way, but I also know that they gave up a lot of things to raise their kids right!

One thing they did right has to do with how they handled my brothers and me. The three of us were born within twenty-one months of each other—and you can imagine the degree of competitiveness inherent in that situation. My parents never tried to squelch a normal, healthy, competitive spirit, but they also avoided making comparisons that would have been very easy to make. Firstborns, for instance, are usually fast achievers, but my parents didn't ask my younger brothers, "Why can't you be more like Dann?" And, in certain cases where my brothers were a lot less compulsive than I was, they didn't ask, "Why aren't you more like your younger brothers?" My parents were too wise to do that.

Instead, my parents encouraged individuality. They did this by not comparing us to each other and by spending time with us individually. They spent a lot of time with each one of us, encouraging our own thoughts and asking us how we felt about things. We never felt we had to compete with one another for our parents' approval or attention. As a result, we brothers are very close. That's one more thing I am very indebted to my parents for.

Another thing I appreciate about my parents is what they taught me about respect. My parents never allowed us to talk back to them. We were taught to obey them—which we did. They definitely didn't spare the rod—but we didn't have to have too much "rod" before we understood that it would hurt if we didn't do what we were told. I guess what made them different from other parents was the fact that, while they expected us to obey them, they also felt that they had to earn our respect just as they had to earn other people's respect (children being people after all!). In other words, we had to obey them, but we did not have to respect them. That respect was something they had to earn.

Even when my brothers and I were too young to understand what respect was, my parents always acted with respect toward us. I remember times when they would come in and say, "Dann, we're sorry"—even when I was five years old! "What are you sorry for, Dad?" He would say, "Well, we were wrong in what we said to you" or "We were wrong about how we punished you." Their manner seemed to say, "That's just the way life is. If you do something wrong, you say you're sorry." It wasn't until later that I realized that saying "I'm sorry" to a child is not a normal mode of operation for many parents. Many mothers and fathers will do anything except say "I'm sorry," admit that they were wrong, and then move on.

My parents felt very strongly that we had to earn their respect and their trust and that they had to earn our respect and our trust. And that's something that will go down through the generations of the Huff clan—I guarantee it! Your children are your children, but they are also people you must respect and whose respect you must earn.

The most important part of the heritage my parents gave me has to do with lessons about God and love. I was raised in a Christian home, but my parents did not hammer religion into me as a young boy. Because they are people who love God and are involved in the church, I received the normal Sunday school teachings about the Bible and the life of Christ. What I remember most about religion can be summed up in one word: *love*. Christ showed his great ability to love in order to validate his existence before the rest of the world. And love is the one thing that sets apart people who know God as a living God. It's our highest calling—and the toughest. It sounds like it's the simplest thing to deal with, but the ramifications of love can be far-reaching and scary.

What I remember most about these lessons on love is the spontaneous way in which my family would discuss this and other aspects of our faith. There were some Sunday mornings when we'd all be dressed and ready to go to church when one of those spontaneous discussions would arise, and before we knew it, we'd missed church and even lunch. When we did go to church, my parents didn't draw church time to a halt when we walked out of the building. Before we knew it, we were home, sitting at the table or sprawled out on the living-room floor, talking about issues that mattered. Whatever was going on in our lives would be linked to compassion, to choosing the most loving option, to the simple question, "What would Christ do?"

My parents were very serious about their faith, and they tried to make it relevant to our young lives. It took time, it took discussing, but through it all we grew to understand that faith in God is not just something you capsulize into a Sunday or an event—it's a way of life. I can see in my brothers—and they can see in me (it's harder to see it in yourself)—a real sense of compassion and a love for people that had to come from our parents. That's how they were and are, and only through a lot of time spent talking about our faith and seeing their example did we ever get to this point. I think I learned more about a godly life from those family discussions than I did from any teaching I ever received in church. I saw my folks live out their faith. I saw the stuff they were doing for people, and I heard the answers to the questions we asked them. I mean, we grilled them—"Why do you do this?"—and they would be very candid.

Besides teaching me about Christ's love, my parents taught me a lot about their love for me. I knew that my parents loved me even during those teenage years when parents seem to always be saying you can't do things. You square off with jaws clenched, and somebody has to win and somebody has to lose. Well, my parents didn't just say, "Look, Dann. You're not going to do this. End of discussion." Instead, our discussions went on and on—and, as a result, we kept close.

When I got to the point one time of saying "I'm going to rebel! I'm out of here! I can't deal with my folks! They don't know what they're talking about!," I remember thinking very specifically, *I can't rebel against them—they love me too much!* And I hated them for that! Now this may sound odd, but at that point I couldn't rebel. I wasn't an angel, but I couldn't turn my back on that kind of love. I wanted to, and that's what made me angry. If there had been any flaws in the way that they loved me or any hypocrisy on their part, any dishonesty or patronizing from them, then I think I would have found my hole and escaped through it. But I couldn't find that hole.

I couldn't fully rebel because I had nothing to rebel

against. My folks kept communication open, and they respected my views about things. They made me explain my ideas and support them with arguments, and usually—most of the time—I was wrong. On those rare occasions when I was right, they would concede to that—but they also might add, "As long as you're in our house, this is the way it is." I understood that and I could deal with it. Taking time to communicate, opening doors, acting with respect and earning respect, teaching me about love—I learned so much from my parents.

Let me close with one statement that says it all: My dad was the best man in his three sons' weddings—and my mother would have been matron of honor had we been daughters.

Growing in the Garden of Grace

F or many of you, the name June Hunt means "Hope for the Heart." Since 1986, June has been broadcasting this award-winning daily radio program. Across the country, people struggling with life's challenges benefit from her biblical and practical words of hope.

June is also the originator and teacher of Counseling through the Bible, a course designed to equip believers with the tools they need to help others through life's tough times. Here, too, June's warmth, insight, and counselor's heart mean biblical hope and practical help for her audience.

In her new devotional book, Seeing Yourself through God's Eyes, *June focuses on Scriptures that offer readers a godly perspective of themselves as the answer to their feelings of low self-worth. Through her three albums, June uses music to express Christ's compassion and care and invite the listener to a closer walk with God.*

After earning a degree in music and serving as a youth director for several years, June began to gain recognition as a speaker at conferences, retreats, and seminars. She has appeared on NBC's Today *show, toured Vietnam with the*

USO, and been guest soloist with the Billy Graham Crusades. She is also a contributor to the Women's Devotional Bible.

Perhaps it's not surprising that the ministry of grace June offers to people today has its roots in the "garden of grace" where she grew up and that she talks about here.

Occasionally when I talk with a young woman, traces of disdain or even hatred for her mother will appear in the conversation. When there are no words of gratitude or grace, my heart is grieved. Sadly I wonder, *Just what type of nurturing did you receive as a child?* With that thought is a wish: *If only you could meet my mom!*

Somehow my mother, Ruth Hunt, is able to disarm the most seasoned cynic and draw the best out of those who appear to be at their worst. People are immediately attracted to her, and I love it. Oh, it's true that I'm unquestionably prejudiced and undeniably biased, but I have every reason to be. My mother has done a lot of things right! As people enter her presence, they find themselves in a garden of grace, and as a result, they feel unconditionally accepted. The word *grace* means "unmerited favor, unearned care." When she extends grace, you receive an undeserved gift—a gift of time, forgiveness, encouragement, or love.

Just how did she grow this refreshing garden for her children? By cultivating seeds of grace right before our very eyes. I watched Mother parent by using five principles, or secret seeds, that have taken root and borne fruit, spelling grace for her four very different children:

> *Give grace instead of guilt.*
> *Refuse to live in Pity City.*
> *Accentuate the positive.*
> *Cultivate the feeling of freedom.*
> *Encourage love for the Lord.*

Give grace instead of guilt.

When I was a student, I loved summers. No cramming for quizzes, no exhausting exams. One summer I decided I'd organize the entire house—every room, every closet, every drawer!

Periodically I found items that needed to be hung on walls instead of buried under beds. Among those treasures was a pair of Dresden sconces that held three candles each. Knowing Mother always loved the beauty of that china, I discovered the perfect place for the sconces in the living room. The problem I encountered was the concrete walls—driving in nails was virtually impossible!

So I went to the hardware store and bought two sets of wall hooks with adhesive backing. When I told Mother about my plan, she asked, "Are you sure they'll hold?" I confidently replied, "Oh yes. Each sconce weighs only eight pounds, but each hook will hold up to twenty."

After hanging the sconces, I showed my mother who—as I expected—oohed and aahed. She did express one note of concern, but I quickly reassured her about the adhesive grip. I *knew* it would hold.

The next day when I walked into the living room, my eyes were drawn to a white area on the floor. My heart sank. A sconce had pulled loose from the wall. I slowly walked to Mother's bedroom. "Mom, I'm afraid there's something you've got to see. . . . I'm so sorry. . . . One of the sconces fell. It's broken. It's beyond repair." Hesitantly, we entered the living room and saw the sea of scattered fragments.

Never shall I forget Mother's first words to me. "Oh, June, things are just things. Now if *you* had been broken, that would be something to be concerned about."

"Things are just *things!*" What a relief! She had given me grace instead of guilt. How easy for her to have said, "I told you so!" Instead, she looked beyond my fault and saw my need, and what I needed was grace. What I received was undeserved, unmerited, unearned forgiveness. Colossians 4:6 says, "Let your conversation be always full of grace" (NIV). In spite of my guilt, my mother extended me grace. What a reflection of the character of Christ!

Refuse to live in Pity City.

For four or five years, my mother was semi-bedridden with a rare bone condition that doctors knew little about. The honeycombing of her pelvic bone made it both excruciatingly painful and very dangerous to walk.

One afternoon I was walking down the upper hallway of our home toward the stairway when I noticed Mother midway up the stairs. She stood still, an expression of severe pain on her face. Rarely had I seen her in such anguish, and I wondered how she would respond if she knew I was present.

Certain she hadn't seen me, I quietly slipped into a

bedroom, turned around, and then marched to the top stair. "How are you doin', Mom?" With the sweetest smile, she answered, "Just wonderful. And how are you, honey?" If ever there was a reason to complain about discomfort, this was it—yet she didn't want her family to feel burdened by her.

I've often wondered why some parents verbalize their problems again and again and why some parents refuse to be forgiving. Psychologists tell us that the issue is *emotional control.* If people are able to evoke an emotional response by rehearsing their pains for others, they feel they are in control. If they choose to be unforgiving, they exercise the power of unforgiveness and feel that they are in control.

But my mother wouldn't play that game of manipulation. When she was in pain, she refused to invite people to a pity party. She would never say, "You just don't know how hard it is for me!" When people hurt her, she refused to harbor unforgiveness. She wouldn't say, "He's hurt me so much that he doesn't deserve to be forgiven." She refused to live in Pity City.

We've all had reversals, and we've all been rejected. Likewise, we all have God-given inner needs for unconditional love, significance, and security. From the beginning, God planned to meet our needs. Philippians 4:19 explains, "My God will meet all your needs according to his glorious riches in Christ Jesus" (NIV). However, if parents don't allow the Lord to meet their needs, they will look to others—especially family members—to meet all their needs for support, significance, and security.

Such parents will seek attention. If they can't get

positive attention, they will often settle for negative attention and become intentionally needy and intentionally dependent. God did not create any person to meet all the needs of another. God himself wants to meet our needs. The wise parent will understand that children are not possessions whom we own in order to have our needs met. Children are gifts from God to love, to learn from, and to enjoy—not to control.

How refreshing to know that if my mother has a headache, it's a real headache. She doesn't use her pain to try to get my attention or control me. She depends on the Lord, not self-pity strategies, to meet her needs. The weeds of self-pity will choke the life out of a loving relationship, but Mother has always shown that seeds of self-pity won't grow well in a garden of grace.

Accentuate the positive.

Ever since I can remember, music—uplifting, fun, and inspirational music—was woven into the fabric of our home. Mother felt that music could literally set the tone of the home. Although Mom was neither soloist nor pianist, she delighted us all when she sang or played, and she always had us singing right along with her.

If I had to choose one song to represent Mom, it would have to be "Accentuate the Positive." It's easy for me to close my eyes and hear her sing, with a twinkle in her eye. Mom not only sang those words— she lived them!

One particular day, for instance, I noticed for the

first time an etching deep in the grain of our dining-room table. This wasn't a decorative carving that would enhance the table; this was the more primitive kind that definitely devalues a piece of furniture. I asked Mom about it, and to my astonishment, she said, "Well, June, that was your little backward *J*. In school you were trying to learn the alphabet, but somehow you got mixed up on the direction of the *J*. You didn't mean to do anything wrong. You were just practicing on the table. I thought that little backward *J* was so cute I wouldn't let the table be repaired."

What an attitude! Instead of dwelling on the negative, she focused on the positive and chose to cherish a child's mistake. How in keeping with Philippians 4:8: "Whatever is true, whatever is noble, whatever is right, whatever is pure, whatever is lovely, whatever is admirable—if anything is excellent or praiseworthy—think about such things" (NIV). Others would say, "But it wasn't right to carve on a table!" Mother would say it's only natural for children to do childlike things. Yet how many people value possessions over people. Since the human being is God's highest creation, Mother felt it only right to put the higher value on the human heart instead of the human error. In doing so, in accentuating the positive, Mother planted another seed in the garden of grace.

Cultivate the feeling of freedom.

After children grow into adulthood and move away, the holidays seem to call them home. Thanksgiving and Christmas are special times, and many a parent feels deeply wounded when children choose not to go home to celebrate. The children's awareness of this hurt can make them feel pressured to go home, but this mixture of pain and pressure can result in anger, estrangement, and children never wanting to go home.

No one could be more family-oriented than my mother, especially during the holidays. Every vacation throughout my growing-up years was spent with lots of relatives—and bushels of fun—at Granny's house in little Idabel, Oklahoma. Even today, it seems only natural to have scores of people home in Dallas for the holidays. So imagine my surprise when, one November, Mother cheerfully called to say, "Now, honey, at Thanksgiving I want you to do whatever you really want to do. If you want to do something special with a friend, you should do it." I already knew that my brother and two sisters would not be with her; only one granddaughter planned to spend Thanksgiving in Dallas.

"No, Mom, I'm planning to be there."

"Now, June," she continued, "I'm going to be just fine. Don't worry about me."

I always appreciate a call from Mom, but how I especially appreciated the freedom this call gave. I wasn't being pressured to prove my loyalty or love. Mother was giving me freedom to show my love in other ways. And I knew that this gift of freedom doesn't come easily for her. She has worked on it. (Three cheers for Mom!)

I think, too, of the many times I've dropped in unexpectedly to see her, and I know that she has been thrilled down to her toes. Yet, after some time, she would interject, "You've been working so hard. You probably need to rest." Mom would give me an "out," which, most of the time I never took. What a gift of freedom!

How many parents make the tragic mistake of using guilt-inducing statements like, "But do you have to leave now? You never come by anymore. Can't you stay a little longer?" Children often feel that no matter how much they give, it's never enough, and they feel guilty trying to pry themselves loose when they do visit.

Second Corinthians 3:6 says that the letter of the law kills. When a parent lays down the law, the child no longer responds out of love. And, sadly, the letter of the law kills desire. When a parent clings to a child or heaps on guilt, the child doesn't feel a greater desire to be there. Instead, the child feels pressure to stay away.

We all would rather express love out of desire, not because it is demanded of us. The wise parent will therefore sow seeds of freedom for the child. I thank God for a mother who does not lay down the law, but who gives me love and freedom. (By the way, I went home for Thanksgiving—because I wanted to!)

Encourage love for the Lord.

Since I've encountered many cynics and various critics of Christianity in my life, I used to wonder why I had never seriously doubted the existence of God. I cannot credit the philosophical argument of "first cause," the eloquence of a gifted apologist, or the support of a dynamic church. I simply credit my mother. From a young age, I knew that she knew God. The relationship she had with him was real and characterized by genuine love.

Even though we kids didn't know it, she sought to make spiritual things a priority in our lives. I remember all of us climbing into her bed to listen to her read from a Bible storybook for children. She would choose books that had inspirational pictures—and I loved those pictures!

Recently I asked Mother how she encouraged us children spiritually. "I tried to fill the house with spiritual music," she said first, "and you children didn't seem to tire of it." She told me how she chose fun songs that taught spiritual truth—she wanted our faith to be a joy. Often she would tell a story that would help us take the words of a song to heart. A tender story about friendship, for instance, would precede "What a Friend We Have in Jesus."

Knowing how uncertain the future is, Mother wanted us to learn to trust in God's promises. Her own experience with pain, pressures, and failures had taught her the importance of such comforting words as these from her favorite hymn "God Will Take Care of You": Be not dismayed what e'er betide, / God will take care of you. / Beneath his wings of love abide, / God will take care of you. God used the promises in such songs to plant seeds of faith in the soil of my young heart.

Mother was not raised in a church or a home where she learned the Bible. She was saved while visiting a friend's church, but she was never discipled. She had a hunger to grow, but didn't know how. One of her great delights was when she finally discovered the treasures of a Christian bookstore. She found children's books and music, pictures and plaques, pencils and pads—and she filled our lives with these wonderful surprises. As we learned and grew, so did she.

Mother also used the walls of our home to influence our young minds. To this day I can remember meditating on the plaque Mother hung by my bedroom door: "Only one life 'twill soon be past; only what's done for Christ will last." God used that saying to plant seeds of surrender deep within my heart.

A surrendered life was what Mother modeled for us. When life knocked her to her knees, she learned that was the best position for prayer. What a comfort to have a praying mother! She didn't just say prayers—she talked to God! And she talked to him about our lives, our needs, our future.

For many years, it was not uncommon for Mother to stop by a church, slip into a chapel, and spend time on her knees before God. One fall afternoon, she did just that, and she prayed so long that, when she got up to leave, it was totally dark and she was locked inside. Fumbling through the darkness, she eventually found a light switch and the pastor's study. She then found his phone number, and he came to her rescue.

When I heard about the incident, I was amused, but more importantly I felt humbled. I knew that some of her prayers that afternoon were for me. Mother believed in prayer and in God's promises, and God used Mother's prayers to plant seeds of hope in my heart.

As an adult, I've thought a lot about why people feel accepted in my mother's presence. Why do so many adopt Mom as their Granny Ruth? I believe it is because she stands with arms wide open and warmly welcomes others into her garden of grace with the prayer that ultimately they will be drawn to the God of all grace.

"Stick wit' Jesus"

❖————————————————————————————————❖

Carman Dominic Licciardello is better known to his fans simply as Carman, a talented singer/songwriter/musician who is also a deeply committed minister of God's Word.

Carman was a nightclub singer in Las Vegas, well on his way towards a career in show business, when, through the prayers of his sister, Nancy Ann, and his attendance at an Andrae Crouch concert, he became a believer. Committing his life to the Lord meant committing his music to the Lord—and that he did.

Carman's debut release, Some-O-Dat, was followed by Sunday's on the Way, Comin' On Strong, The Champion, and A Long Time Ago . . . In a Land Called Bethlehem. The energy of his concert appearances was captured on Carman Live . . . Radically Saved. His latest release, Revival in the Land, offers musical word pictures of Satan's view of impending doom and God's army marching through the land.

Gifted and versatile, Carman sings rap, praise, ballad, story-song, rhythm and blues, and rockabilly, gaining him a wide audience for his gospel message of salvation. As his press release explains, he works to make his live performances evangelistic events instead of mere entertainment; he is interested in producing "sold-out Christians—not sold-out concerts."

As he shares here, Carman credits his mother, a talented musician herself, with encouraging him to take up music and his father with giving him the ability to tell a story. Using both these gifts, Carman shares stories about Jesus through the songs he writes and performs.

In January 1956, Elvis Presley came out with "Hound Dog" and shook the nation. In January 1956, Dominic and Nancy Licciardello came out with a hound dog named Carman who shook up the neighborhood. I was the third of the three children in our family; I was the baby. My brother, Mario, is eight years older than me, and my sister, Nancy Ann, is ten years older.

My parents were born again in the early fifties, coming out of Catholicism. My sister was the one who really stayed close to the Lord, and later she married a preacher. My brother always lived near the edge and often was saved by the skin of his teeth. He was always a roughneck who got into a lot of fights; he was sort of like the Fonzie of the neighborhood. Remember Sylvester Stallone in *Rocky?* That was Mario, and I always wanted to be like him even though my father would say, "Don't grow up to be like your brother." There was something in my brother that was fearless. He was willing to take any chance in the world, and I was very attracted to that. However, I always told my dad I wanted to be like my sister just so I wouldn't get a beatin'.

I was the only child in our family who was born into a Christian home, so my mother used to call me her

Jesus-boy. Because of a birth defect in my neck, my head was permanently tilted to one side. I was prayed for by my parents and my uncle Don and aunt Catherine, all very devout Christians, and God miraculously healed me. It was during this time that my parents held me up in a Bible study and dedicated my life to the Lord so that, whatever happened, my life would be used for the service of God. I guess that commitment really stuck because the presence of Jesus haunted me until I finally succumbed when I was twenty years old.

As I was growing up, my parents had some financial problems. My father went into a business venture that didn't work out so well, and he lost everything. We went bankrupt. But I lived in the same house until I was eleven years old, went to the same school, and had the same friends. I had a very stable upbringing.

I remember going to church when I was a little boy, but because of all the things that took place in our lives, our family began to fall away. By the time I was seven, we were out of church completely. My sister was getting married and moving away to a Christian college with her husband, and my brother was in rare form. He always had stories to tell, coming home with skinned knuckles from a fight he'd been in.

I didn't really have much direction growing up. But I did find out that the most miserable people on the face of the earth are not necessarily the unsaved. They're Christians who have backslidden—they've got just enough of the world in them to not really enjoy walking with the Lord, and just enough of God in them to not really enjoy sin, so they're in a tormented situation.

As I grew up, my mother was the main musical influence in my life. I remember her playing the accordion at family functions and our annual Italian picnics. She would take center stage somewhere, get her accordion, and play all the old Italian songs for hours. She would start in the afternoon and finish at ten o'clock that night. (By that time, everybody had a few drinks in them, and they really weren't listening anymore anyway!) My mother had studied the accordion since she was twelve years old. She had a great career planned, but when she was eighteen, she met my father, a very handsome army man, and was swept off her feet. There went the career, but she passed her love of music on to all of her children.

My father was a great personality, and he could tell stories for hours. Whenever there was a get-together, my father would position himself somewhere at a table, and all the cousins and uncles and brothers and aunts and whoever else was around would sit and listen to my father tell stories for hours. At one end of the building my mother played the accordion and kept half the crowd spellbound. My father would tell stories in the other part of the building, and I'd hear roars and laughter and oohs and aahs. Mom and Dad were quite a pair.

While I was growing up without the Lord, my mother began to play her music in nightclubs, and my father became even more distant because of his failure in business and his lack of commitment to the Lord. There was a definite chasm in our family. My mother used to come home from work at two or three o'clock in the morning with all her band members. I waited up and then we jammed until six or seven in the morning. This got me out of a lot of school because I was too tired. My mother would write me excuses.

By the time I was a teenager, my parents saw that my life wasn't really going anywhere, so they put me in a military school. That didn't work out so well. I remained unfocused, and I got into a lot of fights. I wanted to be more like my brother, but I guess in my heart I was more of a peacemaker and negotiator like my father.

Even though I was directionless, music never left me. My mother always encouraged me to pursue what was deep in my heart, but my father wanted me to get a job, a real job. He used to tell me that if I didn't learn a trade, I'd end up digging ditches. He was a butcher by trade and wanted me to go into meat cutting. It just wasn't there for me. My brother was the same way, except he got married at nineteen and had to get a good job to make ends meet. Slowly but surely he started getting jobs as a security guard and wound up, at age twenty-nine, the youngest chief of police ever in the state of New Jersey.

Just as Mario had always wanted to be a cop, I had always wanted to be a musician. I pursued my dreams with my mother's encouragement until one day, when I was twenty years old, I left New Jersey to go to Las Vegas. I wanted to pursue a career there, but I was going to spend some time with my sister who lived in Southern California and who was the epitome of a Christian. I had been working in clubs for a few years and felt like I wouldn't be that influenced by this Jesus thing she had going on. Well, little did I know that she'd been praying for me for eleven years.

By the time I got to Southern California, I was pretty hip, pretty cool. I always wore my shirt unbuttoned down to my navel, and I knew more than a nineteen-year-old should about life, at least the dark side of life. I was driving back and forth from Vegas to Southern California setting up floor shows and meeting with managers, trying to get my thing going. Things were going pretty well, moving ahead, until I went to Disneyland's "Night of Joy" concert with a girl who was a Christian. I respected her so much that I pretty much went wherever she took me, yet at the same time it bothered me that she was Christian and I wasn't and still she was dating me.

That night, I listened to most of the Christian performers sing, and I really wasn't impressed. They didn't seem to have the tenacity that I grew up with, the dogged determination that I saw in my brother, or even the commitment I'd seen in my sister. I just didn't feel it in the music I heard—until from a distance I heard all sorts of hand clapping and tambourine playing and wild, pulsating music. I turned to the girl I was with and said, "Who is that?" She looked at me with a sort of gleam in her eye and said, "Oh, that's Andrae." I went over and sat mesmerized as Andrae Crouch and the Disciples took what was sacred at the altar and brought it out before the world in a way I could understand. He sang, "It won't be long. Soon we will be leaving here." I felt like I was the only non-Christian in the whole park!

The very next day, having learned what music is really meant to be, I committed my life to Jesus Christ. My mother supported my decision, my managers and agents back in New Jersey went crazy, and my father was quiet. I went through a real difficult time. Sometimes in life you don't know what you should do; all you know is what you shouldn't do. I knew that I shouldn't be in the clubs, and I knew I needed to leave the bars. When my sister said, "Why don't you take Jesus to Vegas?" I knew in my gut that wasn't going to work.

Still, I wanted to go back into the clubs, I was getting ready to go back to Vegas, and I was prepared to take Jesus with me. I had all the rest of those crossover thoughts that I hear regularly from Christian entertainers, and I was about to become one of them. But I was struggling with this decision.

My mother had been a real encouragement through the years, but my dad had never said a whole lot. He had never said much when I decided to pursue music and not a trade; he watched from a distance. But when I was getting ready to take a job in a nightclub, I got a phone call from my dad, and it was a turning point for me. He said something to me that I'll never forget, something that changed my life.

My dad said, "Carm, everything was really going well for me when I was walking with the Lord, but things started to go wrong when I turned my back on God. I went into a business venture when I should have gone into the ministry. And ever since then I've hurt. And I've paid a dear price. You know your dad don't talk much, but I want you to listen to me this time."

He said, "Don't make the same mistake I made. You gotta learn from other people, other people's mistakes, because you'll never live long enough to make 'em all yourself."

He said, "Don't go back into the clubs. Commit your talents to the Lord. Sing for Jesus Christ. All the things that you'll ever want in life God will give you, but you give him yourself first. Commit your way to him. And don't play games with God."

Tears came to my eyes. I was on the phone, and I slumped to the floor with my head hung down. And I began to cry. He said to me, "You know your dad loves you, and I'd never tell you anything that was gonna hurt ya." He said, "But don't do it like I did it. Stick wit' Jesus."

I told him, "OK, Dad, I will." I hung up the phone, called the people at the club, and told them I wasn't going to do it. They called me a Jesus freak. They said I was limiting my talent, that I would only be singing in front of small groups in little churches, that I was a waste. But I remembered my father's words and how he told me to go all the way with Jesus, don't compromise, and don't turn back. "Sing for God. Sing for him." I remembered hearing Andrae sing passionately about the Lord, and I thought about how it affected my life. And that's what I wanted my music to do.

That was sixteen years ago, and I've never gone back on my commitment. Today I consistently stand before ten and twenty thousand people at a time in this country and around the world, telling people, young and old alike, to commit their talent to the Lord and don't turn back. To give their all to Jesus

Tony Campolo
is chairman of the
Department of
Sociology and Youth
Ministry at Eastern
College,
Pennsylvania.

**Tony Campolo with
his mother,** whom
he lovingly describes
as a missionary to
everyone she met

Bart Campolo, like his father, is the executive director of Kingdomworks, a development program for youth and children in partnership with urban churches.

Lisa, Peggy, Bart, and Tony Campolo

Charles W. Colson, founder of Prison Fellowship in 1975, is the author of numerous books and articles.

Chuck Colson with his parents

Dr. Lawrence J. (Larry) Crabb, Jr. is the founder and director of the Institute of Biblical Counseling.

Larry Crabb (right) with his parents and brother

James Dobson as a young
man with his mother

Dr. James Dobson, author
of many best-selling books,
is the founder and
president of Focus on the
Family.

James Dobson as a
child, embraced by
his father

Colleen Townsend Evans, once a movie star, is actively involved in many ministries, including serving on the boards of Presbyterians for Renewal and World Vision, U.S.

Colleen Townsend as a young girl with her mother

Bill Gaither is a well-known musician, songwriter, and businessman.

Bill Gaither, (front right) with his parents, brother, and sister

Gloria Gaither is an author and musician, and the wife of Bill Gaither. The Gaithers have three grown children.

Gloria Gaither with her parents and sister

Steve Green, popular vocalist, has won several Dove Awards and has twice been named Male Vocalist of the Year by the Gospel Music Association.

Steven Green (front right) with his family

Larnelle Harris, dynamic gospel singer, has won five Grammy and eight Dove Awards.

3 yer old.

Larnelle Harris with his father

Florence Littauer is a popular speaker and author, and is the president and founder of C.L.A.S.S.

Florence Littauer with her parents and brothers

Senator Richard G. Lugar is the senior United States Senator from Indiana.

Richard Lugar with his mother

Calvin Miller, former pastor of Westside Church, Omaha, Nebraska.

Calvin Miller
with his mother

Janette Oke is one of the best-selling authors of Christian fiction of all time.

Janette Oke (front left) with her parents and siblings

Dr. Kenneth Taylor, who paraphrased *The Living Bible*, is the founder and chairman of Tyndale House Publishers.

Kenneth Taylor's parents

Sheila Walsh, a talented vocalist, is a former cohost of the Christian Broadcasting Network's *700 Club.*

Sheila Walsh (center) with her mother and sister

Christ and don't compromise the message of the gospel. And to be 100 percent for Jesus.

Two years ago my dad passed away. I was in the hospital room with him when he died. Before he died, he looked at all the people standing around the bed, pointed his finger at each one of us, and said, "Do you glorify Jesus? Do *you* glorify Jesus? How about you? Do you glorify Jesus?" He had had a tracheotomy, so it was difficult for him to talk, but we understood his whispers. He wasn't really asking for a response; he was asking so that we would answer the Holy Spirit inside.

At his funeral, he didn't have any money to leave us. He didn't have any worldly possessions or earthly goods. As a matter of fact, he left a couple of bills that I had to pay. But in his will he told me that he had given me something: He had given me the ability to tell a story.

As the will was read at the funeral, I began to cry uncontrollably as I pictured my father sitting at a table telling stories to all of his friends and relatives. They may have heard the same stories a thousand times, but he had this way of taking you into another world and letting you experience what he had. Sometimes he made the stories up or embellished them. When he was in the hospital dying, he told me about all of the things he had made up, and we laughed a lot together. He not only gave me the ability to tell a story, but to tell a story about *Jesus* and for *the Lord.*

My parents did a few things right. Among those things, they gave me something that has value only as I share it with the world. My mother encouraged my music, and I inherited from her the skills and instincts to craft a song. And my father gave me the ability to tell a story. Thanks to these gifts, I use songs to tell stories about Jesus Christ who has so captivated and enriched my life that it's just an absolute bore to talk about anything else.

Gifts from My Parents

Like so many of the people I am privileged to have contributed to this book, the list of Florence Littauer's accomplishments goes on and on! She is known internationally for her ability to exhort, encourage, and entertain her audience. She is a popular seminar and retreat leader, banquet speaker, talk-show guest, and a widely read author.

Among the eighteen books she has written, Florence has authored Make the Tough Times Count, *her life story,* Blow Away the Black Clouds, Personality Plus, Raising Christians—Not Just Children, Silver Boxes, *and, her most recent,* Dare to Dream, *a challenge to beat the odds and win personal success.*

At the University of Massachusetts, where she graduated with honors, Florence won the coveted "Best Female Speaker in New England Colleges" award. Since then she has been awarded many Angel Awards for her writing excellence and been honored by the National Speakers Association with their C.S.P. (Certified Speaking Professional) Designation and the C.P.A.E. (Council of Peers Award of Excellence). She uses her talents to address such topics as getting along with people, *knowing ourselves, building a strong marriage, raising children ("Are We Raising Christians or Just Children?"), and the Gift of Encouragement (Silver Boxes). Florence is the president and founder of C.L.A.S.S., the Christian Leaders and Speakers Seminars in which she shares her secrets to dynamic communication and successful speaking.*

Many of you know that Florence grew up in three rooms behind her father's store. Here are a few more details of her childhood and the seven principles her parents followed to fill those years with love.

When Gloria approached me at the Praise Gathering for Believers in Seattle and asked if I would write a chapter on what my parents did right, I was delighted. For years I have been speaking about growing up in three rooms behind my father's store in Haverhill, Massachusetts. I have laughed about it and cried about it.

As I raised my own children and gave them more than the necessities of life, I have often wondered how my parents ever raised decent children cramped into those three tiny rooms with the store serving as our living and dining room. How did Mother manage with no hot water, no bathtub, no washing machine, no refrigerator, and no appliances? How did Father keep a sense of humor trying to run a business with little children underfoot, eating, playing, and doing homework in the center of the store? How did Jim, Ron, and I dare set any goals when we had no money, no chance of education, no telephone, no car, and no television?

And how did we think we could amount to anything when we wore other people's hand-me-down clothes and shoes that had holes in the soles?

What did my parents do right in the midst of adverse circumstances and abject poverty?

They spent time with us.

One of the advantages of no money, no car, and no TV is that you can't go anywhere and you're not distracted by desires to do foolish things. We were dependent upon each other for entertainment. Whatever we did had to be done around that one table in the store with an ever-changing audience watching us. There was nowhere else to go. Since we lived in a business that was open from 6:30 every morning until 11:00 at night seven days a week, we always knew where our parents were. They taught us to be presentable at any time of the day or night, to be pleasant to the customers whether we felt like it or not, and to cheer up those who were depressed or downhearted. We learned to sell, bag groceries, add, and make change at very young ages. Whatever we did, we were all in it together!

They stayed optimistic.

In spite of what we lacked in material things, my parents maintained a positive outlook. When they married, my mother, a violin and cello teacher, was almost thirty. My father was almost fifty years old and appeared to be well able to support her in style. When the depression hit, however, the company my father had worked for and was to retire from was closed. At sixty years old, he found himself with no job, no money, and three little children to raise. Almost anyone would have been pessimistic about the future, but my father borrowed two thousand dollars from some friends, bought the Riverside Variety Store, and moved us all into it. Neither parent ever told us we were deprived, and they cheerfully made the best out of a situation neither of them deserved. Because they kept an optimistic attitude, we accepted the store as a plus and not a minus. My school friends liked to come to my home to play with me because, as my father said, "Who else has a case of penny candy and a table piled up with cupcakes in the middle of their living room?"

They kept our minds moving.

Living in the store was like a laboratory course in sociology and psychology, and our parents kept teaching us about people from real-life examples. We never sat passively as people came in and out, but we discussed their various problems and learned from them. My father proposed topics for our dinner conversations, and we would all come up with creative solutions to his hypothetical questions. He didn't look for pat answers but for imaginative responses, and he would challenge our minds to move beyond what seemed possible. My father also made listening to the news and political speeches on the radio an exciting event because he would analyze what was said and ask for our opinions. We discussed world events before some children even knew there were any! Since we had no money for magazines or books, the highlight of the week was the arrival of the library bus. An old vehicle full of books would pull up outside our store every Wednesday afternoon. We could only check out three books, so we made our choices carefully—and we didn't dream of not reading what we'd selected.

They kept us taking lessons.

Even without money, my parents insisted we take lessons and become well-rounded individuals. Mother taught us the violin and gave lessons to our friends in order to pay our other instructors. Aunt Sadie taught us all to play the piano, and I well remember her portable piano keyboard with its removable keys. Each key was labeled, and we would take them all out, mix up the black and white keys, and then put them all back in the proper order. With the challenge of a giant puzzle, it was a fun and painless way to learn what was on each side of middle C. Even though none of us was a gifted pianist or violinist, our home instruction gave us all a basic foundation in reading music and an appreciation for quality. Jim and Ron also took voice lessons, and Ron learned to play the trumpet in the high-school band. My favorite lessons were in elocution, where I memorized poetry and Scripture and took part in school plays. Father had me recite my pieces for the customers and put me in the church talent shows, where he sat in the front row and applauded.

They kept us in church.

From the time we were little, we went to church whenever the doors opened. Our store was across the street from the church, and the only time we closed the store was for one hour on Sunday morning. No one ever asked, "Do you want to go to church?" or "Do you feel like going?" We all just got dressed and went. Our parents had high moral standards, but they were never legalistic, negative, or preachy. I can remember the few times as a teenager when I was tempted to be daring in some direction. I would say to myself, "That would disappoint Father or hurt Mother"—and so I wouldn't do it. Although our church was not evangelistic, it did provide us with moral and spiritual values that have continued as a basis for our adult lives.

They gave us a sense of history.
One of the special times I remember as a child was our yearly "History Day." Even though my father was from England, he very much felt that we should understand American history. We children were allowed to suggest places we would like to go, and then my father would plan an itinerary and surprise us on that day. Because we never had a car, our journey started with a bus ride to the depot and then a train trip to Boston. We then took the subway or walked to each different spot. My father had always studied up on the places we visited so that, even if there were no guides, he could fill us in on the historical background. Bunker Hill Monument was just a picture of an obelisk until we all climbed the stairs to the top. Faneuil Hall didn't sound like a marketplace until we saw the sides of beef hanging on hooks in the open square. Paul Revere was just a name in a history book until we saw his birthplace and traced the ride he took to warn that the British were coming.

Recent surveys show that young Americans are woefully ignorant of American history even though it is taught in school. One major reason is that history out of a book has little meaning, but take a child to see the replica of the *Mayflower* and he will begin to imagine what those months cramped in that little space must have been like! Wherever you live, there is some history nearby that costs little or nothing to visit. As with any meaningful experience, this kind of special day takes time and effort on the part of the parent, but the benefits could stimulate in your children a real love of American history.

They gave us hope.

In the midst of the depression, a college education was a wild dream for poor people and almost an impossibility for a young woman, yet I was desperate to go to college. I started an hourly job in a department store when I was fourteen and saved every cent I could. (I had two dresses that I wore every other day and hoped no one would notice.) When I talked to my father about college, he pointed out that whatever money he could find would have to be saved for Jim, the oldest son—"Boys need an education more than girls because they have to support a family."

My father's thinking was the accepted opinion in those days, but I could not go along with this philosophy. "If I promise to work for four years after I get out and put Jim through school, would you let me go?" He agreed on the condition that I get a scholarship to cover tuition. With his encouragement, I studied so hard during high school that I got all *A*'s and a scholarship to the state university. He gave me what little he could and kept telling me, "You can make it. You are plenty smart."

What a shock it was when Daddy died during my senior year when Jim was in high school and Ron was twelve years old. Even though my father was gone and Jim didn't know about my promise, I felt obligated to fulfill my agreement and I did. Not until April of Jim's senior year did I get married—and then only after I knew his bills were paid. He went on to get a second bachelor's degree, two master's degrees, and an award as the outstanding young chaplain in the Strategic Air Command.

Also, because of my father's death, I returned to Haverhill to teach and become a parent-sister-teacher to young Ron. We entered Haverhill High School together, and I gave him the encouragement my father would have if he had lived. I became Ron's speech teacher and his cheering section, and I felt personally rewarded when in 1990 he won the top awards for best radio personality in the United States from the National Radio Broadcasters, *Billboard* magazine, and the Marconis. His morning show in Dallas has been number one for twenty years, and he has become a legend in his own time.

How did my parents raise productive and positive children in impossible circumstances? They spent time with us, stayed optimistic, kept our minds moving, gave us lessons they couldn't afford, kept us in church, gave us a sense of history, and offered us hope.

I hope I have done the same thing.

That Little Brown Jacket

M ark has been a wonderful addition to The Gaither Vocal Band. He brings to the group an excellent voice and a terrific sense of humor. I've seen his storytelling ability win over audiences, and I especially appreciate his way of inspiring the church community to be encouragers.

Mark has been performing in churches and auditoriums for more than ten years. While in college he felt the Lord calling him to a music ministry, but once he started singing in churches, he realized he had to do something while the sound man was changing sound tracks, so he started talking. That's when Mark's comedy was born. He started talking about his life, his family, and his upbringing. The more he talked, the more people laughed. Soon, Mark was known for his comedy as well as his singing.

In 1988, Mark performed at the Christian Artists' Music Seminar in the Rockies in Estes Park, Colorado. Little did Mark, or anyone else, suspect that ten minutes during a morning worship session hosted by Sandi Patti and Dallas Holm would impact his life the way it has. Several record companies pursued him with recording contracts, but it was

Word Records that signed the young artist six months later. Mark has recorded two live concerts with Word: For the First Time on Planet Earth, and his latest release, "My First Comedy Video." Prior to signing with Word, Mark was invited to join The Gaither Vocal Band, and he now performs 80 concerts a year with the Gaithers as well as 120 solo concerts.

Mark remembers having his life planned—"I wanted a nine-to-five business career like my father. God had different plans for me. After earning a degree in youth ministry from Liberty University, I felt God calling me into full-time ministry."

Read here about how Mark discovered his ability to make people laugh and how he learned about unconditional love. Mark also shares some encouraging words for parents of hyperactive kids.

◆━━━━━━━━━━━━◆

The dark brown, imitation-leather jacket was a couple of sizes too big the first time I put it on. It was a hand-me-down. My older brother had worn it until he got too big, but the first time I put it on, it felt like my own. It had a brown elastic collar and cuffs. It didn't have any pinholes in it—yet. You see, my older brother never came home from school with notes pinned to his lapel; but after a year on my back, that jacket looked like a pincushion!

Like every little brother, I was always proud of my big brother. Mike was my hero. He was very athletic and had no trouble being first pick when it came time for the peewee Little League teams. I was just proud to be his water boy. I had a good head start at running back and forth—I was hyperactive.

But let me start at the beginning. . . . My mother and father were both raised in Christian homes. Very normal. They had hardworking parents who brought them up in the ways of the Lord. They met, were eventually married, and started a family. My older brother, Mike, was a fat little baby, but as soon as he started walking, he slimmed down into an athletic and perfect child. He never gave my parents one minute of trouble. In fact, Mike was so perfect that my parents would remark about the misbehavior of their friends' children. They couldn't understand why their friends' children couldn't sit still. So Mom and Dad decided they should bless the world with another one of their perfectly well-behaved children—and they had me. (Actually, I think the Lord wanted to bring them down a notch or two. Their pride was getting the best of them.)

Well, I was born looking for a party. I was into everything. My father says that when I started to walk, I started to climb. He says I could walk across a room, up a wall, across the ceiling, and back down the other wall. When, on the rare occasions my parents were invited to a friend's house (they weren't invited often because their friends were afraid they'd bring me!), Dad would follow me wherever I went to make sure nothing in my path was destroyed.

I don't remember much about kindergarten, but Mom says I came home after my first day and announced that I had learned all I needed to know and didn't intend to go back. In the first grade, my teacher told me that if I didn't sit still and be quiet, I wouldn't make it to the second grade.

Since I was always moving fast, by the time I made it to the third grade, they had me in an accelerated class. My teacher, Miss Johnston, had long, dark hair and the sharpest fingernails I've ever seen. (These weren't Lee Press-On nails—they were homegrown.) After I came home several days straight with Miss Johnston's fingernail prints on my arms, Mom went to the school and demanded that I be put in a class with a teacher who was also a mother. She thought a mom would relate better.

So they put me in Mrs. Holland's class, and I'll never forget this sweet lady. Mom said this was one of the turning points in my life. Mrs. Holland was a Christian. When I would get hyper, Mrs. Holland would take me on walks around the elementary school campus, and we would discuss theology. She knew that my parents were Christians and that, even though this was a public school, she could discuss the Lord with me and not get in trouble. Mrs. Holland went to the Assembly of God church and I was raised Baptist, so we would discuss the security of the believer. I don't think I ever converted her, but she didn't convert me either! What a wonderful influence Mrs. Holland was!

In the third grade, I was put on Ritalin, a medication to control my hyperactivity. I slept through the third grade. Finally, my mother decided she didn't want a zombie for a son, and she took me off that!

The other grades followed, and my little jacket got

more pinholes. (And I didn't just bring home notes from school—I brought home novels!) When teachers pinned something on my jacket, I knew I was in trouble. Sometimes I'd be in tears by the time I made it to the front door. I felt like a little failure. I couldn't make it through one day of school without getting a report of my behavior hung on my lapel like some kind of document of defeat. Mom would read it first and then would join me in my sorrow, yet I knew my parents always stood behind the teachers—which I think was very important. It made me respect authority.

We had a next-door neighbor named Helen, and Helen had a son about nine months younger than I. His name was Fritzy, and Fritzy and I would get into fights. I would usually win, so of course Helen didn't much care for me. In fact, whenever Helen had the chance, she would let my mother know how much she couldn't stand me. When Mom was pregnant with my little sister, Helen made a point of telling Mother she hoped her next child wasn't like me. My mother swung around—as only a pregnant woman can do— and told Helen that one day God was going to use me.

Mom's belief in me goes back to before I was born. She had miscarried the child before me, and at two months into her pregnancy with me, her water broke. The doctor told her she couldn't possibly still be pregnant, but Mom told him she knew that she was! She was confined to bed for several weeks, and while she was in bed, she told God that if he would let this baby live, she would give me to the Lord. (I hope God knew what he was getting into!)

I started singing in church when I was four. I

couldn't throw a football, but I was a ham. Since athletics weren't my bag, Mom took me down to the local theatre in Houston to audition when I was nine. I got every part in the Houston Music Theatre productions that called for a little boy. My first play was with Hal March in *The Music Man*. My second play was with Kay Starr in *Annie Get Your Gun*. I had just gotten the lead in *Oliver* when the theatre went bankrupt, so instead of doing *Oliver*, we went to Nashville. A friend of ours knew the promoter of The International Song Festival and asked if I could perform. The promoter, thinking we surely wouldn't show up, said, "Sure. Bring him." But he didn't know my mother.

Mom packed up the whole family—Dad, Mike, Missy, and me—and we went to Nashville. The producer of the show put me on for one song. I sang a patriotic medley and received a standing ovation from the fifteen thousand people there that night. The next day Bob Benson and Bob MacKenzie signed me to a recording contract with Impact records. I started traveling around the country singing gospel music. It was a great outlet for my hyperactivity, and an outlet is just what Mom and Dad had in mind all along.

I spent a couple of years going to school by way of American Correspondence courses. By now, the little brown jacket had been outgrown and set aside. One day, though, my little sister, Missy, was diagnosed as having diabetes. She needed our family life to be stable, so I had to come off the road. Instead of singing in the summer of '73, I went off to church camp.

It was at that camp on Tuesday night, June 5, that I realized I had never really given my life to Christ. I had walked an aisle to pray when I was seven, but I'd done so just because my older brother did. I hadn't known the Lord for myself. I knew the plan of salvation, but I didn't know the Man of salvation. That changed on June 5.

You might be thinking, "Well, did *you* change?" Yes, I did, but I was still hyperactive, and I still had a smart mouth. But now when my mother quoted Scripture about obedience to me, I actually felt convicted. And, trust me, when she found out that it worked, she really boned up on her Bible!

So a hyperactive kid has grown into a somewhat hyperactive adult. I've turned any extra energy I have into comedy. Now what I used to get spanked for, I get paid to do.

What would I say my parents did right? Looking back, I'd have to say my parents looked at those pinholes in my brown leather jacket the way a scientist looks at an experiment that fails. Those holes simply represented one way that didn't work. I guess I was just one of those kids who needed many experiments before he got it right. Some kids learn to behave on the first try; it just took me longer. I never felt like I was going to bring home one note too many. I never felt like this note would be the one that would get me kicked out of the family.

I learned a lot about God's love from the way my parents raised me. I know God loves me and that his love is never-ending. I know, too, that even though I fail, he's going to be faithful (I'll never bring home one note too many!). I never could—and I don't have to—earn his love, and I can always feel accepted unconditionally.

Mom and Dad always believed in me. Our next-door neighbors didn't believe in me. My Sunday school teachers didn't. My elementary school teachers definitely didn't—except for Mrs. Holland. And Helen thought I would one day grow up to shoot a president. Mom and Dad didn't always believe me, but they always believed *in* me.

I wish parents of hyperactive kids would understand one thing: Whatever you are now experiencing, IT WILL PASS. Nothing lasts forever except the Word of God and people. And even though that little kid may be a brat sometimes, he's still a person. He won't be a kid forever, so laugh when he's funny. Teach when he's curious. Discipline when he needs it. But always, always believe in him and let him know it. One day, when he grows up, he'll understand that, like patient parents, God is in his corner, cheering him on, loving him, and working in him.

I don't know where that little brown jacket is today, but I'll never forget it. Each pinhole now represents a memory, a memory I'll never forget, and a memory my parents are finally able to laugh about.

A Formula for Parenting

Richard Lugar, a fifth generation Hoosier, is the senior United States senator from Indiana. Americans across the country know of his participation in the Senate Foreign Relations Committee and the Senate Agriculture Committee, and many have seen how his role in politics has given him the means to act on behalf of causes he believes in.

Through the years, Richard has supported legislation to prevent hunger and to mandate the testing and disposal of dangerous pesticides. He has been an important advocate for rural America and, as the former mayor of Indianapolis, is also a leading congressional expert on housing and other urban issues. Richard has also spoken out against tyrannies that suppress democratic freedoms around the world. His 1988 book, Letters to the Next President, offers his insight and perspective on American foreign policy.

In writing here about what his parents did right, Richard remembers their focus on education and health, a focus which indeed shaped their son. A Rhodes Scholar himself, Richard has received many education-related awards, including twenty-three honorary college and university degrees. Richard *also promotes health and nutrition programs, especially for children and senior citizens. Practicing what he preaches about the importance of physical fitness, he is one of the fastest long-distance runners in Congress.* The Roll Call *describes him as "in remarkable physical condition" and "America's fittest U.S. senator"!*

My parents found the optimal formula for parenting. Besides giving me every opportunity for education and providing for my health, they did everything they could to make me feel I was a very special person. And they did this during the Great Depression, World War II, and the many years of my boyhood when my father was not in good health (he died in my twenty-fourth year, shortly after Charlene and I married).

My dad was the fourth generation of Lugars to farm in Grant County, Indiana. Great-great-grandfather, George Lugar, had come from Giles County, Virginia, in 1823 and named Lugar Creek after his family. In my parents' family dining room, George's son, Joseph, peered down from a large portrait. He wore a Civil War officer's uniform and held his hand inside his coat in a Napoleonic pose. Joseph Lugar became one of the wealthiest citizens in Grant County during the natural gas and cattle booms. The fact that each of his several fortunes vanished in various economic cycles does not diminish our admiration.

My grandfather, Riley Webster Lugar, was the coach when my dad moved to Marion County, Indiana, and played basketball at Valley Mills High School. Grandfather Lugar's impact was so memorable that when I started playing freshman basketball for Shortridge High School twenty-five years later, coaches still recalled with amusement the salty language of Webb Lugar and his tendency to always be in search of a spittoon.

As an agriculture major at Purdue University, my dad was an excellent student. He joined Beta Theta Pi fraternity and played on the varsity basketball team under the legendary coach Ward "Piggy" Lambert. I grew up in comfortable residential houses on the north side of Indianapolis with a good feeling about family, basketball, and Beta Theta Pi.

My dad had an older sister and two younger brothers, but my mother was an only child (a sister had died as a baby in a tragic fire). Her father, Thomas L. Green, enjoyed only five years of schooling but possessed an inventive genius and entrepreneurial drive that led to the early founding of a bicycle shop and then a small business specializing in the manufacture of cookie cutters. Three disastrous fires destroyed his businesses before he built Thomas L. Green & Company. With his wife, Anna, and my mother in tow, the family toured America and the world, sketching drawings of biscuit and cracker machinery and bringing back orders for the factory.

After spending her childhood living near the Old German Club in downtown Indianapolis (her great-grandparents had come to the United States in the 1840s), my mother and her parents moved to a lovely home on Fall Creek Boulevard, and Thomas L. Green & Co. flourished. My mother was a campus leader at

Tech High School and later at Butler University. Like her mother, she enjoyed a rich heritage of language and music; she inherited from her father a strong sense of risk taking and a talent for leadership.

My parents, Bertha Isabel Green and Marvin Leroy Lugar, were married at the beginning of the Great Depression, and I was born into a comfortable bungalow situated on a narrow lot. In later years, I learned about my parents' arduous budgeting procedures. My dad's early jobs included a stint as a car salesman—which he enjoyed—and some time in an electrical supply store—which he did not. My first memory of his vocation was his longtime partnership with his dad at Lugar Commission Company. At the Indianapolis Stockyards, he sold the hogs and his father sold the cattle. He was up at four each morning and in the yards before five when the auctions began.

In the summer, Dad took my brother, Tom, and me to the six-hundred-acre farm in southwest Marion County that he had purchased in the early thirties with the help of Webb Lugar and Tom Green. There we discovered a new world of corn, soybean, and wheat fields. We learned to ride a pony and feed the pigs. As we grew older, we worked for ten cents an hour many hours a week pulling volunteer corn out of the fields. We saved our money carefully in piggy banks.

All too often, White River came over the farm levees and flooded a 250-acre bottomland field. Relentlessly, Dad tried to contain the river with thousands of hours of bulldozer work that cost tens of thousands of dollars. Mother often commented that travel plans and other projected expenditures had just been converted into another foot of dirt piled on the levee.

One year Dad allowed us to invest our savings in the purchase of one acre of wheat. We were prepared to double our initial investment of seventeen dollars at harvest time, but White River rose and, one spring morning, ended our dreams and Dad's. There was no restitution of our money. We had taken a risk, and we had lost everything.

A year later we invested again, this time in a heavy sow. Her pigs lived and we were in business, multiplying our money over time and litters. Our education clearly extended beyond the classroom into the real world, the business world of our father.

Our education also extended beyond academics to athletics and music. Since the Indianapolis public schools were adamant against constructing basketball goals in their gymnasiums, Dad helped us construct a backboard against the big maple tree in our gravel driveway. We played during the winter days and even under the lights at night, dreaming of Butler Fieldhouse and the State Basketball Finals.

Mother had another agenda for us. Our routine of breakfast and early-morning practice on our musical instruments made certain that we who walked to school were on time every day. At ages four and five, my brother and I were enrolled in a piano class at Jordan Conservatory of Music. About seven years later, our younger sister, Anne, followed. In due course, we took weekly private lessons at the conservatory.

I displayed an ability to improvise tunes and compose short pieces of music. When I was nine or ten, Mother drove me to Bloomington to visit with Dean Sanders of the Indiana University School of Music. He encouraged me to push ahead with my compositions. Tom and I attended all the Indianapolis Symphony Orchestra's children's concerts. When Arthur Rubenstein and Jascha Heifetz came to Indianapolis, we went to Murat Theatre to see these legendary soloists.

Tom played the violin and I the cello in the School 60 orchestra and later in the Shortridge High School Orchestra. During four years of high-school rehearsals, we managed to protect our instruments from destruction—and we experienced only minor mishaps in our football, basketball, and track practices.

Our home was filled with books that my parents had collected. In our summer book clubs, we won a prize after reading eight books and satisfactorily reporting on their contents. I started to read biographies of generals, politicians, scientists, and educators. With my vivid imagination, I could see myself in all those roles.

On a toy printing press given to us one Christmas, my brother and I started publishing a family newspaper. We sold copies to our neighbors and friends of our parents. One year, we sold fresh eggs from the farm to the same customer list. As a Boy Scout, I sold war bonds and found that our next-door neighbor was patriotic, wealthy, and as loving as my grandfather. He bought a $50,000 bond that made me the top Scout salesman in Indianapolis and earned me a $25 bond award from hotel owner George Marott.

Mother and Dad decided that normal social development also required group activity. They were keen on scouting and encouraged Tom and me to work our way up to Eagle Scout. We went to Sunday school, Methodist Youth Fellowship, church every Sunday, and Boy Scout meetings each Friday. Our Central Avenue Methodist Youth Fellowship meant extensive contact and many friendships with what would today be called "inner-city youth." At church and Boy Scouts, we didn't know the distinction.

We traveled on public buses and trolleys, shopped for Christmas gifts downtown, and pumped Mother for information about her work with the Children's Day Nursery Guild.

All of my education—formal as well as informal— occurred under the watchful eyes of Dr. Louis Segar, our pediatrician; Dr. Russell Sage, an ear-nose-throat specialist; and Dr. William Kemper, my orthodontist. My brother always seemed to be in good health, but I faced a myriad of physical obstacles. And my parents provided for my every need.

From the earliest days, I scared my parents with the frightening sounds of croup. They would rush me to the bathroom and, with the shower and hot-water faucet going full blast, attempt to produce enough steam to loosen up my congestion. In addition to throat and breathing problems, I had severe ear trouble that required lancing and one rupture that produced a hearing loss for several years. My feet were too flat, and my teeth were too large and jumbled. Tests determined that I was allergic to more than a hundred substances, and shots were concocted to tackle the worst.

Endless sneezing, loss of voice, throat X rays, braces, corrective shoes—all of these meant a seemingly endless stream of doctor appointments, tests, shots, and treatments. My mother never stopped pursuing remedies and solutions. She praised me for being so patient and long-suffering. With her encouragement to stay the course, I did.

While my parents worked hard to give me a variety of educational opportunities and the best health possible, what probably meant the most to me was their generous love and attention. During my high-school years, for instance, my dad increasingly stayed home with chronic back and stomach difficulties. But despite his discomfort, he would often drive out to the Shortridge High School practice field and watch football practice from behind the protective closed window of his station wagon. I remember a speech contest for which first prize was a television set. Because we didn't yet have a television, Dad had to go to a TV store that night to watch me give my prize-winning speech. Even during days of substantial discomfort and pain, he drove me to athletic contests, and one time he drove the whole family to hear me speak in a Methodist Church oratorical contest final at DePauw University.

As proud as my dad was of all that his children were doing, he was ultimately pessimistic about the future that lay ahead for us. He told me that economic conditions in the world had gotten a lot tougher and that I wouldn't be able to do as well financially as he had. He espoused such strong viewpoints about the New Deal and what he felt was a tightening noose around initiative and ambition that he would hand back all the Roosevelt dimes that he received as change.

Yet he and my mother were confident that there were great adventures and achievements in my future. They worked hard to make certain that my ego was not inflated and equally hard to make certain that I had boundless self-confidence. Every day they were loving, caring advocates, and I wanted to please them. I tried so hard that on some occasions I found myself in way over my head, but I succeeded often enough to learn more about myself and to like the new avenues that even small accomplishments opened to me.

My mother, now eighty-five, has watched, applauded, and often participated in the adventures of all three of her children and a growing number of grandchildren and great-grandchildren. Her formula is still the same—good education, good health, and plenty of love and attention.

John F. MacArthur, Jr.

The Key Is Love

Many of you who live far away from Sun Valley, California, have undoubtedly been touched by the ministry of John MacArthur through his "Grace to You" radio broadcast. Each day, his teaching educates, encourages, and inspires people around the globe.

At home on Sundays, John is pastor to the more than seven thousand people who attend Grace Community Church's morning worship services and the almost thirty-five hundred people who join him for the evening Family Bible Hour.

John's ministry extends beyond the spoken word to the written word. He is the author of more than fifteen books, including The Gospel According to Jesus, Shepherdology, Our Sufficiency in Christ, and a series of New Testament commentaries. He has also produced a number of teaching films and videotapes.

A graduate of Talbot Theological Seminary, John now serves as president of The Master's College, a position he has held since 1985. A year later, The Master's Seminary opened its doors and began to train tomorrow's church leaders.

John and his wife, Patricia, have four children, Matt (married to Kelly), Marcy (married to Mark), Mark, and Melinda.

It comes as no surprise that a pastor-teacher-writer like

John grew up in a home where his parents clearly loved God, the Bible, and books.

♦————————————————————————————♦

I had just settled into my seat on a cross-country red-eye flight and taken out my Bible to read when the young lady next to me quietly asked what I did for a living.

Thankful for the opportunity, I told her I was a pastor who taught the Bible. "Do you counsel people?" she quickly asked.

I replied that counseling was a standard responsibility for me. She sat up in her seat and said, "Then you'll understand what just happened to me."

She began to tell me how thrilled she was to be working with a new psychotherapist who had just helped her uncover a most liberating fact—she had been abused by her father. "I never realized that before," she said, "but it all came out in counseling. Now I know why I have so many problems."

She felt she had been liberated by being able to blame someone else for her troubles. I don't know about her parents, but there are some fathers and mothers who should be blamed for scars inflicted on their children through abuse. Not mine!

I have no one to blame but myself for my quirks and failures. I was never abused by either parent—only loved, affirmed, encouraged, and trusted.

Mom had asked the Lord for a son who would be a preacher, and I was the answer to her prayer—her only son, born first and followed by three daughters.

I needed—and received—special love as a child because I spent so much time sick and in the hospital recovering from rheumatic fever, pneumonia, several surgeries, and assorted stitches.

That love was tempered by the necessary discipline. I was spanked hard and often with belts, wooden coat hangers and spoons, sticks, and hands. I have no memories of an angry parent who struck me out of frustration, though. There was always the little speech: "This hurts me more than it hurts you"—and looking into their eyes, I knew it was no mere speech. Their discipline was always strong but reasonable. Often I sensed disappointment and hurt as they chastened me, but I never sensed anger.

There was good reason for firm corporal correction in my case because I was quite aggressive and adventurous. When I was healthy enough, I repeatedly tested their parental powers.

My dad has told and retold his cherished and perhaps embellished recollections of my childhood exploits. I certainly provided him plenty of sermon illustrations.

One chilly morning when I was about three, I warmed some couch pillows in the oven and then put them into my little sister Jeanette's playpen so she wouldn't be cold. In the fresh air, the pillows burst into flames. I ran to tell my parents that Jeanette was on fire. Dad says my quick response no doubt saved Jeanette's life. She was singed but fortunately not badly burned.

My dad likes to tell about the time when I was three or four and took a shot at playing traffic cop (probably on a dare). Taking my place in the center of the intersection near my house, I began directing cars until I stopped one with my father in it! That abruptly ended my law-enforcement career. I paid a painful price for that stunt.

Hopelessly curious, I went on many adventurous trips near the house. Frequently I slid down the drain-pipe under the curb so I could get into the big drain wash and run for miles. My mom was so worried about my disappearances that she had my father tie me to the clothesline pole with a long rope!

Unquestionably, the most embarrassing treatment I ever received came after I bit a neighbor boy who irritated me. My dad, wanting to teach me an indel-ible lesson, pinned a sign to the back of my shirt that said, "Don't play with me. I bite." It worked—I haven't bitten anyone since!

As a teenager, I almost lost my life in a car accident twenty-five hundred miles from home. My parents nursed my recovery for several months. To this day, Mom still worries about me, usually punctuating our phone conversations with a reminder not to fly too much.

As I look back and ask myself what my parents did right, the key word is *love*. They love visibly and in several directions.

First, my parents love the Lord. He is the center and circumference of life to them. They live to honor him, teach his Word, serve him, and make the truth about him known. Dad, a fourth-generation preacher, has never done anything else in his adult life but preach, pastor, write, and be involved in ministry. His father taught him by word and example that life is Christ and service to him.

My dad's passion for spiritual service has moved him to travel as an evangelist, preach on radio and television for decades, and write books and commentaries—all while pastoring a church. He is still pastoring, writing, and preaching on radio today—and he will continue ministering until he meets the Lord.

And what my father believes, he preaches and lives. My parents have been the same in church and at home—not perfect, but consistent. From them, I learned devotion to the Lord and his church as a way of life.

Second, my parents love Scripture. My life is set for the proclamation of God's Word—a passion inspired by my dad. He understood that the Bible is God's inspired, inerrant, infallible Word, and he preaches it without equivocation. He is an untiring student of Scripture who spends ample time in his den engrossed in study tools so that he might come forth on Sunday to unfold its riches. I sat under his expositions through all my young years.

When I told him I was called to preach, he gave me a Bible and wrote on the front page, "Preach the Word. Dad." I'm still under that mandate. My love for Scripture was passed from his heart to mine.

Third, my parents love each other with uncommon devotion. This may seem hard to believe, but I have never once heard them say an unkind word to each other or argue in an angry exchange. They are so deeply woven together in a peaceful oneness that their marriage is the best example of devoted love I have ever seen. They seem to always overlook each other's faults.

I believe that the chief ingredient in a fulfilled family is not the love parents give their children, but the love that they have for each other. That love is the most powerful tool they have for helping their children feel secure. And I know that my parents' love for each other set me on a course to love my wife and seek to be a peacemaker in my own home.

Fourth, my parents love their children. The four of us have always been the most important people in their lives. That remains evident to anyone who knows our family today. Still we get hugs and kisses when we see Mom and Dad, and they constantly talk freely of their love for us.

Mom never worked a day outside the home. We kids were her life. The house was always clean and comfortable, and she was always home baking cookies or bread or making something special for us to eat. When I went to college nearby, I could count on coming home in the afternoon and finding her there, cooking, reading, or knitting (needles and yarn were always in her hands or close by).

Dad was always eager to take me with him to church meetings so we could be together. A few times I went forward when he gave the invitation—just to prime the pump. He was there on the sidelines through all my high-school and college athletic endeavors. And he was always eager to tell me what he was learning from Scripture.

I think the four of us children are still our parents'

greatest earthly joy—along with all the new family we have brought home.

Fifth, my parents love books. Both are readers. Mom enjoys historical novels and classics of all kinds. Dad reads everything. Though he is in his mid-seventies, his easy chair is surrounded by books, magazines, and articles. We have had countless conversations, no two of them alike. He is so well read that he is always full of new information and insight. We all know how it is to visit relatives who are still saying the same things they said last time we saw them. That's not my dad.

My dad has given me a love for books and reading that continues to enrich my life and ministry. More of my time is spent reading—the only way to really learn—than any other single thing I do. And whatever richness there is in my preaching is the result of the Spirit stirring the thoughts, ideas, and insights I've gained from reading.

Dad always said, "Don't go into the sacred desk [the pulpit] unless you are fully prepared." He spends hours studying for every sermon. The thousands of books filling his library and stretched across his desk on little racks are his treasured friends—and they have become mine.

My parents' formula is really simple: Love the Lord consistently, love his Word, love each other purely and devotedly, love your children enough to both encourage and discipline them, and teach them to love the great resources that can make them wise.

Frankly, my parents turned out amazingly well—after being so abused by their son!

The Child Sings One Round Silent *O*

Two themes run throughout the writings of my friend Karen Burton Mains. Her ministry clearly reflects, first, her deep commitment to those who suffer and, second, her insistent call to fellow believers to experience the truths of Christianity on an everyday basis. Her writings grew, in part, out of lessons she learned during the years that her husband, David, pastored inner-city churches.

Open Heart, Open Home, *Karen's first best-selling book, challenges the reader to let hospitality become a means of sharing Christ's love.* Child Sexual Abuse: A Hope for Healing, *coauthored with Maxine Hancock, reflects Karen's heart for the hurting. She has also written* With My Whole Heart, *a call to develop the inner disciplines that strengthen the spiritual life, and* Making Sunday Special.

Karen frequently cohosts David's daily "Chapel of the Air" radio broadcasts, and the two have collaborated on several projects. In Tales of the Kingdom *and* Tales of the Resistance, *for instance, they use allegory to teach children truths about the kingdom of God. Their travels to the barrios and refugee camps in fifteen countries of Central America, Southeast Asia, the Middle East, and Africa resulted in* The Fragile Curtain. *The Mains also coauthored* Living, Loving, and Leading *to encourage spiritual growth in the home.*

Perhaps the piece Karen shares here will get you thinking about things you may have learned as a child without even being aware you were learning them.

It's a Sunday afternoon in October, and I sit in a pew in the middle of the congregation, listening to the fulsome sounds of our new organ. The dedicatory prayer and blessing have been pronounced by our Episcopalian rector: "We present this organ to be set apart for the glory of God and the service of Christ's holy church." The response printed in the program reads:

> **Officiant:** *All things come from you, O Lord;*
> **People:** *And from your own gifts do we give to you.*
> **Officiant:** *Praise him with sound of the trumpet:*
> **People:** *Praise him with lyre and harp.*

Then, robed in black with academic colors falling loosely about his shoulders, our pastor prays, "O Lord, before whose throne trumpets sound and angels sing the songs of Moses and the Lamb: Accept this organ for the worship of your temple that, with the voice of music, we may proclaim your praise and tell it abroad; through Jesus Christ our Lord."

Immediately, the festival anthem *Entrada Festiva* op. 93 by Flor Peeters fills my ears; the incorporated *Christus Vincit* melody rolls through our almost-new nave, pounding notes along the pews and into our ears. A small bird of somber satisfaction nestles in my soul, quietly plucking feathers from its breast for brooding. This dedicatory concert is the culmination of two years of steady work. I am the chair of my church's music committee.

People who have heard me sing or are aware of my lack of instrumental skill might wonder how I came to be the chair of this committee. What do I, they might rightfully ask, know about church music? And after two years of serving in this office, I, too, am surprised. It seems I know more, much more, than even I suspected.

I am not the musician in my family. I am the word person, the writer. Seven years of childhood piano lessons immunized me against the desire for musical disciplines. My piano teacher, a well-intentioned maiden lady smelling faintly of middle-age mustiness and lilac water, must have been a paragon of dedication. Undoubtedly disappointed by many students who stubbornly preferred musical illiteracy to skill, she nevertheless persisted despite the finger-stumbling ineptitude of those like myself who benignly rebelled against the rigors of practice. I remember her pointed elbows, sitting so close to them as I did when she shifted around me on the piano bench in order to play first the high octave, then the low. I remember her thin elastic fingers, and I can still hear her sighs.

The dedicatory concert is in honor of our new tracker pipe organ. Tracker organs are unique in their use of direct mechanical action to transmit all stop, keyboard, and pedal action, and they have been built in essentially the same way for the last five hundred years. Our organ is comprised of 772 pipes set in fifteen ranks and controlled by twelve stops. The organ at St. Mark's Parish in Geneva, Illinois, was designed and built by the Martin Ott Organ Company of St. Louis, and Mr. Ott is a guest this afternoon.

I am amazed that in our world of production-line technology, all handcrafting is not extinct. Martin Ott, a comparatively young man, was born in West Germany to a family of organ builders. He apprenticed with an uncle and spent his journeyman years with his father, a master organ builder. Some thirty-six hundred man-hours have been invested in creating this instrument. The wood pipes, expression louvres, and case work were all crafted from select top-grade Missouri oak and walnut. The manual keyboards are covered with grenadilla wood and ivory.

An organ committee, donating hours of time, chose the organ and raised thousands of dollars for this quality instrument of worship. My responsibilities had included finding an organist, determining whether we needed a choir director (in Episcopal churches, the choir director and organist are often the same person), establishing a church music philosophy, steering the music committee through defining our mission statement and writing our general objectives, and determining how we would relate organizationally to the church governing body, the vestry.

So listening this afternoon to the soaring melodies of Peeters, Bach, Widor, and Boëllmann, I think with satisfaction of a job well done. Interviews and choir and organ laboratories had revealed which organist and which director would best serve our purpose. The choir had been included in the evaluation process, and we had taken profitable learning detours into the history of liturgy and its meaning. Working together on a common task, the music committee members had also become friends. The gifts of the instrumentalists in the congregation had also been called forth, and the choir had begun to blend and find depth in tone and range. Our new organist and choirmaster were working comfortably together. Time and again, I was to hear after the Sunday service, "Oh, the music this morning! The music! How it lifts us to worship!"

The magnificence of this rich sound frees my mind, and I think back to Sunday afternoon suppers. My father gathered his family to these meals. There, in those after-church discussions, he unintentionally gave me, his nonmusical child, lesson after lesson in music theory, the philosophy of church music, the choir's function, voice technique, and the psychology of inspiring volunteer workers. My father was a church musician (the music director in every childhood church I attended except one), and I, unknowingly, absorbed his philosophies while chewing Mother's braised pot roast and slurping her molded strawberry Jell-O salad. He might as well have sat me in the classroom he taught at Moody Bible Institute and given me academic credit! I remember his lessons well:

"A good church music program will bring at least fifty, seventy families to any church. It is an unfailing stimulant to church growth.

"One must respect the common musical language of the people of any local congregation. One honors their preferences first and then builds an appreciation for a wider or a better quality of musical expression.

"When it comes to church music, the most musically illiterate lay person in the pew considers himself an expert. His opinion is the sole arbiter of good taste and, in churches, he thinks his opinion determines what is spiritually correct as well!"

There were many pronouncements about church choirs and many technical evaluations of this soprano's vibrato or that contralto's breathiness. I sang in my father's youth choir throughout high school. We would gather at four o'clock before our youth meetings. After practice, our mothers served us tuna, ham, or egg salad sandwiches made with white bread. But it was mostly at the dinner table that I unwittingly served my musical apprenticeship.

One regular discussion between Mother and Father took the form of disagreement. "Dick Burton," she would chide, "don't lecture the choir members who come on Sunday about those who attend practice and then didn't make it for worship." Faithful attendance was what he demanded, as well as good workmanship and regularity without excuses; he was not above lecturing the faithful about the faithless. Fidelity to the task at hand was what he himself gave and what he modeled to an observant child.

Members of St. Mark's have commissioned an original composition for our dedicatory concert, "Sing to the Lord a New Song (Psalm 89)" by Howard Whitaker. I listen to the chords in this piece—it is a musical challenge for our choir. But somehow the sounds meld, the proverbial soprano, who usually strains shrill, modulates her tones, and the bass section blends with the tenors. The composer sits several rows behind me. How lovely to hear one's composition performed!

Memory makes an entrance, and it's an emotional memory because my father is dead. In memory, I am a teenager with him in the aisle of the balcony in Moody Memorial Auditorium during Candlelight Carols. I sit on the steps. My father stands back here, tense because his body needs to be active in the music. Other members of the faculty direct the women's glee club, the male chorus, and the chorale. It is the first time I have heard antiphonal singing. The voices toss music to one another, calling and echoing, singing in our-turn-our-turn time. Feeling my father pace—the body marking the rhythm, his ear cocked to the sounds, his mind concentrating intensely to determine the effect of his musical program—I understand that he is an artist, that passion blows alive a flame in his soul that stays unlighted in the soul of others.

Another memory pushes aside the first. I am a child again, sitting on a hard bench in the hallway of the Music Conservatory in downtown Chicago. My father, in the nearby practice room, is giving voice lessons, coaching a student in vocal exercises and breathing techniques. I am an outsider to this camaraderie: I am without musical speech. My feet swing, heels knocking against the wooden brace beneath the bench, but I hear the shared language. . . . The rushed snatches of piano practice . . . the pause, the repetition, the two-finger and three-finger chords . . . the singer's scales copycatting the rigorous piano scales . . . the crescendos and decrescendos . . . From somewhere close, behind another door, a cello laments. I hear the *click/click/click/click/click/click* of a metronome. My father's hand pounds time woodenly on the surface of the piano, heavily accenting the second beat, his voice counting . . . one and two and three and four . . . one and two and three and four. . . .

Silence. The music lesson is over. I hear muffled voices, grace notes of laughter. My feet plop to the floor in expectation. The door opens. My father smiles and says good-bye to his student. "'Lo, Sweet," he greets me. "You can come in." An outsider, shy and alien, I move hesitantly into the music room. Stacks of sheet music, corners crumpled and spines showing their irregular order, are piled on chairs, on book-shelves, and on the wide windowsill. Natural light falls from the tall arches in rectangles on the scratched wood floor. The radiator in the corner cranks. The music cabinet, of shellacked yellow oak, breaks the horizontal line above the wide grand piano. Atop this file perches the bust of a Dutch boy: His eyes are tightly closed and his lips form a perfect *O*. He is frozen, forever singing a perfect round *O*.

And I, sitting at the organ dedication concert, am

surprised. I have been a good church music committee chairperson! Like Martin Ott, I spent my journeyman years tutored by my father, a master church musician. My father had studied opera, but nodes on his vocal cords destroyed that dream. So he expressed his artistry through the sounds of others. The transepts and choir lofts of churches became his stage, the faculty meetings he directed were his dramas, and the concerts and recitals were the events he produced.

So it is that I love church music, all types and kinds, with an aching fondness. My father's lectures, the choir robes, the music files, the music stands, the overused sheet music, the batons—these were the props that grabbed me and excited my imagination, but I have only now discovered it.

We stand to sing the final number, Wesley's "All Hail the Power of Jesus' Name." Our children's choir sings the second verse, their little voices strong. Men's voices command the third stanza. The organ and trumpet play a duet. A brass fanfare flares. The congregation and choirs raise the last line—"We'll join the everlasting song and crown him Lord of all."

I have been party to creating this moment, pacing figuratively in the aisle in the balcony. My music has been committee work, all informed posthumously by my father. Something lost inside me has been found, something I misplaced as a little girl sitting in a practice room and hating my piano lessons. But I have found it now, and I am surprised. I am forming a perfect round frozen *O*. It is silent, wanting to be sung.

The bird in my soul stirs in its nesting, perched on the edge, finds wing, flaps. I hear my father saying,

"'Lo, Sweet. Come right in." The bird flies. "O Lord, before whose throne trumpets sound and saints and angels sing the songs of Moses and the Lamb: Accept this organ for the worship of your temple, that with the voice of music, we may proclaim your praise and tell it abroad; through Jesus Christ our Lord."

Ralph Martin

Strong and Sacrificial Love

R *alph is one of the most prominent laymen in the Catho-lic charismatic renewal going on today. A graduate of the University of Notre Dame, he has been active in this renewal since its beginning back in 1967.*

Ralph is also the founding editor of New Covenant, *a magazine for Catholic charismatic renewal, and is presently a consulting editor. He directed the International Catholic Charismatic Renewal Office for five years, first in Ann Arbor, Michigan, and then in Brussels, Belgium. While in Brussels, he worked closely with Cardinal L. J. Suenens to promote worldwide charismatic renewal, foster Christian unity, and build Christian communities.*

A popular speaker, Ralph has also written more than a dozen books, among them Hungry for God, A Crisis of Truth, Called to Holiness, The Return of the Lord, *and* Husbands, Wives, Parents, Children.

Recognized by the Vatican as an international leader among the laity, Ralph has traveled throughout Europe, Africa, Asia, North America, and Latin America. For more than seven years, he has also hosted the weekly television program "The Choices We Face."

Ralph is currently a coordinator of The Word of God, an ecumenical Christian community in Ann Arbor where he resides with his wife, Anne, and their six children.

Two things Ralph especially remembers about his growing-up years are the "purity and single-mindedness" of his childhood devotion to God and the example of genuine faith his parents offered him.

There were six children in our family, and I think we would all agree that, because there was so much right about who my parents *were* (and are), so much of what they *did* was right in raising us. While our lives have not been problem-free by any means, today all six of us are following the Lord and living lives of love and service according to our different circumstances.

My father and mother—who are celebrating their fiftieth wedding anniversary this year—met in New York City at a wedding. My mother's parents had come over from Ireland when they were teenagers, married in New York, and raised their children as Catholic Christians who were strong in the faith. Two of my mother's brothers even spent time in a seminary exploring the possibility of a call to ordination. My father, also a Catholic from New York, was raised in the faith and educated at Catholic schools.

We six children were raised just as our parents were. I clearly remember having a strong and definite relationship with the Lord as a child; I loved him sincerely. I really wanted to obey him and not depart from him in any way through sin. The relationship was not formal and objective, but close and personal. I knew and experienced his love as well as his truth. As I moved on through high school, though, I began to encounter more of the intellectual challenges to the truth of the Christian faith, and a gap began to open up between the Lord and me that widened in college, even though I attended the University of Notre Dame.

It was on a retreat during my senior year at Notre Dame that I rediscovered in a deep and powerful way the awesome truth and love of the person of Jesus and the whole Christian faith. I was reconciled with him and with the Catholic Church and have spent the subsequent years following him and serving him as best I can. But even today I wonder if I've yet regained the level of purity and single-mindedness that I had in my devotion to the Lord as a child growing up in our family.

At that time, the Catholic church had a lot to do with my upbringing and my childhood faith. The church had not yet experienced the confusion and ambiguity about living the Catholic faith on a practical level that occurred in the seventies and eighties. But the example of my parents was really the key to my convictions. Let me share some of the areas that my four sisters, my brother, and I identified when together we reflected on what our parents did right.

First of all, both of my parents had a very genuine faith in and devotion to the Lord. This devotion was not ostentatious or self-conscious, but it was clearly visible to us and made an impact on our young minds. Furthermore, the Christian worldview was the operative worldview in our home. We knew of the reality of heaven and hell, the mercy of God in sending us his Son, and the importance of faith in and obedience to him in this life and for the life to come. My parents lived out these basic truths in so many ways, from their faithful church attendance every Sunday and holy day (with all of us in tow!) to their sacrificial commitment to send all of us to Catholic schools when they never had much "extra" in the way of income. (My father was a steel and wire salesman for most of his working years, and my mother was a full-time homemaker.)

I remember my dad coming home from work early on Good Friday. As a family, we would observe a certain silence and sobriety during the three hours from noon to 3:00 P.M. in honor of Christ's sacrifice for us on the cross. We would read together a gospel account of Christ's passion and death, pray together, and refrain from normal activity.

I also remember Christmas morning. My parents would ask us to kneel before the manger we had set up and wish Jesus a happy birthday before we rushed to the Christmas tree and the marvel of presents for all.

The habit of prayer before bedtime was instilled early, and occasionally we would watch a Christian television program or say the family rosary together.

I also remember my parents' quiet, more private devotion to God. I remember my mother's bedside book—the one with the green cover—that she read from often. I later found out that it was Thomas à Kempis's *The Imitation of Christ*. I remember my father's occasional blessings when he left for work or we left on a trip. I've also learned about their quiet and almost continual intercession for all of us and others as well, and their constant prayer continues.

My parents' life was based on clear and correct priorities. Their life was definitely centered on God, and their chief goal was to live the Christian way of life and pass it on to us. They highly valued education, but education for life always took place within the framework of education in the faith. My parents were and are remarkably free of the power of materialism, knowing both how to "abound and abase." Though we never had much, we never felt poor, and we never developed an anxiety about money. My parents knew—and we also knew—that God would always provide what was needed if we did our part. With what little they had, they were always generous with us and with others. I remember how carefully they prepared the collection envelope for church and how they taught us to do the same. Besides that, they regularly wrote out checks for the missions to the American Indians, for some African missionary work, and for the Lenten "widow's mite" boxes.

Their attitude of trust and generosity extended beyond material things to "forgiving and forgetting" and not holding grudges. They were also remarkably free of prejudice, accepting people who were different from us Irish Catholics and teaching their children to do the same. We grew up in a New Jersey suburb of New York City in a town that was predominantly Jewish and had a growing black population. I don't think I ever heard from my parents a negative word about someone who was different from us.

For years my parents subscribed to the *Christopher News Notes,* and they taught us all to emulate their motto, "Better to light one candle than to curse the darkness." They taught us not to complain about a problem but to do something towards a solution.

And, yes, we were spanked and yelled at occasionally; discipline and correction were certainly some of the important things we received from our parents. My parents kept an eye on our friends, inquired about where we were going, and set curfews for when we were to be home. They also kept an eye on what we wore, being sure it was modest. But as we got older and moved into young adulthood, they also knew how to appropriately "let go and let God," persisting with their intercession for us and with their advice.

Another key to what my parents did right in raising us was maintain their honor, love, esteem, and affection for one another. My father would often affirm members of the family with "What a great girl Mary is!" or "What a great woman your mother is!" My mother would gladly "look after" my dad, whether that meant fixing his meals, screening his phone calls, or doing anything else that would be helpful to him. She would and does submit to him and defer to him, not in a servile way but with the freedom that is rooted in mutual love and respect. Sure, they had tensions in their own relationship from time to time (and sometimes we would see that), but they always remained loyal to each other. The hallmark of their relationship was strong mutual and sacrificial love for one another.

This love for God and for one another resulted in the strong sacrificial love they had for their children. We always knew that, even when they disagreed with what we were doing, they were always for us. They were able to distinguish between the sinner and the sin in us. And still they deeply love and faithfully pray for us as well as for their twenty-four grandchildren.

Perhaps there is no more striking example of their devoted love than their ongoing care for my brother Andrew, who was born with serious handicaps twenty-seven years ago. (I'm the oldest of the children, Andrew is the youngest, and my four sisters are in between.) Without complaining, and by constantly drawing on the Lord for strength and wisdom, my parents have cared for and loved Andrew no less faithfully than they have any of us. Without drawing attention to it in any way, they have lived out the saying of Jesus: "If any want to become my followers, let them deny themselves and take up their cross daily and follow me" (Luke 9:23 NRSV). They have borne the pain, anxiety, fear, and disappointment of life, all the while trusting God and persevering in faith, hope, and love.

My mother, now seventy, and my father, who is eighty, keep on loving God, each other, their children, their grandchildren, and others. They keep on giving, keep on trusting, and keep on following Jesus in the circumstances of their lives, an example to us all. Thanks be to God for the gift of such parents!

The Greatest Thing Was Love

◆──◆

Tony gained national recognition in September 1987 when he played his guitar for Pope John Paul II in Los Angeles. Born without arms, Tony touched the hearts of people across the country when he sang "Never Be the Same." And those who saw it will long remember the Pope approaching him from the stage and kissing him in appreciation.

Tony was a "thalidomide baby" born without arms because his mother was prescribed that drug during her pregnancy. His parents took him from Nicaragua to Los Angeles to have him fitted for artificial arms. He wore those until he was ten—and then he'd had enough. "I didn't feel comfortable," he explains. "I used my feet more."

During high school, Tony began "playing around" with the guitar and writing his own songs. He also became very active in the Catholic church, performing in as many as five services each Sunday. Someone planning activities for the Pope's visit asked Tony to an audition, and he was accepted.

Since that special September day, Tony has traveled across the United States and overseas. He has recorded the albums

Never Be the Same *and* Ways of the Wise *and written his autobiography,* A Gift of Hope. *Various civic and charitable organizations have recognized Tony as a role model and inspiration.*

Here Tony talks about the love and support he found at home, love and support that undoubtedly gave him the gift of hope that he now shares with others.

What did my parents do right? I have no trouble answering that question. Let me first share with you about my mother. She was a soft-spoken lady, but you knew that if she looked at you a certain way, you'd better watch out. She was a fun lady, always laughing and doing things with friends. She worked very hard, either going to work, baking a cake, cleaning the house, or helping out a friend. She was always doing something. She didn't spend time just sitting around.

Born in El Salvador, my father was an adventurer. He was involved in agriculture, and he was also a veterinarian. He loved animals, and many times played with snakes and alligators. He loved dangerous animals that most people—even the rest of my family members—would avoid.

His family was very important to my father, and he worked hard for us. For fun, he played the guitar and even serenaded my mom when they were young. He had a trio and performed a lot with his friends.

My parents worked at everything together. Except for their individual jobs, they didn't do anything apart from each other. And when it came to family, we were first. There was no way around it.

My parents were firm without being overbearing. Whenever my mother was displeased, we knew it. My father was more authoritative. He laid down the law and told us how it was. My older brother, my two younger sisters, and I were allowed to learn from our mistakes, and we received a tremendous amount of support from both of our parents. They showed us a lot of good things by their example and the way they lived their day-to-day lives.

We lived in the Los Angeles area, and every three years all six of us jumped in the car and drove to Nicaragua where my mother was born. Even though the car trip lasted seven days, we loved it. We'd spend several months in Nicaragua, and when it was time to come home, we all cried. We loved it that much.

We often did things with relatives. Every weekend we got together with family. Sometimes we just sat around and talked. We enjoyed being with each other.

Unless my father had to work late, all of my family would share mealtime. When everyone was home, we ate together. No one would just grab a sandwich and run out the door. We always sat down around the table for dinner.

My parents taught us to stick together. If I was away from home and found out that something had happened at my house, I ran home. All of us wanted to be there for each other. If anything happened at home that led to bickering between us kids or with our parents, we tried to find out what was wrong and help if we could.

Although there were many good things about my parents, we were not without our problems. My father was an alcoholic, and his heavy drinking eventually led to his death. From the time I was about eight years old through my teenage years, my father drank. We wanted to help, but we never knew what to do about it. Anyone who has a family member with an alcohol or drug problem will understand. You just don't know how to help.

Through all of this, my mother's love for my father never waned. I watched her go through a lot of pain and suffering, but she loved my father even when he drank. Although we kids loved our father too, we wanted to leave. One day we went to our mother and told her so. But my mother said no. She said that our father loved us and reminded us that there was always food on the table and clothes on our backs. She also brought up the good things that he did for us. She said that we were not leaving; we were going to stay. My mom was very married; I never saw her run away. I will always carry with me her example of love.

Last but not least, God was very important to my family; our Lord gave us everything. My mother took us to church, but we were inconsistent. It was an up-and-down relationship with the Lord. Some years my parents would not go to church, and some years they would. But as we got older, we four kids took our parents to church. Even though we did not attend church faithfully, my mother read her Bible every day. She also prayed every night. I will never forget her reading the Bible and praying. When we were little, she would sit us down and make us pray. We would sit there and roll our eyes. But now I look back on that and realize what an important example it was for me. My mother was so beautiful.

Whenever we attended church, my father would want to help serve—whether that meant taking the collection or fixing something over the weekend. That was his way of serving God and helping the church.

The greatest thing that our parents gave to us, their children, was their love. They loved each other, and they loved their family. I love my dad dearly. I love my mom dearly. They were the greatest parents a son could ever want.

Good Proverbs and Good Parenting

It is not surprising that, when he thinks back to his growing-up years, a gifted writer like Calvin Miller remembers the proverbs he learned from his mother.

Calvin was born and raised in Enid, Oklahoma. After graduating from Enid High School, he attended Oklahoma Baptist University and then went on to Midwestern Baptist Theological Seminary in Kansas City. There he earned a Master of Divinity degree and later a Doctor of Ministry degree.

His first full-time pastorate was Plattsmouth Baptist Church in Plattsmouth, Nebraska. Since January 1966, he has served at Westside Church in Omaha and has seen the congregation grow from ten members to more than twenty-five hundred.

Through his writings, Calvin reaches thousands more parishioners. He has authored twenty-six books of popular theology and inspiration. The Singer, The Song, *and* The Finale *trilogy in the late seventies introduced him to readers. Among the titles published since then are* If This Be Love, A Hunger for Meaning, The Legend of the Brotherstone, A Requiem for Love, A Symphony in the Sand, *and, most recently,* Apples, Snakes, and Belly-aches. *Calvin's poems and freelance articles have been published in journals and magazines such as* Christianity Today, Campus Life, Leadership, *and* His.

In his pulpit as well as his writing, Calvin seeks to be a contemporary apologist and to equip the church for missions and evangelism. In what he says is his primary rule for life—"time is a gift"—we see his mother's love for brief statements of profound truth.

So often in the counseling room I hear some member of our "psychologized" generation blame their parents for their own erstwhile state of life. "My parents raised me wrong," they say, thus exonerating themselves of the responsibility of achieving less than they should. That situation is very different from my experience. All my mother did right stands above me and trumpets so loudly that the smaller concert of her mistakes is inaudible. At all the important "change points" of my growing up, Mother was there and so very right that her lessons always hurried me on toward God's best purpose for my life.

Several of these major change points need to be experienced before we settle, at last, into marital stability and a steady career, and all of these change points have to do with leaving home. Consider starting school (leaving home for a few hours a day); getting a driver's license (gaining some independence from home); going off to college (leaving home for long intervals); finding that first job (becoming responsible for your own home); and getting married (building a home for your own family). Into this general list of change points I always insert conversion to Christ. If all the other steps signify leaving home and becoming independent, conversion represents our full admission that, once we see life through the eyes of faith, we do not want to be totally independent; rather, we want the security of depending on Christ. Somehow at each of these successive steps, Mother couched her wisdom in proverbs (some from the Bible; some not) that remain, like the experiences from which she drew them, very real to me.

It was my feet I remember most. They were bare on the oak floor of Mrs. Duerkson's first-grade classroom. Ours was the poor end of town. Some of the kids had shoes, and some did not. My mother worked hard, and my eight brothers and sisters laid as many demands on her excellent but meager financial management as I did. We Millers had no "live-in" father. He left home when the last of his covey were still preschoolers, and since money was often short, so were shoes. Shoes and fathers always come in the same family—this truth had become clear to me quite early in grade school.

So there in Mrs. Duerkson's classroom, it was easy to look under the desks and determine which kids were from two-parent families. Under the rows of desks, some short legs dangled naked feet while others dangled shoes. I complained one night about not having shoes, knowing Mother would have given me shoes if she could have. Since she couldn't, she gave me a proverb: "I wept because I had no shoes until I met a man who had no feet." It was heady stuff for a six-year-old, but for me her adage was the beginning of a covenant of thankfulness in which I would ever after try to remember that God does provide (Mrs. Duerkson found me not only shoes, but galoshes as well within the next week) and always meets our needs (Phil. 4:19). Often God's provisions arrive later than we hope, but sooner or later, there are many things to be thankful for: Shoelessness, for instance, is much better than footlessness. In giving this gift of a positive outlook, my mother did something right.

My mother's wisdom overrides the sociologists who would not list conversion as one of the critical events of life. Conversion was a significant change point for me as I was growing up. I looked at my sin as most children do (not in an "Al Capone" sense, but in the sense of neediness), and I knew I needed "saving." When I came home from a Pentecostal tent revival one August, my mother seemed pleased that I had "found the Lord." I think she secretly found my "hypervibrancy" "hypervibrating," yet she never put down my enthusiasm for the sheer joy with which it had infused my life.

She seemed secretly glad that I never learned to talk in the "unknown tongue" (a frequent practice in our church), preferring that I work on what she called "the King's English." She liked to see me reading the little Gideon New Testament we were given at school. (I never knew exactly where those folks with the Gideons came from, but every three years they showed up at the school door with a couple of cases of little maroon Bibles.) While I still preferred *Tom Sawyer* to the Gideon Bible, I nonetheless read and grew in my understanding.

Mother wanted me to "stay balanced" in my reading habits, so she gave me a second proverb: "Son, never get so holy you can't look up at the sun." I had no idea how holy that would be, but once more her proverb stuck. I wanted to make Christ Lord of all I touched, but at her urging I wanted to touch more widely than the world of churchy things. She wanted me to read the Bible along with the best of English literature. Thus she taught me to enjoy many worthy books. She urged me to try *The Three Musketeers, The Count of Monte Cristo,* and *The Corsican Brothers.* She moved me gently through any number of classics, which made me far richer in many ways than the gift of tongues alone would have.

The third proverb came when Mother did right concerning my driver's license. Mother didn't drive, and we couldn't afford to have a car anyway! So we Millers were walkers. We walked everywhere! In addition to the usual lust with which most fifteen-year-olds look forward to their driver's license, the issue became a passion *in extremis* with me. Of course, a driver's license is of no use without a car, and since the Millers owned none, I began saving to buy a car so I'd have a reason to want a driver's license.

By my sixteenth birthday, I had saved three hundred dollars. I drove a friend's car when I took the test to obtain my license and then walked to a used car lot with a wad of fifteen twenty-dollar bills to buy a 1939 Plymouth coupe convertible with a rumble seat. You could buy a new 1952 Plymouth for one thousand dollars, but I only had three hundred dollars—not that I complained! Three hundred dollars was something by 1952 standards! The roadster coupe was apple red with a white canvas top. It looked good, but it wasn't as good as it looked. To blight its shiny reputation, it had a lot of miles. You couldn't start it (the starter was defective), and you couldn't stop it (the brakes were defective); and since I had spent my entire wad to purchase it, I had no money left to repair, insure, or maintain it.

My mother seemed unimpressed as I drove up our unpaved driveway looking like the Great-but-over-spent Gatsby. I stopped the car, smiled proudly, and killed the engine—just as I remembered I wouldn't be able to start it again.

"Wanna go for a ride?" I asked Mom.

"How much did it cost?" she asked.

"It's got a new top. . . ."

"How much did it cost?" she asked again.

" . . . and a rumble seat . . ."

"OK . . . OK," she said, getting in and closing the door.

I hit the ignition. Nothing happened.

"Mom, would you help me push it down the drive? It starts with only the tiniest push."

"How much did it cost?"

She got out of the car, and we pushed it along until

we were going about five miles an hour. Then I jumped in and kicked in the clutch. It started right up just as I had said.

"See there!" I said to her as she straightened up from her two-hands-on-the-back-bumper-Triple-A-towing position.

She walked around the car and got in, and we roared off until we got to the 10th Street stop sign where the pavement began. I stomped on the brakes, crimped the wheel, and spun into the street as the stop sign whizzed by like an octagonal encouragement to speed onward.

"You can't stop this car, can you?" Mom challenged.

"It's the brakes, I think," I said.

"Let me out—now!"

As soon as the car came to a level place, I let it roll to a stop. Mom got out.

"We're taking this to the dealer and getting your money back!"

"Why? Don't you like it?"

"You can't start it and you can't stop it and you have no money left to buy either a starter or a stopper, do you?"

"Well, I'll save some more and then—"

"Let's take it back to the used car lot."

"OK, OK. Jump in and we'll take it back."

"You drive; I'll walk," she said.

"We can't get the money back," I argued, hoping to dissuade her. "A deal's a deal!"

"Oh no! Watch me," she said.

I did watch her and discovered her to be a little woman of considerable strength. Like God at the

Judgment, she wagged her finger in the face of the used-car salesman (whom she called a "used-car shyster") and shouted, "How would you like to explain to the county attorney how you took the entire savings of a minor for a piece of junk that won't start and can't stop?"

He got her point.

She got the money.

I put it back in my pocket with my new but useless driver's license, and we walked home. "Son," she began, "Mohammed once said, 'If you have only two pence, spend one for bread and the other to buy hyacinth for your soul.'"

I got her drift. I had spent both pence on hyacinth, on that unstartable, unstoppable car. Together we car-shopped, and I purchased a '37 Chevy for thirty-five dollars. The car had almost no class, but it did have a starter and brakes. And I had—to quote Mohammed—money for bread safely stashed away. From that day to this, I have kept a savings account and tried to remember this wonderful principle of survival that Mother taught me.

There is a general proverb circulating that says every boy marries his mother—or tries to. My mother's opinion meant a lot to me, so one by one, like Penelope waiting on Ulysses, I introduced her to any prospective wife. It has been more than thirty years since I brought by the date who would later become my wife. My mother took one look at Barbara and later said to me, "This is the one!"

"How do you know, Mom?"

"Look how she loves you. Son, I've loved you for twenty-three years. Look at her. She loves you, too. Son, you're creative and artistic, and believe me, you're going to take a lot of special understanding. Son, I'd like knowing that when I leave you someday, you'll be all right in the hands of someone who feels about you exactly as I do!"

"But Mom—"

"Son, every poet needs a pragmatist to keep his feet on solid ground."

How wise she was. How much my wife, like my mother before her, has loved me richly and practically. Offering this counsel was one of the wondrous and important things my mother did right.

The job I might have selected, selected me. God called, and I became a pastor. I was older then. School was behind me; I was "saved," married, and could drive. Mom was older, content, quiet, and seemingly—at last!—out of proverbs. From time to time she came to visit the little church where I was pastor. She was never the kind to say it out loud, but I knew she liked my sermons. I wrote books. She bought the books and gave them to church libraries (whether or not they wanted them), and thus I knew she liked my books, too.

At each of the four or five major steps I took in leaving home, Mother proved herself helpful and wise. Nobody is ever right all the time, but she was right so much more than she was wrong—and the things she did right became a powerful force that still talks to me, even after all these years. Good parenting has a way of crossing generations to inspire its children's children. I pray that the best of all she did right has spawned a force in me that is even now taking root in our children.

My Parents Loved Me

Today she is widely known by children and adults alike, but popular author Janette Oke didn't try writing for publication until her own four children were teenagers. Since her first book, Love Comes Softly, was published in 1979, she has written more than thirty others.

In talking about her writing, Janette says, "Christian fiction is just one more way to share the gospel of Christ with a needy world. Even though the characters of the story are fictional, biblical truths can be presented, and each book can be a little missionary sent out to speak to a reader somewhere."

Janette was born in Alberta, Canada, and raised on a farm in a family of seven girls and one boy. Upon graduating from Mountain View Bible College in Didsbury, Alberta, she married Edward Oke. After he completed his training for ministry in the Missionary Church, the Okes served in churches in Elkhart, Indiana, and in Calgary and Edmonton, Alberta, before he became president of Mountain View Bible College.

Janette and Edward have three sons, one daughter, and

eight grandchildren. Here, Janette shares some of her own thoughts as a parent as well as some special memories of growing up with firm guidelines and a lot of love.

I just spent the last two weeks with my sisters dismantling the family home. It was not an easy task. Dad has been gone since October of '84, and Mom, who has been in a wheelchair for a number of years, has now come to the point where she can no longer manage on her own.

"I'd like one more summer in my own home," she had told us at the beginning of June, and we had agreed, taking turns staying with her from June to October. But the time inevitably came when we had to make the difficult change.

Mom booked herself into a new extended-care facility in the little town where she lives, and we gathered to help her make the move. But after she was settled, all of her things needed to be sorted and cared for.

She wasn't interested in the dollar value—she never had been—but the sentimental value she placed on her many treasures made our task difficult. She dispensed with some of the items herself, giving "memories" in the form of small items to family and friends.

And now, we sisters and our one brother had the huge and final task of caring for the houseful of things that remained.

In spite of our tears and our task, the days spent together were good days. Tucked away in this corner or that closet were memories, and for us who have been blessed, they were good memories.

I do not claim that my parents were perfect. I only know that we were loved. And in their wisdom, they realized that love and discipline are not only compatible, but indeed, that each is an important component of the other.

I don't recall when I first realized that my father expected to be obeyed—immediately and without question—but I knew it. *How did he do it?* I have sometimes asked myself. *How did he get across the message that he was in command?*

I don't know. Nor do I know when it began. As far back as I can remember, I loved him with a deep devotion, and I also respected him with a reverent fear. Yet my father never spanked me, never shouted, never even threatened. I do have a dim recollection of getting my ears boxed once when I was acting up at the table. I chalk that up to getting what I justly deserved.

My father had wonderful blue eyes. They could hold warmth and love and teasing—but they could also be piercing. I remember how he looked at me when he had to correct. He didn't raise his voice, though it held authority, but instead he fixed on me those cool, probing eyes, and I knew instinctively that I'd better obey—and quickly!

"He ruled with his voice and his eyes," one of my sisters commented as we waded our way through a box containing his little mementos.

She was right—but he also ruled with his love.

I would never have challenged my father—not because I greatly feared the consequences, but because I did not want to jeopardize in any way the love relationship we had. As a small child, I knew without a doubt that he loved me. And I also knew that I was always welcome on his lap to snuggle up closely against his firm chest. He wasn't in the house two minutes before I had claimed my rightful position. So it was the great love that I felt for him that made me respond quickly to his commands.

But Dad also ruled by example and expectation. His mother had taught him to be a gentleman, and for that I will always be grateful to the grandmother whom I scarcely knew. She had raised my daddy to doff his cap when greeting a lady on the street, to rise from his chair when a woman entered the room, to give up his seat quickly and without comment, and to put the comfort of others before his own. I was proud of my daddy.

And Dad expected no less from his offspring. Selfishness, pettiness, and rude and improper behavior were not acceptable. We knew that by his example. We also knew that he had higher expectations for his children.

My father, in his quiet, gentle way, made it awfully easy for me to accept a heavenly Father who expected both love and obedience from his children. After all, I had learned that love and obedience fit together naturally.

My mother—and we are thankful to still have her with us—is a totally different personality. From things that I have gathered, she must have been an outgoing, vibrant, pert, and sometimes saucy child and teenager.

She was the kind who brought home strays—both animal and human. She was daring and giving and people oriented. She was quick to speak her mind and just as quick to share anything that she had with others.

She carried the same qualities into her marriage. There were never so many in her home or around her table that she couldn't make room for one more or two or . . . She was never so busy that the task couldn't be set aside to make a cup of tea for a drop-in neighbor or a complete stranger.

People were always coming to our house and taking away my mother to nurse the sick, to comfort the mourning, to minister to the dying, even to prepare the dead for burial. As a child, I suppose I resented this at times, but that's just the way she was and it was to be accepted.

Like Dad, Mom expected obedience, but her manner of seeing that it was obtained differed from that of my father. She wasn't above using some force to get it, and often—with me and with other family members—she had to do just that. I remember more than once being unceremoniously turned over her checkered apron and given a good reason for listening to her instructions. There were always hugs and kisses and a few tears afterwards, but we paid better attention—at least for a little while.

Having been raised as I was, do I believe in spanking? Yes, I do. I do not believe in violence. I do not believe in abuse. But I do believe in spankings when they are needed to enforce the laws that have been established in a home. However, I do not think that spankings should be used for any other reason than deliberate disobedience. Children are perceptive. They know when they have "earned" a spanking, and I know that I never got a spanking that I did not deserve. Those spankings might have smarted for a season, but they never caused me harm, nor have I carried any resentment or bitterness toward my mom because of them.

I don't think that children should be spanked for breaking rules that have not been clearly established. Nor for accidents. Nor because of a parent's impatience or anger. And never when the child doesn't realize the offense committed. I believe that much of the trauma and pain that result from physical punishment come when the child is unaware that he or she has committed a violation of the rules. Confusion results. Either the parent is wrong, or the child must be wrong. To see the parent as wrong betrays the child's trust in the role model, the caregiver, the one who should be most concerned about the welfare of the child. Most children opt to assume that the fault must have somehow been their own. It follows that the child will lose self-worth and feel unwanted and bad without understanding why.

I pity children raised in such circumstances. But we must not throw out all physical correction because some people misuse it. To do that is to deny many children the solid understanding of right and wrong that they deserve to have established for them.

And my brother and sisters and I had right and wrong clearly defined for us. We were also taught that there was no room in our home for defiance or self-rule. I suppose as a child I might have wished that I could have had my own way now and then, but I think that even as a youngster, I was smart enough to realize that I did want guidelines. And I was bright enough to understand that consistent discipline is hard work and that, if my parents cared that much, they must really love me.

Also, because the guidelines were very firmly established and never altered, we always knew what was expected of us. We also had a firm base to fall back on when temptation came our way through our peers. "We can't do that," we could truthfully say. "Our folks won't let us."

We never did use the familiar expression, "They'd kill me," but I sometimes think that we might have feared that our fate would be even worse than death! Actually, it wasn't that we feared we'd be physically beaten within an inch of our lives nor that our parents would be so angered that they'd withdraw their love. No, we knew with certainty that their love was constant. But we also knew that because they loved us unconditionally, we had the awesome ability to hurt them deeply. I think it was this reason that held us on track. We honestly feared causing inner pain to those whom we loved and who loved us.

My parents loved us, and they taught us probably the most important lesson in preparation for our Christian walk: We learned from our parents that a God who loves us, and who demands obedience because of that love, is not only a biblical truth but also an incredibly reasonable arrangement. Love and discipline go hand in hand, and I thank God for giving me a father and mother who taught me it was so.

Never Too Old to Say "Daddy"

◆—————————————————————◆

Twenty-nine prestigious Dove Awards, two platinum albums, six gold albums, and five coveted Grammy Awards—quite a list of accomplishments for someone whose ambition in life was to teach a high-school music class! I'm talking about my friend Sandi Patti.

The daughter of a music minister, Sandi gave her life to the Lord when she was eight years old. As part of her family's singing troupe, she toured the country with her father, mother, and two younger brothers, singing in revivals, camp meetings, and crusades. While studying music at Anderson College in Indiana, she met and married John Helvering.

Sandi made her first recording in 1979 called "Sandi's Song." She then joined The Gaither Trio with whom she traveled for one year. It wasn't long, though, before audiences began to recognize Sandi as a uniquely powerful communicator in her own right. She embarked on her first major nationwide solo tour in 1984 after the release of Songs from the Heart. Since then she's recorded Hymns Just for You, Morning Like This, Make His Praise Glorious, Sunshine Company for Kids, *and, her most recent,* Sandi Patti and the Friendship Company.

Sandi is the mother of Anna, born in May 1984, twins Jonathan and Jennifer, born in November 1987, and Erin, born in January of 1990. Their births have caused her to take her music and her life much more seriously. Says Sandi, "A tremendous responsibility has been placed in the hands of John and me, a responsibility not just to sing the words that are in my songs, but to live them out. Although I've always taken my relationship with the Lord seriously, it has taken on new importance because I realize it is now my responsibility to pass on my faith to my children."

Also important to Sandi is her relationship to her father. She shares here a letter she wrote to him on Father's Day 1990.

Father's Day—June 13, 1990

Hi, Daddy!

Sitting here in my hotel room in L.A., I suddenly realized that Father's Day is coming up. I'm not so good at remembering much in advance, but I don't ever forget altogether!

I was wondering what I could give you that you don't have or don't need, when so many thoughts came to me about how I feel about you that I decided to give you some of what's in my heart. I began making a list in my head about you and why I'm thankful for how you've helped me grow—

and I very much want to share with you these pearls.

1. I'm glad I have a daddy. So many kids, young and old, don't even have a daddy for one reason or another, and my life seems less fragmented because I do.

2. I'm glad I have a daddy who wanted me—and still wants me—for his child. To be wanted is a most precious gift.

3. I'm glad I have a daddy who loves me with his whole heart.

4. I'm glad I have a daddy who was never too busy—and still is never too busy—to stop what he's doing and give a hug, fix a bike tire, take a little girl with a broken arm to the hospital, cook breakfast in the desert on a Saturday morning, hang up some pictures in his grandchildren's rooms, or stop and listen to a grown woman—who's still his daughter—talk about some things that are hard in this process of growing up.

5. I'm glad I have a daddy who loves my mommy—a man who treats his God-given mate with tenderness, love, and humor. These days, it seems so rare for parents to be together and stay together, and I'm glad for your example.

6. I'm glad I have a daddy who is crazy about my children. How lucky they are! You give them access to so much of yourself. Right now it's "flips" and "walks" and "hits" and "swings," but what you are saying to them is that they matter a great deal to you. I believe that you have anchored them with love and acceptance so that, as they grow and the world begins to tug all the more at them, they can stand confident in knowing who they are.

7. I'm glad I have a daddy who has made effort after effort to connect with John, the other man in my life. My heart is so full when I see the two of you growing closer together. Thank you for not giving up.

8. I'm glad I have a daddy who trusts me and has always been in my corner saying, "You can do it! Hang in there!" And I'm glad you trust me even when we don't agree. I suppose that's the truest test of trust. I'm glad you let me grow and even mess up sometimes. I know you are always there and will never say, "See, I told you so," but will let me rest on your shoulder and swing on the back porch without having to say anything.

Life and time change a lot of things. They change people, relationships, and attitudes. But one thing that can never change is the fact that you are my daddy. I love you with my whole heart and, on this day to honor fathers, you are honored among men.

I love you today and always.

Sandra Faye

Frank Peretti

My Two-by-Twos

F*rank Peretti is a twentieth-century Renaissance man. Consider his resume—banjo player with a bluegrass group, studio musician, student of playwriting and film at UCLA, associate pastor at an Assembly of God church, employee of the K2 ski factory in western Washington State, storyteller, and author. Add to this his list of personal interests: carpentry, construction, repair, plumbing, banjo making, toy making, sculpturing, bicycling, and hiking.*

We the reading public know Frank best for the phenomenally best-selling This Present Darkness *and its sequel,* Piercing the Darkness. *In the first, Frank addressed the pervasive threat of humanism and the New Age movement; in the second, he focused on the power of the Cross to give people victory in the spiritual warfare of everyday life. Both feature an exciting narrative, solid characterization, and strong Christian teaching, his trademarks.*

Frank is also the author of the Cooper Family Adventure series, written specifically for ten- to thirteen-year-old readers. He addressed the abortion issue in Tilly, *a book that reflects his desire to help equip believers for dealing with contemporary issues that call for a solid Christian response.*

In his writing, says Frank, he wants to share a world based on God-given ethics and philosophy. That world comes to life through true-to-life characters and easy-to-read plots that keep readers glued to their seats.

Read here how Frank's parents never discouraged or stifled the wonderful imagination we his readers so thoroughly enjoy.

You know, it never entered my mind that I might not succeed in building a full-size blimp in the backyard, and Dad never flinched at the idea.

"Just be sure to get the grass cut, and don't leave nails and boards lying around," he said, and he went back to painting the porch.

I had plenty of nails and boards. The previous summer's twenty-foot model of the *Titanic* hadn't quite gotten past the keel-laying stage, so behind the garage there was a sizable pile of two-by-twos bristling with nails. My brothers and I pulled out all the nails, pounded them straight on the patio, and put them to work holding the two-by-twos together again, only in a different shape.

What a feeling, driving in that first nail! It was the same feeling I had when we started building a mad scientist's lab in the basement—complete with a monster on a slab—so we could make a blockbuster movie with Dad's old Standard 7 spring-wound movie camera.

Or when we started making hot-air balloons out of laundry bags and raining them down on the neighborhood . . .

Or when we bought two old lawn mowers at the Goodwill so we could use the engines to power the two airplanes we were building in the garage out of the two-by-twos that would soon become the keel for the *Titanic* . . .

Or when I built that robot . . . well, actually the secret lab where I was going to build the robot . . .

Or when we made an eight-foot giant to wear on our shoulders so we could stalk the neighborhood and scare everybody (we made it out of the two-by-twos because it was more fun than the blimp) . . .

Or when we dug up the alley because we were going to build a World's Fair . . .

Dad never flinched. He never said, "It's a dumb idea" or "It'll never work" or "Remember the last project?"

No, he just let us use his tools and the same old nails, and as long as we put the tools back and didn't kill ourselves, he just watched.

Our old Tower portable typewriter really did belong to Mom, even though I kept it in my room and used it more than she ever got the chance to, hunting-and-pecking out reams of stories, poems, and essays suitable for sticking on the refrigerator but that no one ever saw.

I hid most of my stuff. Too self-conscious, I guess. Whenever Mom got her paws on something I'd written, it would end up in the hands of friends and relatives. They'd all be reading it and praising it, and I'd be embarrassed.

But sometimes—not often, just sometimes—I'd

purposely leave something on the dining-room table so she'd see it. Maybe sometimes—not often, just sometimes—I liked being embarrassed.

And Mom never said a word about the typewriter.

I was going to be the future Walt Disney and learn to draw cartoons and make great movies. My folks bought me a huge drawing pad, two charcoal pencils, a book on how to draw heads, and a big, gum art eraser.

I liked being a ham and making people laugh. My folks bought me a Jonathan Winters album, and I wore it out. Then I wore them out: "Hiya, honey. I'm Maude Frickert!"

I was going to be a great singer—I was a pretty good soprano anyway! Mom played the piano, and we all sang.

I could make anything out of empty cereal boxes: a toy jetliner, a huge mansion for my rubber animals to live in, even a scale model of the 1962 Seattle World's Fair. Mom kept me well stocked with Wheaties and Cheerios boxes and Elmer's glue, and when I think of all the glue she had to wash out of my jeans. . . .

You know, it has recently occurred to me:

My older brother is a missionary in a land hostile to the gospel. He's gotten one church well established, and now he's getting ready to plant another one.

My younger brother used to feel sorry for everything, even rocks he'd kick on the way home from school. He coupled that compassion with years of hard work, and now he's a licensed family counselor.

My sister used to dream about being an actress, a

singer, and a poet. For a while, she was a teacher who acted, sang, and wrote poetry, but now she's pursuing a ministry in theater arts. She says it's something she's just got to try.

I finally got my own typewriter, kept banging away, and saw my first novel published when I was thirty-six. Now I'm all set to write another.

I think the four of us kids just assumed all along that it's OK to dream, to aspire, to try and fail but then to try again. We don't whine much. We don't hear little phrases in our heads such as "That's a dumb idea," "It can't work," or "Remember that last project?"

No, we just keep building our blimps and airplanes and *Titanics,* pulling the nails out of the last dream's two-by-twos and building the next one. We're bound to succeed sooner or later.

Mom and Dad always knew that.

Two Very Special People

W*hat are the issues that matter to Ron Sider? The answer becomes clear with a glance at the titles of his writings and a list of the positions of service he has held.*

Consider the following books and articles to Ron's credit: Rich Christians in an Age of Hunger: A Biblical Study; Evangelism, Salvation, and Social Justice; Cry Justice: The Bible on Hunger and Poverty; Nuclear Holocaust and Christian Hope; Completely Pro-Life; Non-Violence: An Invincible Weapon?; "Mischief by Statute: How We Oppress the Poor"; and "Jesus' Resurrection and Radical Discipleship." We learn much about the man from this brief survey of his writings.

Not only does Ron share his ideas through the printed word, he also acts on those ideas. Currently, he is executive director of Evangelicals for Social Action, a member of the National Association of Evangelicals' Social Action Commission, and professor of theology and culture at Eastern Baptist Theological Seminary. He has served on the boards of Bread for the World and the Mennonite Central Committee. A graduate of Waterloo Lutheran University, Ron went on to graduate work at Yale that included a master's degree, and a Ph.D. in history.

Here, in the warm memories of his childhood, Ron talks about his parents and their "appealing and joyful Christian faith" that was "their best gift to me."

Dad put his arm on my shoulder as we stood together looking out the barn window at a torrential August thunderstorm. We had worked that day repairing the combine. As threatening storm clouds rolled eastward, we hurriedly brought the cows inside a bit early for evening milking to beat the storm. Successful and dry, we stood together for a quiet moment watching the lightning pierce the black sky and the heavy rain pound the ground.

Suddenly there was a flash and a crack of thunder that knocked us to our knees. As we got to our feet, frightened but instantly thankful that we weren't hurt, we saw that some of the cows had also been knocked down. Almost immediately we smelled smoke. Seeing nothing in the barn, I ran toward the house and then the toolshed. Both were fine. When I rushed back to the barn, Dad told me to check the loft, which held the summer's hay we had cut, baled, hauled, and stacked together.

The hayloft was ablaze! Together we rushed madly to untie the cows and drive them from the barn. Next we moved the tractor and combine to a safe distance away. Then, since there was nothing more we could do, we watched in sad silence as the raging fire devoured the summer's hard work.

That fire ended the first—and very happy—period of my life. We did rebuild the barn, but the fire made it easier for Dad to sell the farm a couple years later when he was called to pastor in another part of Ontario.

I am sure I romanticize a bit now, but living on a farm with a wonderful Mom and Dad was a fantastic way to grow up. I was born in that farmhouse. Mom and Dad carried me to the barn in a basket while they milked the cows together. I remember boiling apple butter in the fall, working hard with Dad in the fields, and being given time off while Dad finished the chores so I could skate on the frozen creek that meandered along the line of willow trees Grandpa had planted.

Mom and Dad were really very good parents. Of course all parents—even a holiness preacher and his sanctified wife—make mistakes, but they got it right most of the time without benefit of Dr. Spock. I suspect it was partly the inherited wisdom passed down by devout Christian ancestors over hundreds of years. I have no doubt that the single most important factor shaping who I am today is my parents—who they were and how they parented. And their most significant gifts to me were their faith, their integrity, and their love for each other.

Christ was the center of their life. From Mom's regular prayers, to going to church by sleigh after blizzards, to Dad's willingness to risk economic disaster for his beliefs, they communicated by example that trusting and obeying Christ is by far the most important thing in life. A little plaque they hung in my second-floor bedroom describes how they lived (and prayed I would, too!): "Only one life, 'twill soon be past;/ Only what's done for Christ will last."

When I was small, the local farmers joined together to do their threshing. (That's not a whipping; that's harvesting the wheat!) Often they worked late into the evening, but never on Wednesday. Everybody knew Mom and Dad always went to the Wednesday evening prayer meeting. So come 5:00 P.M. every Wednesday, the whole neighborhood threshing crew stopped early because, in their words, "Jimmy goes to prayer meetin'."

I also remember how Dad struggled with whether it was wrong to send milk to the dairy on Sunday. We had a good milk contract, and the money from the milk we shipped every day was by far the most important part of the family's income. After a lot of prayer, Dad decided God was calling him to stop shipping milk on Sunday. Even though he feared he might lose his whole milk contract, he told the dairy he could no longer have them pick up milk at our place on the Lord's Day. As it turned out, the dairy was cooperative, and we did not suffer much financial loss. But Dad had been prepared to lose a lot of money rather than disobey the Lord.

Mom and Dad's deep, genuine, and all-encompassing faith permeated every corner of our family life. I don't know what it means to struggle with religious hypocrisy in one's parents. Certainly they occasionally—very occasionally, I must say—failed. I remember the time when Dad, in frustration and anger at the death of a very good cow, uttered an awful word—*Damn.* He felt like a terrible sinner. I felt a bit relieved that he at least was not *entirely* sanctified. (I was never sure about Mom. I have sometimes wondered if she just may be the one known example of what the Wesleyan Holiness tradition that Dad preached has meant by "entire sanctification.") Day by day, year by year, Mom and Dad lived an appealing and joyful Christian faith. That, without doubt, was their best gift to me.

Also crucial were their love and respect for each other. From my earliest recollections to this most recent Christmas, it has always been obvious that their mutual affection and respect were deep and strong. Perhaps one small factor was their long, eager wait of more than five years during the depression until they could find enough money to marry. I cannot remember hearing them quarrel, although I'm sure they must have on occasion. (Perhaps it would have been instructive for us to see how they resolved their problems.) At seventy-eight this past Christmas, as he retired—for the third time—from his last pastoral assignment, Dad told me that he and Mom looked forward simply to being home together for more evenings. They have always loved being together.

And they have always made decisions together. They respect each other's judgment and talk everything through. To be sure, they lived in a time and context when nobody yet questioned the husband's role as final decision maker, nor had biblical feminism yet brought its very significant challenge to one-sided female submission. But Dad's leadership was a gentle headship exercised in a context of mutual respect, mutual decision making, and mutual love.

Mom's and Dad's love for God and each other provided for me an atmosphere of security that many children today never know. Only with great effort can I imagine what it would mean to live with the gnawing anxiety that comes with alcohol abuse, parental neglect, or divorce. Secure in their unshakable and powerful love for God and each other, I was able to grow up with a sense of security in my world. Just by being who they were—devout Christians in love with each other for a lifetime—they gave me a valuable gift.

The way they did their parenting was also important. Mom and Dad did their parenting as a team; they did it together. They demanded obedience, work, and responsibility. They also gave me increasing space to mature and decide for myself. They taught me how to confess when I blew it. And they communicated unconditional love. They enforced the same rules, supported each other's decisions, and checked with each other if any of us children was foolish enough to try playing one of them against the other. They never undercut each other even in subtle ways, and neither ever said negative things about the other.

Mom and Dad insisted on obedience—not harshly or rigidly—but firmly and consistently. I once managed to get spanked for misbehaving during church revival meetings on three successive Friday evenings. And my oh-so-gentle mother was quite capable of washing out my mouth with soap and water when I uttered bad words or told a lie. The discipline was not harsh. It was never done in anger. And it was always surrounded with an overarching, unmistakable love for me. But it was there—clear, firm, and consistent.

My parents also taught me how to work. As the oldest child (until we adopted an older sister when I was about twelve) and first son, I worked with Dad in the barn and the fields. As a teenager in high school, I found that one or two hours of work in the barn each evening blew away the academic cobwebs. And the summers were full of vigorous activity driving the tractor, combining the grain, and doing chores— hard work that, as well as I can now remember as a fifty-one-year-old city dweller, I thoroughly enjoyed.

The call to work and to responsibility, however, was always mixed with wise and caring concern. Whereas some fathers demanded that their high-school sons help with the milking both morning and evening, my dad did it alone in the morning so I could get a little more sleep. When our creek froze over during hockey time in rural Canada, Dad even let me miss the evening chores sometimes.

Mixed with the work was a mutuality and partnership that both taught and empowered. Long before I was old enough to have anything significant to contribute, Dad would discuss with me what crops to plant in our fields. Mom and Dad gave each of us our own calf to raise and sell. And when my parents wanted to decide whether to adopt an older sister who had been living with our family for several years, they made that a family decision we all discussed together. In the process, they taught us not only what it means for parents to make children partners in decision making, but also what it means to love one's neighbor.

They also taught us to save money. It was never in a boastful way, but Mom told us how she used to walk across the Peace Bridge separating Fort Erie from Buffalo to save a dime. (That was back when a dime was still worth at least two large ice cream cones!) And she cut my hair at home until I got too self-conscious to allow it.

I'm especially grateful that Mom and Dad taught me how to confess my sins regularly to God and, when appropriate, to neighbors. On just a few occasions— and no more were needed!—they insisted that I return something I had wrongly taken or go back to a teacher and confess a lie. Undoubtedly that was easier because Mom and Dad apologized to us children and asked for forgiveness when they believed they had made a mistake in their parenting. That was not necessary very often, but the few times it was made a deep impression on me. And my parents also made it crystal clear that we could fail and still be loved and accepted.

Finally, my parents had an uncanny wisdom about when to transfer responsibility for decisions to their growing children. While we were young, they insisted that we do what they believed was right. But every year brought more freedom to decide things for ourselves.

When I was young, our church was socially conservative. Men often parted their hair in the middle and almost never wore neckties. But when I wanted to part my hair on the side at the beginning of ninth grade, Mom and Dad talked with me about the issues without pushing me one way or the other. The decision was clearly up to me. They offered me the same space to mature as an independent adult on far more significant issues. I did not feel much need to rebel in order to establish my own identity and independence. They gave me that freedom step-by-step, usually at the right time.

Two very special people . . . James Peter Sider. His father's early death meant that he had to drop out of school at the end of eighth grade to care for the family farm, but he became a successful pastor and church leader in spite of that. One of my favorite comments about him is that he did not speak often in church gatherings and boards, but when he did, people listened. . . . And Ida Grace Cline. Her farm parents' greater economic stability enabled her to finish high school. Her deep faith was always beautifully obvious as she served with Dad as a gifted partner and church leader in their joint ministries. My most powerful sense of what it means to be radically, unconditionally committed to Christ above everything else, I owe to her.

They are two wonderful people who passed along a vision of what it means to be Christian parents. For that, and for their daily prayers for me for more than fifty years, I will always be grateful.

Gary Smalley

Tools in God's Hands

• ─────────────────────────────────── •

*A*s *Gary Smalley states here, his mother and father—* "whether they were aware of it or not"—*taught him much about what it means to be a successful parent. And Gary has gone on to share those lessons with thousands of people through his books, seminars, and appearances on radio and television talk shows.*

Gary is the author of several best-selling books including For Better or For Best, The Key to Your Child's Heart *and, with John Trent,* The Blessing, The Gift of Honor, The Language of Love, Love Is a Decision, *and* The Two Sides of Love.

During his more than twenty years of family research and counseling, Gary has spoken to people throughout the United States, Canada, and parts of Europe. The powerful and practical principles he has developed have helped restore and heal countless families. In his "Love Is a Decision" seminars, for instance, he shares ten vital elements essential to making the home a place where each family member is valued, honored, and loved.

A graduate of the California State University at Long

Beach, Gary is currently president of Today's Family, a Phoenix-based organization dedicated to the enrichment of families everywhere. He is also presently working toward his doctorate degree in Marriage and Family. He and his wife, Norma, have three children, Kari, Gregory, and Michael.

Here, Gary shares principles he learned from his parents that served as the basis for the parenting he and Norma have done.

If you've been to one of the "Love Is a Decision" conferences John Trent and I do across the country, you've probably heard me joke about having grown up in a very permissive home—so permissive that I wasn't allowed to start my formal dating until the third grade!

Rules were hard to find at the Smalley house, partially due to my parents' personalities and partially due to a tragedy that forever changed the way they dealt with their children.

My oldest sister, my parents' first child, died needlessly at the age of six. One day when she was on a playground, a splinter from a wooden slide imbedded itself under her skin. A few days later, my mother lost her patience with Laurna and spanked her for something minor, unaware that the splinter was causing an infection that would soon take her life. Those were the days when doctors didn't understand that much about antibiotics, and within three weeks my sister was dead from blood poisoning.

As you can imagine, my mother was devastated. She was haunted by the horrible thought that, somehow, she had contributed to Laurna's death or had made her last few days on earth needlessly harsh. For her, my sister's death was something Dr. Trent and I call an "emotional freeze point," a traumatic experience that caused a permanent change in the way she dealt with her children. She vowed she'd never again spank any of us, and she made my dad promise the same thing. From then on, any form of punishment was an unwelcome visitor at our home.

Unfortunately, while my mother's intentions were good, her reaction to my sister's death had exactly the opposite effect she intended. The stability and security she thought she was giving us by avoiding discipline actually deprived us of those things and made us yearn for the discipline we knew we needed.

I can remember several occasions when I was caught red-handed doing things I knew weren't right. Once my father caught me in the middle of a very serious wrongdoing; another time a teacher caught me violating a major class rule after I had been told repeatedly to stop. In both cases, I was let off with a warning—and I can remember being disappointed that no one seemed willing to follow through with the punishment I knew I needed.

There is no doubt that my parents' inability to look past the tragedy of my sister's death and lovingly provide the discipline I needed had a negative effect on me. Even as a young adult, I had a hard time abiding by the rules—whether it was a No Parking sign on the curb or "We do not accept checks" printed at the bottom of a menu.

But, remarkably, I look back on those growing-up years with a deep sense of gratefulness. Why? Because, whether they were aware of it or not, my parents taught me much about what it means to be a successful parent. Were it not for experiences I had with them, the lessons God has taught me about parenting wouldn't have been nearly as significant. In a very real sense, my childhood was a rich greenhouse that nurtured the growth of two key parenting principles that changed my life and the lives of my wife, Norma, and our children. Over the years, virtually everything Norma and I have done with the kids has been based on these two principles.

The first is that every home needs clearly defined rules that, if violated, involve consequences. Study after study has demonstrated that children need boundaries in order to grow up with a healthy sense of stability and security. By providing that for them, we give them one of the greatest gifts any parent can give a child. (As Proverbs 23:13 says, "Do not hold back discipline from the child. . . ." (NASB).

As I mentioned, this principle was lacking in my home. But because it wasn't there, I developed a deep hunger to know and understand what it means to have a healthy family, and that hunger is still with me today. Had I grown up in a home that provided this discipline, I might have taken it for granted and never had the desire to learn and share with others what it means to be a successful parent. I'm convinced that many of the opportunities I have for ministering to families today are a direct result of the experiences I had thirty and forty years ago. I owe my mom and dad sincere thanks for that.

The second key principle is that, as parents, we must be committed to love each of our children in a warm, affectionate, and supportive way. This involves such actions as openly expressing our commitment and love to our children, being available to them, listening intently to them, and giving them the physical affection they yearn for. In doing these things, we add to clearly defined rules the second key ingredient that makes for blue-ribbon parenting.

As is the case with many parents who have a hard time establishing and enforcing rules, my mom was very warm, affectionate, and supportive. While my father never learned the secret of communicating his feelings to us, she worked overtime to make sure each of us knew we were loved. Regardless of what I was into or interested in, she was there—supporting, encouraging, and helping in any way she could. Like the times I'd awaken her after a date and watch her eyes light up, lift her arms toward me, and say excitedly, "Come on, sit next to me and tell me all about tonight."

Her model of tenderness and caring helped shape the convictions I have about the four key ingredients for a loving relationship: unconditional security, meaningful communication, shared experiences, and healthy touching. Over the years, I've done my best to learn more about what it means to include these ingredients in my relationships with the people I care about, always remembering the way Mom offered them to me and my brothers and sisters.

Another result of Mom's warm, supportive love was that I grew up with a very healthy sense of self-esteem. I was encouraged to go, to do, and to explore. I learned quickly that there was very little I couldn't do—and that, with a little practice and training, there was virtually nothing I couldn't do. In fact, as my employees, family, and friends will attest to, one of the things I'm fond of saying is "There is virtually nothing you can't do—all you need are the knowledge and skills to do it."

Finally, my mom's encouraging love taught me to be creative and enterprising. I learned that boundaries are not so much obstacles as they are opportunities, and that just because something has been done one way before doesn't mean it has to be done that way again. That understanding has led me on some wild adventures, but it's also given me the ability to look at things from a different perspective, approach things from a different angle, and come up with a new solution. Mom taught me the value not only of asking "Why?" but also of asking "Why not?"

My parents weren't perfect. In many ways they could have done a better job of helping prepare me for adulthood. As I've shared, some of the mistakes they made have presented some real challenges for me.

But there is much about what I learned from my parents, especially my mom, that makes me thankful I grew up in their home. In many ways, God used my experiences there to mold me into his image and prepare me for the work he wanted me involved in. Without them, I could not have had the rich, full life I've enjoyed—something I'll always be grateful to them for.

So if you come from a home where everything wasn't perfect, take heart. Whether they were aware of it or not, your mom and dad were important tools in God's hands for making you who he wants you to be. And that makes your parents—like my mom and dad—very special indeed.

A Strong Foundation for Life

W hen asked what's important to him, Norm Sonju responds without hesitation—"My three priorities are my faith in Jesus Christ, my family, and the Mavericks." Norm, a committed Christian, husband, and father of three children (Lynne, Scott, and David), is also the chief operating officer and general manager for the Dallas Mavericks basketball team.

From 1976 to 1978, Norm was president and general manager of the Buffalo Braves. When that team moved to San Diego as the Clippers, Norm began working to bring a basketball team to Dallas.

A graduate of Grinnell College in Iowa, Norm served a stint in the Air Force before receiving his M.B.A. from the University of Chicago. Norm worked at ServiceMaster Industries in Downers Grove, Illinois, before getting involved with professional basketball.

Norm has directed the Camp of the Woods basketball clinic for twenty-seven years. He founded the clinic, located in the

Adirondack Mountains of upstate New York, in 1963. Norm heads up the annual Christian Leadership Golf Classic and is also active in Urban Alternative, a weekly radio ministry headed up by Dr. Tony Evans, the Mavericks' chaplain and counselor. In July of 1990, Norm shared his testimony at the Billy Graham Crusade at Knickerbocker Stadium in Albany, New York.

Read here how his parents taught him to value the family, giving him the motivation to speak up for a strong family unit—an endangered species today.

I'm concerned about the state of today's family. If we in America don't change our ways, I believe we will become weak and ineffectual like so many previous civilizations. Historically, most civilizations don't last much beyond two hundred years, and our 215-year-old nation appears to be on a course that could be devastating.

A few years ago, I went with my family to the Masi Mara region of eastern Kenya and was amazed to see so few rhinoceroses. The species is virtually extinct because of the damage done by poachers. There were only three in the entire region when, only a few years earlier, there were thousands in that same part of Kenya.

Our families face the same danger that the rhinos do: Our kids are being poached by every pressure imaginable. We as parents must provide the necessary character building from within our own family units;

the positive lessons and examples children need won't come from without. If we as parents don't make the effort, I'm afraid that the well-adjusted, under-control young person will became as rare as the rhinoceros of East Africa.

I am grateful for my parents. They taught me a lot of good things, and much of what I believe so strongly today was instilled in me when I was young.

My parents, Marinius and Anna Sonju, were born and raised in Norway. They immigrated to America in the twenties, as did so many Europeans at that time. They wanted an opportunity to live in a country that provided hope, and the United States did just that. Still, when my mother said that final good-bye to her parents on the dock in Balestrand, Norway, it was painful because she probably suspected that she would never see them again. She didn't; her parents died many years prior to her being able to return to Norway.

Neither of my parents went to high school, and the lack of opportunity that resulted seemed to be the driving factor in our lives. Having not received all the formal education they wanted, they made certain that their children did. As early as I can recall, we all knew that we were going to college. It was never really an option for us. The importance of a good education was instilled in us very early, and my two sisters and I all graduated from college and went on to earn master's degrees.

Besides learning early the value of a formal education, I also learned that common sense and wisdom do not come because of an earned degree. My parents had great wisdom despite very little formal education, and understanding this reality has been invaluable throughout my business career. Many people whom I considered wise and who seemed to have a lot of common sense have not necessarily been college types, though some were. Common sense and wisdom are not guaranteed results of formal education, and my parents helped me understand this.

Years ago, prior to my entering the National Basketball Association (NBA), I headed a division of a major firm in the Chicago area. I was responsible for thousands of workers, most of whom were hourly employees and many of whom lacked much formal education. I respected many of them and appreciated their willingness to work hard and their ability to do quality work. They knew I cared for them, and we all had a good time even though we worked long hours and, at times, in difficult situations. Because my parents had been good models for me, I could appreciate how hard the hourly employees had to work.

Today, my mother is ninety-two years old. Though her body is aging, her mind is alert, and she still continues to be an encourager to me. When we were children, she never allowed us to say or believe that we couldn't do something. She was always a very positive person, and no matter how difficult the challenge might have been, she made us feel that we could meet it. She had great tenacity and strength. She also held the genuine belief that her God was sovereign and in control of all things. These qualities—her optimism, tenacity, strength, and faith—gave me a strong foundation for life.

In 1980 when I was working around the clock organizing the Mavericks and trying to find investors, the odds against success seemed insurmountable. Here I was in Dallas, well known for its football but not for its basketball, trying to form the ownership foundation for a new NBA basketball franchise! Furthermore, interest rates were well over 20 percent, and the Iranian crisis had many people thinking negative thoughts. It was not a good time to be trying to put together a sports franchise.

At times everything seemed to be going wrong, yet when things appeared hopeless, I would remember verses I had learned from my mother when I was young. One of those was Jeremiah 33:3: "Call to me and I will answer you and tell you great and unsearchable things you do not know" (NIV). The truth of God's Word made such a difference in my attitude: I knew that he was in control of all things even when, on the outside, things looked so hopeless. God's promises were reassuring to me.

One of the chapters that my mother had committed to memory was Romans 8. I can remember her reciting from it day after day. It made a strong impression on me. I can still recall how I felt as a youngster when she would emphasize that nothing can separate us from the love of Christ (v. 39).

Even today, my mother continues to uplift and encourage me. This year we all expected our team to play well during the regular season, make a strong run in the play-offs, and compete aggressively for the NBA championship. We had made some dramatic trades over the summer and had signed a high-scoring free agent, so we truly expected to be one of the better teams.

Our season started well. We were in first place with a 4–1 record, but during our fifth game we lost our best player for the entire year. Another key player was lost for the season as well, and all of a sudden our plans and hopes were shattered. Yet each time I talk with my mother, she only sees the good that is still to come. I feel blessed to have such a positive influence in my life.

My father passed away in December 1967 when he was eighty-two years old. A carpenter, my father often left for work before I was out of bed. Yet whenever I would sneak up to his bedroom early, I'd invariably find him on his knees praying. And never have I heard a man pray like my father did. He had a strong Norwegian accent, and he normally prayed out loud. And my father spoke as if he were talking to his closest friend; he prayed as if he knew Jesus intimately. That legacy and the example he set is one that I will cherish forever.

When I was in school, all the basketball games were played immediately after school in the middle of the afternoon, not later in the evenings as most schools do today. Because of this, it was impossible for Dad to see me play without missing work. Since he was paid on an hourly rate, missing work would have meant missing out on needed dollars for the family. I understood that, and I never felt deprived as a youngster. Now as a father, though, I try to do everything possible to attend all of my children's events.

Attending my children's sporting and music events requires planning. It might mean not accepting a speaking engagement or even missing a Mavericks home game, but I want my children to know that they are a priority. I remember once missing a Lakers game to go to my daughter's game instead. Her coach chose not to play her that night, but it didn't matter. I was there at the game to support her no matter what, and later that night we had a great time at dinner together. I wouldn't trade that time alone with her for anything.

Another time when my oldest son was struggling with some things, I decided to miss our only home game with the Celtics to see his game instead. He didn't know I was there until afterwards. We had a wonderful meal together, and then we went to our practice gym where I rebounded for a good hour while he worked on his shot. We listened to our game with the Celtics on the radio. That evening was a terrific time with my son. The Mavericks will have a lot more Celtics games, but now my son is grown and away at college. Those times with him cannot be recaptured. How glad I am that I took advantage of those precious moments before it was too late!

My father's inflexible work schedule has encouraged me to, whenever possible, take advantage of the opportunities to support my children in their activities. It's one of the best uses of time that I know. I want to be an encourager and a support for them. I believe that if we can instill confidence in our children—confidence in themselves and the assurance that we love them—they will be more ready to face the many poachers that prey on our families.

Dr. Kenneth Taylor

Looking Back

D r. *Taylor is probably best known as the paraphraser of* The Living Bible, *but he was the author of children's books long before that.*

He and his wife, Margaret, have ten children, and you can be sure that books such as The Bible in Pictures for Little Eyes, Stories for the Children's Hour, *and* The Living Bible Story Book *were forwarded to the publishers only after the children gave their approval! Ken undoubtedly wrote his more recent publications—*Wise Words for Little People, Big Thoughts for Little People, *and* Giant Steps for Little People—*with his many grandchildren in mind.*

A graduate of Wheaton College and Northern Baptist Seminary, Dr. Taylor is the founder and chairman of Tyndale House Publishers and the author of more than thirty books. He is also the recipient of numerous awards, among them the Christian Booksellers Association's 1980 Achievement Award, The Committee for International Goodwill's 1983 Man of the Year Award, and the Evangelical Christian Publishers Association's 1984 Gold Medallion Achievement Award. He was named Alumnus of the Year by Northern Baptist Seminary in 1973 and by Wheaton College in 1977.

Dr. Taylor has served on various boards of directors, many of those reflecting his interest in publishing, evangelism, and the Bible. What he writes here suggests that those interests have their roots in the home in which he was raised.

I'm glad I was invited to write this chapter because, after so many years, it has been good to remind myself of my parents' many positive qualities. My folks did a lot of things right.

Dad and Mother were quite different in temperament. Dad was jovial and warm; Mother was quieter and more serious, but still able to enjoy the family fun. Both were people of piety—in the best sense of the word—and consistent in their kindness and their concern for others and their three boys. I don't remember any sharp disagreements between them. If there were any, we children were protected from the confusion we would have felt.

The love in our home was strong, and we felt it even though my parents were not demonstrative. Hugs were not shared much and kisses seldom—except for good-night kisses from Mother when we were little. Perhaps this is a negative, but my brothers and I knew how much they loved us.

Discipline was minimal mostly, I think, because we didn't need it. Somehow we all had a clear understanding that obedience to parents was a fundamental obligation, so we obeyed without thinking about it.

I do, however, have a couple of painful preschool memories. Once when my brother Doug and I were outdoors playing, I deliberately used my tricycle to run over and break one of his prized toys. At the ensuing commotion, Mother left the parlor and her duties as gracious hostess, came out to investigate, obtained the facts, and took me up to my bedroom to do her duty as mother. On another occasion when I was angry about something, I sawed a branch from an ornamental tree in the front yard. Dad used it on my britches—just one whack but it was hard enough that I still remember it! How grateful I am that some of my bad tendencies were nipped in the bud.

I am also thankful that my parents had a family prayer time every morning after breakfast before we children rushed to the school bus. My brothers and I went into the day with our parents' blessings and prayers. At family prayers, there was also a Scripture reading and an explanation from Dad when the passage was hard to understand. Then each of us prayed about matters of personal concern and for one another. Dad's prayers were often long as he prayed for his family, for missionaries, and for his work.

A prayer I remember him praying more than once was that God would protect his sons from "that moment of temptation that could ruin their entire lives." I am glad to say that God answered this prayer for all three of us. Immorality was not an option in our family.

As we children came to an age of understanding, we didn't have the feeling that our parents were on one side of a great gulf and we were on the other side until we said the right words about "accepting Christ as our Lord and Savior." No, it was assumed that all of us together were loving Jesus. No formula had to be said first, yet it was very clear to us how we had been saved from God's anger toward our sins. We gradually learned the details of Christ's death on the cross for us, and we were very grateful.

I'm glad that we grew up as a family that prayed together, and I'm also glad that we were a family that ate together at the dinner table. In those days, it was normal. Only as I see what is happening in homes today do I realize the wisdom of this practice. We didn't eat until everyone was at the table. Even Mother sat down for the prayer before eating, getting up again afterwards to tend to the final details of the meal.

As I grew up, I saw Mother and Dad reading their Bibles frequently, and they encouraged us to get into this habit. Dad used to tell us, "You fellows will never amount to much for God unless you get into the Word and the Word gets into you." Although I was troubled for a long time by the difficulty of some parts of the King James Version—which was all we had in my growing-up years—I am glad to say that since the advent of *The Living Bible* twenty years ago, a regular private prayer and study time is now a normal and important part of my day.

Something else I look back on with appreciation is that Dad, a United Presbyterian pastor, sometimes took me along when he was visiting parishioners. I learned a lot about the importance of his work. My hardworking dad also taught me to work. When my older brother and I were in our early teens, he gave us a summer assignment of two hours a day cutting trees and brush from the back of our acre, blasting stumps, and cutting and splitting cordwood for the wood-burning furnace in our home. It was hard work—but fun too.

Dad was a great personal evangelist for his Lord. As often as possible, he told people about what Christ had done for them. For a long time, I was too timid to appreciate his zeal. I recall as a child getting on my hands and knees in the backseat of our Model T Ford when Dad picked up a hitchhiker. I knew what the topic of conversation would soon be, and I was embarrassed! Since then, Dad's example has helped me be bolder.

In summary, what my parents did right was to be right in their own lives and so attract me to our Lord.

A Favorite Song

She has done everything from street evangelism to singing in coffee shops, from interviewing heads of state to performing before millions of people. I'm talking about Sheila Walsh, the talented singer and former cohost of the Christian Broadcast Network's popular "700 Club."

Born and raised in a small mining town in Scotland, Sheila was raised to love God by her Baptist parents. By the time she was ten, she had two major interests—her faith and opera. When at seventeen she heard a group of young people singing gospel music with a contemporary beat, she headed in that direction musically.

Sheila's albums have been nominated for both Grammy and Dove Awards, and she was named the Gospel Music Association's International Artist of the Year in both 1983 and 1985. Her first album, Future Eyes, was followed by three critically acclaimed albums—War of Love, Triumph in the Air, and Don't Hide Your Heart. During this time, Sheila was asked to host the British Broadcasting Company's "The Rock Gospel Show." She hosted the show from 1984 to 1987, appearing before a weekly audience of more than 5 million people. The mid-eighties also marked the release of Shadowlands, Say-So, and Simple Truth.

Her most recent release was an a cappella project simply called Hymns & Voices.

Sheila also cohosted "The 700 Club" with Pat Robertson. This weekday program reached more than 20 million households. Sheila had her own daily show on The Family Channel called "Heart to Heart with Sheila Walsh," and 1990 saw the publication of her best-selling book Holding onto Heaven with Hell on Your Back.

It's hard to know where to begin and how to catalog the things that my mother did right. As I look back today, in the warmth of the friendship that we both continue to cherish, so many pictures dance before my eyes. I remember the summer of '72 when I was sixteen years old. . . .

Each year, Queen Elizabeth's husband, the Duke of Edinburgh, presents his gold award to a few high-school students in Great Britain. It really is a heady occasion to be invited to the palace grounds for a garden party and reception in your honor. The awards are given to those who have completed three years of extensive community service, survival expeditions in rugged terrain, involvement in the arts, and baffling initiative tests.

As the dog days of summer approached, I was almost at the end of this journey. I could taste the cucumber sandwiches! I had survived several nights of numbing cold at the top of a lonely Scottish mountain in a one-man tent and had returned with nothing more serious than a bite from an irate goat with an attitude.

My final project was to live in a community of mentally handicapped adults and assist the nursing staff for the summer. I was moved by the unconditional love and acceptance offered me by some of the Down's syndrome adults. Each evening we would gather in the sitting room, sing some well-worn chorus, and offer God thanks for life and friends. And yet, in the midst of the love and joy, I encountered someone who made me want to run a million miles away from it all.

A new matron had recently been appointed to the home, and she was the most cruel, heartless person I had ever met. It broke my heart to see the way she rebuffed the spontaneous affection of the residents as they reached out to her. I could see the confusion and hurt in their eyes as she physically pushed them out of her way. It was too painful to watch, and I wanted to leave.

One evening after dinner, I went to the local village telephone box to call my mom. I told her that I was miserable and wanted to come home. I asked her to come get me. What she said to me that day has stayed with me like a favorite song, and I've replayed that song many times in my heart. She told me that she would certainly come get me if that was the only option I felt I had, but she asked me to stand back for a moment and think. She said, "There will be many times in your life, Sheila, when you feel like running away because nothing makes sense anymore. These moments can crush you or strengthen you—and you alone can choose."

She helped me to see that, for a moment, the Lord had allowed me to bring a little joy into the confusing world of my new friends and that, if I chose to leave, I would take that joy with me. I remember her words: "Sometimes to love means to embrace pain."

As I wandered down a country lane on that dusky summer evening, I asked God for the strength to stand when I felt like falling. As I stayed through the summer, I sang a melody I had learned from my mother and which she had learned from hers.

I went on to college and encountered terrifying academic challenges, but I kept on singing that familiar melody. I moved into married life and faced a time when everything within me screamed to give up and walk away, but the song had lived with me for so long by then that I had to listen. . . .

Unconditional love is a mystery to me. I have always known that no matter how I choose, my mother's heart towards me remains unchanged, and yet that very love that throws open the doors to opportunity causes me to choose the narrow path.

(Oh, by the way, I did win the award, and personally, I think cucumber sandwiches are overrated!)

Grace Encountered

A writer's inspiration can come from many different sources, and the source of some of Walter Wangerin's writing is his inner-city parish ministry. He worked with Grace Lutheran Church in Evansville, Indiana, from 1974 until 1985, serving officially as pastor from 1977 on. He and his wife, Thanne, are the parents of four children.

After earning a Master of Arts degree in English from Miami University (Oxford, Ohio) and a Master of Divinity degree from Christ Seminary-Seminex in 1976, Walter began serving God and his people through both a parish ministry and a writing ministry. He occupies a Chair of the University at Valparaiso University, Valparaiso, Indiana. He speaks "on matters literary, theological, sociological, homiletical, faithful, and human" at seminars, workshops, and retreats.

Walter's writing has earned him many awards and much professional recognition. The Book of the Dun Cow was named the New York Times's Best Children's Book of the Year and received the American Book Award in 1980. Potter received the Gold Medallion Book Award in 1986 and the CSIA C. S. Lewis Award in 1986. Among his other popular books are Ragman and Other Cries of Faith, As for Me and My House: Crafting a Marriage to Last, *and* A Miniature Cathedral and Other Poems.

Here Walter, the oldest of seven children, looks back at an unexpected gift of—and lesson in—grace.

Grace: Ever since Sunday school I've known that word.

God is gracious: In confirmation class I memorized the meaning—"showing undeserved kindness, forgiving." So Luther said.

The grace of God: This, I learned, is more than an attribute; it's an act of God. But I received it neat in a doctrine, which itself is not an act but a definition: "God loves me when I'm unworthy of love and grants me salvation I could not purchase. Forgiveness is a perfectly free gift of Jesus. And grace transforms the sinner, or God's love makes the unlovely lovely indeed."

"What is grace?" Pastor Schoepf demanded at my public confirmation. And standing in the chancel, shaking, gazing at two hundred faces, I recited rightly:

Ephesians 2:8-9: "For by grace you have been saved through faith; and this is not your own doing, it is the gift of God—not because of works, lest any man should boast" (RSV).

I was a smart kid, the darling of my teachers. And yet I did not in fact understand grace. Oh, I knew what I was talking about, as one might talk about aerodynamics (which I did, being at least as interested in flight as in salvation). But I wasn't struck dumb by the impossible beauty of grace—no, not until I actually experienced a love I knew I didn't deserve.

Doctrine may teach us the names of our faith's most fundamental truths; God bless doctrine. But the truths themselves we meet in our own experience, meet them, greet them, and are borne aloft by them. Then we know what hitherto we only learned by rote. *Grace:* This is how I first encountered it. . . .

We lived in Canada, my family and I. Winter was hard in 1957. Life was hard in general. But I felt it right that I should shoulder my load in life, for I had become an adult. I was thirteen. I had been confirmed the previous spring—initiated into independence. I accepted adulthood solemnly.

To me it meant that you did your duty solitarily, without complaint. Certain honors were accorded the adult, but certain obligations were required in return. The honors sounded like this: "You're free, young man." I could, for example, choose what time I went to bed. But the obligations sounded like this: "Young man, you're on your own." I was alone.

So I shouldered responsibility in the family. I was the oldest of seven children. I began to see to their welfare. I bossed them. I made sure they went to bed.

My mother said, "Who died and left you boss?"

I said, "Yeah, but . . ." like any debating adult. "Yeah, but they ought to be quiet," I said. "Yeah, but they need their sleep. I'm only doing what's right."

"And why aren't you in bed?" she asked.

"I'm grown now, Mom."

"Ah, grown," she said. "My son is grown." She folded her arms and stood back to get a better look. "And can he reap the whirlwind too, this man of mine?"

My enigmatic mama. I knew what she meant: *You're on your own.*

But I had good and grave reasons to boss the others, though I couldn't tell them to my mother: I was protecting *her.* In those days she and my father were suffering the malice of bitter people. A scourge of gossip cut the city against my parents, and I saw the hurt in their faces. I took it upon myself to make at least their home a peaceful place: I bossed the kids to silence and to bed, and I myself withdrew.

Winter was hard in those days. I felt lonely in adulthood. But I accepted loneliness as due an adult.

And then one night late I couldn't sleep. My stomach knotted in spasms I didn't understand, and by 2:00 A.M. I'd dampened the sheets with sweat. There was a wind outside. It whistled with the sort of scorn that made this corner of my bedroom truly dark and solitary.

Now I expected absolutely nothing. It never occurred to me but that I'd handle this misery alone. I was adult. Free. On my own. But I must have been groaning out loud.

For suddenly the hall light burned outside my door. The door swung inward. And there stood my mother, silhouetted in her diaphanous nightgown, utterly beautiful.

"Wally?" she whispered. "What's the matter?"

I was stunned by her coming. "Wally—?" Her voice, the mere voice of my mother, was so deeply familiar to me that I started to cry.

"My—stomach," I sobbed.

"Ah," she murmured. She floated toward me and

sat on the edge of the mattress, which sank to her weight. She put a cool hand to my forehead. She whispered (how holy the homely remedies), "Pull your knees up to your chest. The warmth will ease your tummy."

I did, and I cried and cried—for none of this should have been. I never thought that I could be a child again. Oh, I thought I had lost all that.

But I had a mother after all, and she came to me. I was protecting her in those days, not she me—yet she came to me. I was adult, independent, brave, a reaper of the whirlwind, acceptor of the consequences; I had forfeited the mercy of a mama in the nighttime. Nonetheless, she came to comfort me—and like a baby I curled in the crook of her arm and wept.

Grace: This was the first time grace embraced me. In the face of my mother was the love of the healing God, all undeserved but visible. And behold: My stomach hurt no more. And behold: My mother's son was lovely, lovely indeed.

Dr. Robert Webber

A Father's Influence

R arely do I see in people the heart for worship that I see in Robert Webber. An Episcopal lay theologian and professor of theology at Wheaton College in Wheaton, Illinois, Bob conducts seminars on worship, spirituality, and evangelism in denominational and ecumenical settings across the United States.

Bob's heart for worship has been behind such publications as Worship Old and New, Worship Is a Verb, The Book of Family Prayer, and Celebrating Our Faith: Evangelism through Worship. Also to his credit are Evangelicals on the Canterbury Trail: Why Evangelicals Are Attracted to the Liturgical Church and The Majestic Tapestry: How the Power of Early Christian Tradition Can Enrich Contemporary Faith. He has also written about church and society in The Church in the World and The People of Truth.

Recently, Bob completed the book Signs of Wonder: The Transforming Power of Worship and the video "New Directions in Worship". Currently, he is working on a multi-volume Encyclopedia of Worship.

Besides working to enrich the worship life of today's believers, Bob has been active for more than twenty years in those movements that have given shape to an ecumenical Christianity. He lends his knowledge of the historical church and his love for God to these efforts to join the evangelical spirit with the universal message of the gospel and a concern for social outreach.

Here, this hardworking professor and prolific writer shares a little about how he learned to persevere.

On the day that I began writing this piece, CBS aired a special called "Arnold Palmer: The Man and His Legend." The opening question addressed to the famed golf star went something like this: "Arnie, you are a man whose influence and leadership have been felt around the world. If there is one thing that has contributed to the making of Arnie Palmer and to the respect that you command everywhere, what would that be?" Without hesitation, Arnie Palmer answered: "The influence of my father."

My father was born in 1900, the second child of hardworking Midwest farmers. His own father, a risk taker, decided to move his family westward in hope of a better life. Boarding a covered wagon in the first decade of this century, my grandparents traveled to Billings, Montana, where they farmed for a short while before making the rest of the journey to LaGrange, Oregon, where they settled.

As a boy, my father had no religious training or

Christian upbringing, but he had a longing in his heart to know God, a troubling that remained persistent, a yearning that sought to be fulfilled.

One day when he was fifteen, he was plowing the field. The desire for God within him became so strong that he stopped the mule and dropped to his knees. There behind his plow, he called out to God, whom he did not know, to come into his life. The next Sunday he made his way to a local church where he found Christ. In a few short years, his entire family became Christians. To this day, the Webber family, which has grown into a tree with many branches, remains faithful to the Lord.

After attending Moody Bible Institute and Northern Baptist Seminary, my father went off to Africa with the Africa Inland Mission. He married Harriet Russell, another missionary, and served the Lord at Mitulu station in the Belgian Congo. I was born on furlough and returned to Africa to live at Mitulu.

For Christmas in 1987, my older sister sent me a picture from Africa that now hangs on the wall of my home office. My dad had felled a huge elephant, and my sister, my brother, and I had gone into the jungle to see the catch. The picture shows the elephant lying on the ground with its long trunk stretched out over the trampled elephant grass (so-called because it stands more than six feet high). The gun is perched against the head of the dead animal; behind the trunk a native stands, holding my two-year-old brother in his arms; and there in the forefront of the picture, sitting on the trunk of the elephant is my dad wearing Banana Republic–type rumpled trousers and shirt, combat boots, and a safari hat. His left arm is perched on his left leg, and his right arm is extended over the trunk toward the head of the elephant. And there I am, six years old, wearing shorts and a turban on my head, snuggled up against my father's right side.

When my sister sent me this enlarged picture, now a prized possession, she said, "I thought you would like to have this because it symbolizes the close relationship you had with your father." Indeed, when I want to get in touch with my childhood, all I have to do is spend some time looking at that picture. Through it, my heart and mind become flooded with memories of my father's influence. Let me share two stories from my childhood that I carry with me today.

The first story comes from my early days in Montgomeryville, Pennsylvania, the place where we settled after returning from Africa when I was about nine. Our small home opened up to a field belonging to the next farm, and many blackberry bushes grew on our property and the farmer's. I loved blackberries, the picking as well as the eating!

On one occasion when I had nearly filled my ten-gallon pail, the farmer came out of his back door and began yelling at me for picking the berries on his property. "Get out of my field!" he cried. "And don't let me catch you on my property ever again! Do you understand me?"

Afraid of the man, I ran to the house to tell my father. "Give me the pail of blackberries," my dad said. "We're going to go next door and talk to that man."

"Good," I said to myself. "My dad will show him a thing or two!"

"Mr. Farmer," my dad said calmly, "I'm sorry my son was on your property." Then, handing the pail of blackberries to the farmer, Dad said, "Here, I want you to have these blackberries."

The farmer, completely disarmed by this unexpected gesture, waved his arm and said, "Hey, I'm sorry I yelled at the boy. I don't want the blackberries. I don't even like blackberries. You keep them. And you can pick all the berries you want from my field. It's OK."

As we walked back home, Dad turned to me and said, "The Scripture says 'a soft answer turneth away wrath.' Remember that, Robert." I've not always lived up to that Scripture, or to the example of my father, but I've never forgotten those words or my dad's action that gave those words meaning.

A second story comes from my days as a student at Bob Jones University. I had had a very difficult time adjusting to the rules of that institution and to the watchful eye of students ready to report their fellow students to the dean for what seemed to me inconsequential matters. After repeated skirmishes with the dean, I decided to give up and go home. (To be honest, I was about to be expelled for what they called a bad attitude—i.e., disagreeing with the institution.)

But one did not simply pack up and walk off campus. There were even rules about leaving: A student could not leave without written permission from a parent. Not knowing what my father would say, I took the risk of calling and asking for a telegram granting me permission to leave. Now that I am a parent of college-age children, I am even more amazed by my father's response. He listened; he really listened, and he understood. The next day the telegram was in my hand, and I left.

I knew this was a crucial time in my life, and so did my father. But he waited patiently for the right moment to address the issue.

When I arrived home, there was no yelling about what a failure I was and how I would never graduate from college or do anything decent with my life. Instead, my father said, "What can I do for you?"

"I'd like to look at some colleges in the Philadelphia area," I told him. Without any fuss, my father dropped what he was doing. For the next three or four days, we visited various colleges and universities, inquiring about their programs and the possibility of a January admission. After all these visits, nothing seemed quite right for me. I went into a state of despair and frustration. I retreated to my room, where I spent hours in quiet solitude.

One day a knock came on my door. My father entered and sat by my side. Finally he spoke: "I've been thinking about you, and I have some thoughts I'd like to share." My father had won my confidence by not badgering me, so I was ready to hear what he had to say.

"I think," he said tentatively, "that the best thing for you to do is to go back to Bob Jones University and make good."

"Why do you think that?" I asked, astonished.

"Son, you need to learn that life is not easy and that, whatever you do in life, you will be working with people who don't agree with you. Go back to Bob

Jones and learn how to function in a context that is difficult for you."

I was thinking about what he said and how much sense it made when he added, "Besides, you quit. You ran away from a situation that was difficult. If you run away completely, you will set a pattern that will be hard to break. You may end up being a quitter all your life."

I knew that he was right and that returning to Bob Jones was exactly what I should do. I felt almost an instant peace about my decision. That very afternoon I picked up the phone, called Bob Jones University, and asked if I could return. The answer was "We all breathed a sigh of relief when you left." I responded with words that Bob Jones, Sr. often said: "If a boy has a good father, we'll let a student come back to BJU on the strength of his father's character." I then told the dean about my father's advice, and I was allowed to return.

Returning wasn't easy, but it was right. In the next six months, God began to work in my heart in many ways, one of which was to lay total claim on my life for ministry.

Since then, in the nearly four decades of training and work in ministry, there have been many difficult times—times when I have wanted to throw in the towel and give up. Every time, though, the words of my father have come back to me, and in my heart and with my lips I reaffirm, "You are not a quitter."

Life is difficult, but it is also an adventure—and an exciting one at that. I'm persuaded in my own life that God's calling demands steady, unmoved perseverance. This lesson—a lesson that lies at the heart of Christian discipleship—is one that I learned from a father whose wisdom in dealing with a rebellious son opened my heart to hear the call of God, "Come, follow me."

Kenneth T. Wessner

An Example
to Follow

◆────────────────────────────────────◆

Ken Wessner joined ServiceMaster in 1954. Since then, he has served as regional manager, field sales manager, and general manager of the western sales and service division. In 1962 he established and developed the company's health-care business, and he served as its general manager until 1972. He was named president in 1973, chairman of the board and chairman of the executive committee in 1981, and retired as chairman in June 1990. Ken has been a member of the board of directors since 1965, and he was the company's chief executive officer from 1975 to June 1983.

Through the years, Ken has been recognized with a variety of awards. In five consecutive years, he was named top CEO in the industrial services industry by The Wall Street Transcript. Financial World named him the outstanding CEO in the service industry for 1980. Religious Heritage of America selected him as a business and professional leader for 1981. He was inducted into the American National Business Hall of Fame in 1991. Ken has also received honorary doctorates from Wheaton College, Wheaton, Illinois, and The King's College, Briarcliff Manor, New York.

As Ken's climb through the ranks of ServiceMaster suggests, his parents taught him about responsibility and the power of self-confidence. Ken describes how these and other lessons shaped the four objectives of ServiceMaster.

I was born in the small Pennsylvania Dutch town of Sinking Springs, the first of two sons born to Thomas and Carrie Wessner. I grew up during the depression. We were poor, but so was everybody in our neighborhood. Through junior high school, I had only one shirt to wear, but it was always clean. My mother would wash, dry, and iron it each night and have it ready for me to wear the next day.

Although my boyhood and youth were spent in difficult economic times, I learned important lessons about integrity and high standards from my parents during those days. People of their word, my mother and father were 100 percent honest in their dealings, and they paid all of their bills on time. Their example of this kind of discipline has had a lasting influence on my life. As I have grown in my business career and been involved in sales, operations, and management before becoming president, chief executive officer, and chairman of ServiceMaster, these values have remained with me and have served as a daily yardstick for me.

One of the things my parents taught me was a work ethic. I learned that it was honorable to work. I also learned that work did not bring dignity to the individual, but the individual brought dignity to the work.

Along with this work ethic was the principle of discipline and shared responsibility practiced by our family. As a boy, I had to take care of the large yard and garden we had. The yard was beautiful, and the garden provided vegetables for us to eat not only during the summer but, because my mother canned, during the rest of the year as well. I was not paid an allowance or an hourly rate for my work. We all worked for the good of our family. We were a true family unit, and everyone was important.

Two of my early childhood memories involve lessons learned at the dining-room table, a gathering place for us. My father taught me how to make change even before I had started school or learned to read. We would sit down at the dining room table and play games of making change with real coins and dollars. He had me buy things and pay for them and then sell things and be paid for them. This early exercise taught me the difference between spending and investing and offered simple but practical experience for life.

Later, when I was five or six years old, I sometimes responded to instructions—as children often do—with, "I can't." My father didn't like hearing this. I remember how he sat me down at the dining room table and asked me what I was. My answer was "I'm a boy." He said, "Yes, that's true, but you are an American." He then took a piece of paper and wrote on it: AMER-I-CAN. He said, "When you are an American, you always say, 'I can.'" That simple lesson instilled a spirit and mind-set of "I can do it" that has served me well throughout life. It helped me through college when I worked in the dining hall thirty-five or forty hours a week in addition to carrying a full schedule of classes. It helped me in my ServiceMaster career as I joined a small company with a revenue of less than one million dollars a year and helped it become the $2.25 billion company it was the year I retired as chairman.

My mother instilled in me a sense of pride and was always encouraging me to excel. She believed in me, and her confidence generated my self-confidence. My mother always had a vision for the future, and she was always looking on the bright side. She could think, plan, and talk about the better things to come. At the same time, she was very practical and realized that only with work and commitment would a dream become reality. Her positive attitude was contagious and has influenced me throughout my entire life. I, too, have become a visionary and have dreamed dreams, but at the same time I've been aware of the work and commitment necessary to accomplish the goals I set.

During my teenage years, my mother made a confession of faith in Jesus Christ as her personal Savior. This good woman became a very godly woman, and her example had a profound influence on the family. Her love for the Lord Jesus and for her husband and her sons was evidence of a changed life. She expressed her loving concern in many ways. Numerous times, for instance, she welcomed into our home a boy who was beaten by his drunken father. She also cared for her sick stepmother—who had greatly mistreated my mother in earlier years—during the last years of her stepmother's life. My mother did what she thought she ought to do, and that went beyond what she was expected to do because she had a special love for God and for people. My mother's life gave me a service attitude in my thoughts and actions.

My father, brother, and I became believers and followers of Jesus Christ because of my mother's faithfulness and godly life. This new dimension of our family had a far greater influence than any other lesson my parents taught me. My decisions and actions became Christ-centered and gave every word and action greater value. It is the basis of my personal and business philosophy, which is expressed in the four objectives of ServiceMaster: To honor God in all we do; to help people develop; to pursue excellence; and to grow profitably. When we realize that each person is created in the image of God—each person is unique and has a contribution to make—our values come into true focus.

I met my wife, Norma, at college, and we have been happily married for forty-six years. We have two children: our daughter, Barbara, is married to Ross E. Anderson, M.D., and they have four children; and our son, David, a health-care executive, and his wife, Patti, have three children. Norma and I enjoy visiting our children and grandchildren as they, too, build strong family units based on the heritage provided by my parents.

My mother and father are now deceased. They were loved by everyone who knew them, and their Christian living made them an example to follow and a pleasure to know.

You Can Break
the Cycle

N ot all of those people who were invited to write about
what their parents did right were able to respond with
a lot of positive statements. A few well-known leaders spoke
with reservation about their upbringing; some had childhoods that were painful. What intrigued me, however, was
that each of these people told a story of God's intervention,
healing, and grace and invited me to contact their children
about a contribution for the book.

Sociologists and psychologists say that the healing of family dysfunction may take three or four generations. The Bible
tends to support this finding when it says that the sins of the
father are visited upon the third and fourth generations. Yet
statistics were defied by those who had been—to use a C. S.
Lewis phrase—"surprised by joy."

And here is the great variable: The grace of God and the
intervention of Jesus Christ in the life of a person committed
to him actually stopped the cycle of dysfunction and brought
wholeness to homes in only one generation.

If dysfunction is a part of your childhood, perhaps these
personal accounts will encourage you to believe in the miracle
of forgiveness and the possibility that, with the power of the

Holy Spirit, your home can be a place of hope and peace despite the pain you have known.
—Gloria Gaither

Lee Ezell

God's Parenting Guarantee

Lee Ezell has come a long way since being raised in Philadelphia's inner city, the child of alcoholic parents. Today Lee is a devoted wife and mother, a popular author and lecturer, and a sought-after speaker at colleges, conventions, and special events across the country.

On her national radio program "Reflections," Lee uses her background in musical comedy to communicate truth and share messages of hope. She entertains as she informs and so gains an attentive audience for her practical ideas about improving personal relationships. Lee speaks with empathy, spiritual sensitivity, and a lot of common sense.

Lee has also won acclaim as a well-informed author on women's issues. Her first two books—The Cinderella Syndrome *and* The Missing Piece—*won Angel Awards and have been translated into seven languages. A film based on* The Missing Piece *tells the story of Lee's life and the special reunion with her daughter, Julie Makimaa. (I am privileged to share in this book Julie's side of the story as further testimony of God's providential love.) Lee's most recent book,* Private Obsessions, *encourages women to overcome hidden addictions and the habits that control them.*

In her characteristically upbeat style, Lee speaks from experience as she offers this encouraging perspective that God our heavenly Father can—and does—heal and complete the work that earthly parents often fail at.

With the inadequate role models I had for parenting, I felt doomed to having my own children grow up to wear nylons over their faces and rob 7-Elevens. But take a deep breath, parents. God the Father is still in the parenting business!

My mother is still alive. Now she is quite feeble, but I choose to remember her as strong. She had to be; she was the thirty-year wife of a violent alcoholic. Mother built a shield around herself to protect her from the emotional wounds her husband would inflict. Being open and vulnerable was much too risky. But her Great Wall also kept her five children at a distance from her, and as the years rolled by, her armor became impenetrable. This, coupled with her German heritage (her name is Gertrude), made her a veritable fortress. In my home, there was never any expression of caring or love; I knew only defensive survival tactics.

My earliest childhood memories are of the family running for cover as my crazed father climbed the steps from his basement dwelling. After physical abuse, screams, and cries, one of us would make it to the phone and call the police for help. Language was vile, and tempers ran hot in our household. This was the climate I grew up in deep in Philadelphia's inner city. When I graduated from high school, I climbed aboard a Greyhound bus and headed west for a new life in sunny California.

Light in the Darkness

My hope for a new start didn't come from a firm foundation provided by loving parents. It was born out of an experience I had shortly before I left Philadelphia. I stumbled upon a religious meeting, something that was all new to me. The preacher's name was Billy Graham—and you can imagine the rest! That night of simple surrender to Christ convinced me that I was no longer alone in my struggle. Now I had a real Father.

I am sure the process of restoring my soul began with my willingness to forgive. My parents were the first on a long list I had made of people I needed to forgive. I believe this process of forgiveness is well worth the effort it takes to yank our wills to that painful point of obedience. Only when we are able to forgive can the doors to emotional wholeness swing open and the healing process begin. Restoration of the spirit and emotions is not an overnight or instantaneous event. God is not a fairy godfather who goes "bibbity-bobbity-boo" and erases all the past. Instead, he works like a skillful surgeon in the reparenting process.

To use the terms of pop psychology, I would say that I am a codependent ACOA (Adult Children of Alcoholics) in recovery from a dysfunctional family whose inner child was apparently adopted out. While these terms might explain my behavior, they don't excuse my behavior. I can't blame my mother for my cellulite because she was the one who taught me to swallow my feelings and chase them down with a milk shake. And, yes, my earthly dad was a poor model of a father, but I do not have to be crippled in my relationship to God the Father all my adult life because of my earthly father. I believe my parents were responsible for what they did then; I am responsible for what I do now.

As a daughter, I am able to view my parents as the biological instruments God used to give me the gift of life. Impaired and disabled as they may have been, they did what they could to parent me. My parents are not responsible *for* me.

But today I am also a parent. As a mother, I believe I am accountable *to* my children before the Lord, to train them up in the ways of the Lord, to be an example of a follower of Christ, and to ask their forgiveness when I fail to parent well. I view myself as responsible to do my best and leave the rest to God the Father.

I am through playing the Blame Game. I believe my parents were pedaling as fast as they could; they were doing all they were capable of doing at the time. By today's enlightened standards, they failed at parenting, but they cannot be held responsible now for what they didn't know then. Truly, a parent cannot take either the credit or the blame for their children's choices: The Bible teaches us that each person will give an account of himself before the Lord (Rom. 14:12).

Raising Daughters

And in my own parenting? I could whine and say that Dr. Dobson's writings were not yet out when I raised my kids, or I can trust God the Father to assist my own kids by correcting any wrongs I inadvertently committed during my mothering. I know from my own experience how capable my heavenly Father is in superseding any harmful parenting.

By the miraculous grace of God, though, the two little girls who grew up under my care—Pamela and Sandi—are well-adjusted, beautiful people today. Even more miraculously, the same is true of my third daughter, Julie, even though I never laid a hand on her. My three children, yes—even though I never got to diaper or name any of them.

My first two daughters came to me by way of their birth mother, Helen Gaffney, who died of a brain tumor when the girls were only three and six years old. Their dedicated Christian father, Hal, remarried only to witness the death of a second wife. So I am the third woman to try my hand at mothering these sweet girls who were ten and thirteen when I married Hal. (I've learned to take my vitamins!)

My third daughter introduced herself to me on the telephone just a few years ago. She was the result of my being raped as a teenager—and brand-new Christian. It was only the parental guidance of my heavenly Father that led me to decide to give life to that child rather than abort her. She was born in a Los Angeles

County hospital and adopted immediately after her birth. I never got to hold her or see her. I had to trust her parenting to the Father above.

Our reunion, the subject of my book *The Missing Piece,* has been more delightful and satisfying than I can say. Just as God chose a new mother for baby Moses, he also chose a mother to care for my baby, Julie. He had a plan.

God's Parenting Plan

And I've learned that God's parenting plan is the same for each of us, regardless of the earthly parenting models we grew up with. God says, "I know the plans I have for you. . . . They are plans for good and not for evil, to give you a future and a hope" (Jer. 29:11, TLB).

We must submit even the good parental images we have to our heavenly Father for his input and approval. Our job is to accept his role as Father in our lives and receive his forgiveness even as we forgive our parents who trespassed against us. Then we can rejoice in his parenting guarantee in Matthew 7:11—if we as earthly parents know how to give good gifts to our children, how much more will their Father who is in heaven. What a truly heavenly Father!

The Greatest Gift of All

Julie's story is a wonderful testimony to God's sovereignty and a dramatic illustration of how God can bring good out of evil.

Adopted as an infant, Julie later decided to search for her natural mother. After three and a half years, Julie found her. At their reunion in 1985, Julie learned that she was born as a result of a rape.

An important ministry has grown out of this discovery. Julie is now president of Fortress International, a group organized to defend both victims of sexual assault pregnancies, the woman and the preborn child. Fortress is committed to changing the public bias against women and children in hopes of ending society's tendency to treat these victims as if they were the criminals.

Julie is also taking a strong stand against abortion. Firmly believing in the gracious sovereignty of God, Julie, together with her natural mother, Lee, and her adoptive mother, Eileen Anderson, encourages women that abortion is not the answer even when the pregnancy resulted from rape or incest. Julie and Lee have told their story on television and radio talk *shows, and they have been featured in various newspapers and magazines.*

Julie and her husband, Bob, are the parents of two children, daughter Casey and son Herb. Here, in "The Greatest Gift of All," Julie writes about "the knowledge of how important a right relationship with God is," a gift her adoptive parents gave her as she was growing up.

My parents gave me the greatest gift that any parents can give a child. It was not having all the toys I wanted or never being punished for doing wrong. It was being raised attending church and learning the truth about God's love and salvation through his Son, Jesus Christ. The greatest gift a parent can give is the knowledge of how important a right relationship with God is. This gift, above all others, has affected every area of my life and will continue to for the rest of my days.

When I was a child, I was adopted by a family that had two sons but wanted a daughter. When I was five, my parents started attending an Assembly of God church. We attended almost every service—if the doors were open, you could find us there! At that church, I learned the special stories of the Bible. As a great lover of animals—all kinds of animals—I liked Noah's story best. I had a plastic ark with a complete menagerie of plastic animals, and I would walk them up into the boat two by two. (I always wondered how Noah got all those animals onto the ark.)

One Sunday night during a worship service, I went

forward to ask Jesus to come into my heart and forgive my sins. Salvation through Jesus was a normal thing to me. Everyone at church was saved, and I knew that giving my heart to God was the right thing to do. I was just a little girl, but I knew that I had made a very important decision. (Just to make certain of my commitment, though, I raised my hand on a few other occasions at church when there was a call to accept Christ.)

When I was seven, a girlfriend told me I was adopted. I didn't know exactly what that meant, but I knew that adoption was different. I never thought that my parents loved me less than my older brothers, but I knew that I was unique. I never much thought about my natural parents, but I sometimes wondered if I had ever unknowingly seen them or passed them on the street.

I joined the church's missionettes group and began to read and memorize Scripture, not realizing how much these passages would mean to me later in life. I simply enjoyed memorizing Scripture and receiving the awards and prizes. When I was eleven, I attended a statewide missionettes camp and was awarded a trophy for the most verses memorized. It was very scary to stand up in front of all those girls, but I felt good about the work I had done.

As I grew older, I began to see the importance of God in my family's life. I had always felt that I would someday be a missionary or travel around and tell people about God. One day while I was sitting in church, an older lady sitting beside me bent down and told me that God was going to use my life in a very special way. I didn't know what to think, but I never forgot those words she spoke to me.

In 1980, I met a very special man who was a Christian, and we felt that the Lord had brought us together. The following year we were married, and we moved to a small town in northern Michigan. As we started our home together, I began to realize that I could no longer rely on my parents to show me how to follow Christ from day to day. Instead, I had to take responsibility for my relationship with God. I started putting into practice scriptural principles, and I began to really see God working in my life.

As my husband and I grew in our relationship with God, we felt led to become involved in three specific areas of ministry: political issues, the fight against abortion, and prayer for our country. When we began to be involved in these areas, we never imagined what the Lord was preparing us for. During this time, some verses of Scripture became very special and very personal to us:

> *Rescue those who are unjustly sentenced to death; don't stand back and let them die. Don't try to disclaim responsibility by saying you didn't know about it. For God, who knows all hearts, knows yours, and he knows you knew! And he will reward everyone according to his deeds.* (Proverbs 24:11-12, TLB)

> *The good influence of godly citizens causes a city to prosper, but the moral decay of the wicked drives it downhill.* (Proverbs 11:11, TLB)

These verses would become foundational in the work God was calling us to.

As my public ministry was taking form, something very important was happening to me personally. When I was married, my parents gave me my adoption papers. I wanted to find my birth parents. I wanted to share with them my faith in Christ, and I wanted a chance to tell them that, no matter what they faced, they could find comfort in God's love and the fact that all things work together for good for those who love God. How thankful I am that my adoptive parents supported me as I began to search for my birth parents! It was a real encouragement to know that they did not feel threatened by my search. I think they know that I consider them my "real" parents, that nothing will ever change that, and that there could never be anyone to take their place.

After three and a half years of searching, I found the couple whom my natural mother had stayed with when I was born. I wrote to them, and they called my mother and informed her of my search. The next morning I received a call from my natural mother. It was numbing to speak for the first time with my mother—whom I had never met! Lee and I talked cautiously, but my mind raced to all the questions I wanted to ask. I thought I might never speak with her again, and I wanted to tell her about the Lord and my relationship with him. Hesitantly, I told her about myself and some of my interests. With most of my conversation centering on my involvement with church, I was thinking, *This might be a good time to find out if she has ever heard about Jesus,* when she began to tell me about her relationship with God, her speaking ministry to women, her radio program, and the writing of her first Christian book. Lee was already a follower of the Savior!

I had always thought that God needed to use me to save my natural parents. It had never occurred to me that they might already know Jesus! It's strange how sometimes we think we need to help God out, as if he can't do things without us. After learning that we had Jesus in common, Lee and I excitedly made plans to meet, and we set a date for eight weeks after this initial phone call. It was bizarre to think that I was really going to meet her. Would she be like the person I had imagined? What would she think of me? How I hoped that she would like me!

Even with those questions on my mind, I couldn't help but rejoice! What wonderful gifts God had given! Things had worked out so much better than I could ever have imagined. I had found my birth mother, and—it was almost unbelievable—she was already a Christian!

One afternoon as my husband Bob and I sat at home, we received a call from Lee's husband, Hal. I answered the phone, but when he asked to speak with Bob, I knew something was wrong. At first I thought Lee had changed her mind about the reunion. As I listened to Bob, I had a hard time piecing together the conversation, but I could tell that the news wasn't good. There was something they wanted to tell Bob first so that he could decide whether or not to tell me. After the conversation, Bob explained to me that the circumstances of my conception were not unblemished and that, if they were to take place today, my father would probably be put in jail. At that time, Bob and I didn't know if Lee had become pregnant as a result of rape or incest, but we understood that either situation would have been very devastating for Lee. I was sure our reunion was off.

Never had my faith been so tested. This was a time when I had to decide whether I really believed in and trusted God. As a little girl, I had been taught that God was in control of any and every situation, so why had he allowed me to find my birth mother only to not be able to meet her? I know that God is sovereign in our lives, so I had to believe that no matter how I was conceived, God had a plan for me. He was my real Father, and I was born because of his love and not by accident. During those days of struggling with my faith, I rediscovered some verses in the Bible that were old friends:

> *You made all the delicate, inner parts of my body and knit them together in my mother's womb. Thank you for making me so wonderfully complex! It is amazing to think about. Your workmanship is marvelous—and how well I know it. You were there while I was being formed in utter seclusion! You saw me before I was born and scheduled each day of my life before I began to breathe. Every day was recorded in your book! (Psalm 139:13-16, TLB)*

> *And we know that all that happens to us is working for our good if we love God and are fitting into his plans. (Romans 8:28, TLB)*

I wondered if Lee could go through with our meeting; I wondered if she could bear the emotional stress. I realized that seeing me would bring back difficult memories, and I certainly didn't want to cause problems for her. You can imagine my relief and excitement when I got a call from Lee asking if everything was still on for our reunion. She told me that the assault was in her past, that God had healed her hurts from that experience, and that she still wanted to meet me. What a confirmation! God was still in the driver's seat!

With our husbands at our sides, Lee and I met for the first time in a Washington, D.C., hotel. Conflicting emotions—fear, joy, excitement, hesitation—churned inside me. How could I make this reunion comfortable for Lee? Should I be exuberant or reserved? Cautiously, my husband expressed for me how truly important this reunion was. He also told Lee how grateful he was that she had not had an abortion, but that she had given of herself to carry me to term, allowing me to share a lifetime with him. It was a very special moment.

Later that night, Lee and Hal told us how she had been raped and become pregnant with me. We talked about how I felt knowing the circumstances of my conception, and we discussed Lee's feelings about our reunion. There was no doubt that, after twenty-one years, God had brought us together and that he had a special plan for us. That night, Bob encouraged Lee to write a book about her experiences and our reunion to show how God works in our lives for good, even in the toughest of times.

When we left Washington, I never imagined how much my life was going to change. In the car on the long drive back to northern Michigan, Bob and I talked about our experience. We sensed that the Lord was preparing us for something, and we strongly felt that his plans would take us away from our home.

Before my reunion with Lee, Bob's and my involvement with pro-life activities had increased, but we had never decided how we felt about pregnancies that resulted from rape and incest. Now we had to ask ourselves whether we could accept abortion in those situations, especially after knowing that I was the result of such a pregnancy. If God is in control of my life and if he is still working things out for my good, then I had to believe that he would do the same for others. So I began to speak out against abortion, sharing my convictions—which were now stronger than ever— that every preborn child deserves the right to live. Jeremiah 1:5 says, "I knew you before you were formed within your mother's womb; before you were born I sanctified you and appointed you as my spokesman to the world" (TLB).

This verse was a new confirmation for me: God had a special plan and purpose for my life. I was a prophet called to speak out for the preborn who had been conceived under circumstances similar to mine. Many times I felt like Moses: I was not a good speaker, and there were so many other people who, in my opinion, could do a much better job. But I also realized that if I trusted him, God would give me the words that he wanted me to say.

Again and again, I have seen God's faithfulness; he

has always done what he said he would do. Now I feel that the Lord has led me to work specifically with women who have become pregnant as a result of sexual assault. These women need to know that the sexual violation was not their fault and that they are not dirty because of it; they need to realize that they are victims just like the child whom they conceived. Many of the women who are supported and encouraged as they carry their child to term decide to raise that child. Adoption remains a viable option for women who feel that they are not prepared to raise a child.

I feel confident that I am where God wants me to be right now, and where I am has everything to do with my lifelong relationship with him. Knowing God and wanting to do the things that he has planned for me has affected every area of my life: how I dealt with my adoption when I was a child, my choice of a marriage partner, my reaction to learning that I was conceived in rape, and now my work with women who are victims of sexual assault and with children who have been conceived during rape or incest. I believe that if I had not been raised in a Christian home, my life today would be much different. I feel I was spared prolonged periods of hardship and pain because, at a young age, I learned right from wrong from my parents. And, although there have been many times when I failed to do the things I know I should have done and many times I have let the Lord down, it is great to know that no matter how many times I mess up, he is there ready to forgive me when I ask.

Having God in my life is the greatest gift my parents could have given me. I am thankful that my mom and dad raised me in a home where I learned the importance of a strong relationship with God. Now my own children are being raised in the "nurture and admonition of the Lord," and it is exciting to teach them the stories of the Bible and to watch them begin to follow the plan that God has for their lives. Now that I know how my life began, I am especially thankful for life itself and for Lee who chose to give me life. How grateful I am that she prayed I would be adopted into a Christian home and that God was indeed charting the days of my life when, "in utter seclusion," I was being formed in my mother's womb.

My Roots

◆————————————————————————————————◆

*T*he Reverend Jerry Falwell is a man with his roots in Virginia—as his story here reveals—but more important are his roots in the Lord.

A graduate of Baptist Bible College, Jerry founded Thomas Road Baptist Church in 1956. The initial thirty-five-member congregation now numbers more than twenty-two thousand. And Jerry reaches even more people through "The Old Time Gospel Hour," one of the most watched religious television programs in all of North America.

Jerry is also founder and chancellor of Liberty University and Liberty Baptist Theological Seminary, accredited institutions that offer programs for bachelor's, master's, and doctoral degrees. The Liberty Home Bible Institute has offered a home Bible study program to more than seventy-seven thousand students.

Jerry is the author of eleven books, including Listen, America, When It Hurts Too Much To Cry, Champions for God, *and* Strength for the Journey. *The focus of national headlines in the eighties with Moral Majority, an organization he founded in 1979, Jerry has also been the topic of three books—*Aflame for God, Jerry Falwell and the Jews, *and* Falwell: Before the Millennium.

Jerry and his wife, Macel, have three adult children, Jerry, Jr., Jeannie, and Jonathan.

The Falwells have been in Virginia since the early 1600s. Apparently we sailed from England with the pioneer settlers and established our foothold in the new world on Chesapeake Bay near the mouth of the James River. Each Falwell generation moved farther inland up the James from Goochland to Buckingham to Campbell counties. In 1850, my great-grandfather, Hezekiah Carey Falwell, and his brother, John, were the first Falwells to move to Lynchburg. Before that, the history of our ancestors is sketchy.

As best I can determine, the Falwells have long been a commercial people. Originally, they were successful farmers and retailers. Well before the birth of my twin brother, Gene, and me in 1933, the Lynchburg area was dotted with the business enterprises of the entire Falwell clan. That is still true.

While the family has always been deeply committed to the work ethic and free enterprise, I find little evidence that my ancestors were very interested in church or spiritual matters.

My father, Carey Hezekiah Falwell, arose before sunrise every day. After reading the newspaper and eating a hearty breakfast prepared by my mother, he was in the office before 8:00 A.M. He did this six days a week. While he didn't work on Sunday, he still arose very early, read the newspaper, and then had his driver take him on a personal tour of all his businesses and properties.

During his business life, Dad owned and operated The Merry Garden, the largest nightclub in the area and a regular stop for many of the big-name bands. He was in the oil and gas business, both wholesale and retail. He owned Virginia's first motel as well as restaurants, retail outlets, and several farms. In addition, during the Prohibition Era, Dad was a very large dealer in illegal whiskey.

Dad was very intelligent. He would not tolerate slothfulness. He demanded diligence, honesty, and commitment from the many persons who worked for him.

Unfortunately, my father began drinking early in his business life. Although alcohol never adversely affected his business acumen or activities, it did damage his health. He died at age fifty-five of cirrhosis of the liver.

Dad loved Mom and his five children. He provided handsomely for us, and he set a great example with his commitment to honesty (in spite of his whiskey dealings), the work ethic, and personal competitiveness. I personally owe much to my father in this area. I learned from him my dedication to hard work and my habit of rising early each morning. If I know anything about leading people, raising money, setting goals, and persevering, I owe it all to Dad.

It brings me joy to know that a Presbyterian minister and a Christian layman led my father to Christ on his deathbed in 1948.

My mother, Helen Beasley Falwell, came from a

totally different world with totally different standards. Her people were Baptists from the beginning of time. Reading the Bible, praying, going to church, giving a generous offering, working in the Sunday school, and avoiding places like The Merry Garden were as natural and habitual to my mother as sleeping or eating. She was born in Hollywood, Virginia, a town of just one hundred souls. In earlier America, the Beasleys lived in gracious colonial houses on plantations farmed by slaves, but the Revolutionary War and the War between the States impoverished the people of eastern Virginia, including my mother's ancestors.

The Civil War destroyed the Beasley plantations and killed or wounded many of the Beasley men. Thomas Davidson, my mother's grandfather, was killed in the Battle of Petersburg on June 15, 1864. Great-grandmother Rhoda Ferguson Davidson moved in with her daughter Sarah Ann, her son-in-law King David Beasley, and their sixteen children.

Mom's parents were dirt poor, but every Sunday Mr. and Mrs. Beasley loaded the family wagon with their sixteen children and drove them to the Hollywood Baptist Church for Sunday school and morning worship.

Sunday mornings at the Beasleys must have been a fascinating experience. All sixteen children took turns bathing in one tin tub and then dressed in their Sunday best. Each of the nine girls had her hair brushed and braided. Each of the seven boys was spit-polished and gleaming. Each child had a well-marked New Testament, and each could pray out loud, quote long Bible passages, and sing at least a dozen hymns by heart.

The sixteen Beasley children sat beside each other in two long pews in the old Hollywood Baptist Church. Mother Sarah Ann Davidson Beasley sat proudly beside her husband at the end of a long family pew. Helen Virgie Beasley, my mother, sat among them until she moved to Lynchburg in search of employment.

When she arrived in Lynchburg, she went to work for Craddock Terry Shoe Corporation. I don't know how she met my father in 1913. He was already prospering in the business world, but somehow they met, fell in love, and married.

My sisters, Virginia and Rosha, were born in 1917 and 1921. Lewis was born in 1924. Gene and I were born in 1933.

While Dad never attended church in his life, Mom never missed. Every Sunday morning, Dad's chauffeur transported us to Franklin Street Baptist Church. Mother could not convince Dad to attend, but she had no difficulty dealing with the children.

Mom read the Bible at home. She also worked in the home from morning till night. She loved Dad and showed it in so many ways. While Dad was loud, bombastic, and short-tempered, Mom was the most patient, serene, and self-giving person I have ever known. I never saw her lose her temper, and I never heard an unkind word come from her lips. She was submissive to Dad, and he respected her above anyone else he knew. In the end, it was her exemplary Christian life that brought him and all the children to Christ.

Humanly speaking, I owe my salvation to the fact that my mother lived Christianity before me all of my young life. Even after I stopped attending church, Mom would leave the radio on at home while she attended. From our beds we heard Dr. Charles E. Fuller and the "Old-Fashioned Revival Hour." Through that broadcast, I came to Christ while I was a sophomore in college.

My mother was nearly eighty-two when she died in 1977. She was my first church member when I started the Thomas Road Baptist Church in 1956. She was my first Faith Partner when I started our television ministry. For Macel and me, she was a parent to be emulated. For our three children—Jerry, Jr., now a lawyer; Jeannie, now a medical doctor; and Jonathan, a preacher—she was a wonderful grandmother.

I owe so much to my mother: love for people, gentleness toward others, and patience in tribulation.

Perhaps Macel and I will be as well remembered by our children. I pray so.

Jeannie Falwell Savas

God's Plan

J eannie was named one of the Outstanding Young Women of America in 1985 and has been listed in Who's Who among Students in American Colleges and Universities (1984-86 edition). Since then she has gone on to graduate magna cum laude from Liberty University in Lynchburg, Virginia. During her undergraduate years, she spent one summer studying at Oxford University in England.

After graduating from Liberty, Jeannie went on to medical school at the Medical College of Virginia in Richmond. While there, she was active in the Christian Medical and Dental Society. Upon graduating in 1990, Jeannie continued on at the Medical College as a resident physician in general surgery.

Jeannie is married to Paul Savas, a fourth-year medical student, also at the Medical College of Virginia. And, although she's not yet a parent herself, Jeannie has done a lot of thinking about parenting, its demands, and the blessing her good parents are.

How valuable good parents are! Only now that my friends are beginning to have children am I realizing what a never-ending task parenting is. In retrospect, I'm gaining a deep appreciation of the commitment my parents had to parenting all of us. My brothers and I were our parents' top priority.

My mother and father knew—and I learned from them—that spending quality time together is an important part of building a family. Now that I am on my own and am dealing with conflicts between work and family, I am realizing how much time and sacrifice it takes to make a family work. Deciding what is most important is no easy matter.

When a person becomes a Christian, he or she decides to make God top priority. It is not a onetime choice, but rather an ongoing process. The choice to follow Jesus in a secular world will eventually result in conflicts that must be resolved. Likewise, once a husband and wife decide to start a family, that commitment will mean conflicts and choices about priorities. There will always be important meetings on the night of your son's first school play or a club meeting scheduled during the mother-daughter banquet. "What matters most?" will be the constant question.

As I look back on my childhood, I realize that my parents' decision to make God and our family their top priorities demanded many personal sacrifices. My mother quit work when my older brother was born so that she could be at home with us. Maybe "quit work" isn't really true—she simply took on a different job description. She became maid, cook, teacher, referee, and taxicab driver, on call twenty-four hours a day. My dad arranged his schedule so that he traveled only during the day so that he could be home for dinner each night—and on call for thousands of church members. What he's done all these years makes my thirty-six-hour shifts as an intern at the hospital seem easy!

As busy as my parents were, they taught us children that we were important to them. I always knew I could depend on my mom whether for help with a last-minute school project—even if it meant reading an entire book to me the night before a book report was due—or for a manicure. Whatever I needed, she was there for me.

Dad was there, too. It never mattered whether he was watching a football game or needing to leave for a meeting at church. If we needed him to go to the store or to talk something over, he made time for it. One time my dad even canceled a meeting at the White House because it fell on my birthday. When I found out he'd done this, I tried to talk him out of his decision. I assured him that I understood, but he would not reconsider. He insisted that he would not miss my birthday. He also made time to attend my annual piano recitals and any important sports event or award ceremony—not to mention our weekly Sunday lunch at my aunt's house. This family ritual was and still is a time for our extended family—aunts, uncles, cousins, nieces, and nephews—to get together for fun. Everyone talks and no one listens, and it's the place to find the best food in town.

Other fun times for the Falwells were vacations which, with Dad's schedule, often had to be spontaneous. Sometimes we would wake up in the morning and decide to go on vacation that day. Once we borrowed a friend's camper and drove across country; on Sunday Dad flew back to Lynchburg to preach. One vacation was partially planned by my older brother, who was twelve at the time. My dad and I had left for the Holy Land with a tour group. While stopped in the airport in Zurich en route to Egypt, we phoned Mom to tell her how beautiful Switzerland was, and she said she wished she'd come along. My brother heard her say this, so while she was at the hairdresser, he booked flights for Mom, himself, and Jonathan and packed all the bags. When she got home, he hurried her to the airport. At first she thought they were playing a game and—good sport that she is—went along with his plan. But soon she realized he was not playing! The next thing she knew, they were with us in Egypt.

While the family knew how to have fun together, we also knew how to work hard. Mom always pushed us to excel in school as well as in our other activities. She began reading us books before we were out of diapers. She drilled us with word and number flash cards every afternoon once we started school. I remember coming home from elementary school one day with an exam grade of 97 percent. My mother's first response was "What did you miss?" Also, at our house, it was unheard of to miss school for any reason. If we were sick enough to miss school, we'd better be sick enough to have to go to the doctor. But I believe it was because my parents held up such high standards for us that I now have high standards for myself. They expected me to always work hard, to always strive to do better, and not to boast about what I had done.

Besides teaching me high standards, my parents gave me the gift of optimism and the faith that life with God is a series of exciting challenges rather than an endurance race. My dad was forever the encourager. In his eyes, I could do no wrong. He always introduced me as his only perfect child. Everyone who knew me knew that wasn't exactly true, but I always knew Dad would believe in me and support me in anything I wanted to do. (I'm sure that when he thought my plans weren't the greatest, he prayed that God would change my mind.) Dad's commitment and his incredible faith in God have been most helpful in my development and faith. At age five, I remember him announcing to Mom and me in the car that he was going to start a college. I thought, *That's a great idea. I can't wait to go there myself.* My mom asked how he was going to do such a thing—not an unreasonable thing to wonder!—but I knew if my dad set out to do something, it would happen somehow.

My faith in my father didn't end when I was no longer a naive child. There have been so many occasions through the years when I have seen the impossible become reality. Of course, the source of these miracles was not my dad at all, but God. What a coincidence that it has never rained on commencement at this same college in the many years that the activities have had to be held outdoors. Then there was the Easter sunrise service—also scheduled outside—when the rain stopped only minutes before the program began. Thousands were amazed. Also, my dad's knowledge that God is working everything for good helps him, and now me, to endure life's inexplicable circumstances and have hope when all seems lost. There is a plaque hanging in my dad's study that reads, "Life is continually filled with great opportunities brilliantly disguised as insolvable problems."

Growing up, I also learned that a good family is not a family without conflict. We have had our share of arguments, and there were times when I was convinced that my mother, the disciplinarian, hated me. But now I understand the truth of her words, "I'm doing this for your own good because I care about you"—although sometimes I wished she didn't "care" so much! In spite of the correction, or maybe because of it, my parents are now my best friends. They are the first ones I turn to when I need advice or help, and to this day, when I visit, we often stay up until two or three in the morning just talking.

One reason my parents and I are friends—even after the healthy amount of conflict we've faced—is their commitment to God's plan for the family. God's perfect plan for a family is well documented in Scripture and is a model for our individual relationship with God. The mother and father, husband and wife, are to be devoted to God, the Word, and their children. Parents are instructed to discipline their children and teach them how to live. Children are to obey their parents and show them respect as, together, the whole family reverences the Lord. Of course, parents and children are not perfect. Parents get weary of correcting their children, and they sometimes fail to discipline themselves, setting a poor example. Children see these inconsistencies and learn to discredit their parents' authority. This is reality. But when God is a vital member of the family, when he is the head of the household, he becomes the source of love when your daughter makes you late once again, your eight-year-old son pulls the fire alarm in a crowded convention center during your sermon, or your teenager misses curfew and forgets to call. Forgiveness—not bitterness—is the key to resolving these situations, and only God can give us the kind of patience and forgiveness that family pressures require.

The biblical principles of family living I saw practiced at home were, for me, an example of what my relationship with God should be like. I learned that just as my parents forgave my insufficiencies and supported me in spite of myself, so God was ever loving and always with me. I was able to be confident that, though life is tough at times and my knowledge and strength are inadequate, my life is in my heavenly Father's hands, and he has a plan for me. He is there to guide me or carry me each step of the way. Just as a young medical intern needs practical experience to really apply the principles of medicine, so practicing God's principles in the home as a family is the best way to learn how to live. It is amazing that Scripture written thousands of years ago is so relevant and applicable to each one of us today.

Now, working in a busy urban medical center, I come into contact with diverse family structures, many of them far from the Bible-based model I experienced. I have seen fourteen-year-old single mothers who share the same commitment to their children that my mother had. I've seen mothers at their wit's end who, without a family to support them, choose to abandon their children. I've seen the breakdown in family structure result in unwanted pregnancies, drug use, and many psychological illnesses. My heart aches for those who have had no home in which to learn the basic principles of life.

So when my husband and I think about the responsibility of having our own family one day, the task of raising, nurturing, and teaching children seems overwhelming. But we know from experience that God will be with us, and we ourselves are proof that upholding his principles does not go unrewarded. At times, raising my brothers and me must have been a struggle for my parents; it was often a thankless job, I'm sure. But when I see the joy in their eyes whenever we succeed, I know it is true that though parents "hold their children's hands for only a little while, they hold their hearts forever."

Phyllis Jenness

A Witness to God's Grace

S ome of God's special people are the "wounded healers" within his body—and Phyllis Jenness is one of those people.

Today, Phyllis is a facilitator for Overcomers Outreach, a Christ-centered support group for people from dysfunctional backgrounds and people who are dealing with present-day dysfunctional circumstances. Based on Scripture and focused on Christ, Overcomers offers healing and wholeness to those who suffer the effects of alcoholism, drug dependencies, workaholism, addictive behaviors, and abuse in the family.

Phyllis also works with Survivors of Incest and Sexual Abuse, another Christ-centered support group. She has much to offer these support groups because she has experienced for herself Christ's healing touch of wounds too deep for human hands to heal.

She has shared her testimony through various publications, and she continues to offer her story of hope to many more people through her speaking engagements. She is an active member of East Side Church of God in Anderson, Indiana, and she is the mother of two and grandmother of three.

In "Gifts of Grace," Phyllis talks about growing up in a family dominated by alcohol, yet her message is one of hope and assurance that Christ can and does bring restoration to those who turn to him. Phyllis's son Jeff offers further testimony to God's healing presence in her life in "The Fabric of Our Home."

Forgiveness, healing, and restoration are three of the most beautiful gifts of God's grace. When we accept these gifts from the Lord and let him work in our heart, he does a life-changing miracle. He performed such a miracle in me in January 1988, and with it came the freedom and maturity to share my story as a witness to God's grace.

I was raised in a family of five practicing alcoholics, including my mother and my father. This disease progressed until it took their lives. From birth, I was its innocent victim. Living in an alcoholic home is not a spectator sport. Everyone in the family is involved to one degree or another. Tragically, alcoholism is definitely a family affair.

The alcoholic family functions according to two unspoken laws: "Don't talk, don't trust, and don't feel" and "There is nothing wrong with this family—so don't you dare tell anyone about it." Life in the home becomes one big secret, and as someone has said, "You're only as sick as your secrets." Growing up as I did, I had secrets that made me a sick individual.

More than any other family member, Mother had the

greatest adverse effect on my life. Coming from chaos and dysfunction herself, she was a deeply wounded and very unhappy person. She was rigid, unbending, unable to show love, unfeeling, and incapable of expressing joy or happiness. Her means of coping was alcohol, and she clung to this as a tool of survival, a tool she continued to use until the time of her death . . . from d.t.'s.

At age five, I was given many of my mother's household responsibilities and family chores. Typical of children of alcoholics, I complied with mother's controlling demands and performed all these tasks without question. But it was more than a child doing chores for a family of six men. Soon there was a role reversal: I became a mother to my mother and took care of her needs when she should have taken care of me and my needs. Consequently, I was virtually robbed of my childhood. I was an adult as a child.

Alcohol controlled every aspect of Mother and Dad's being. They had no energy, either physical or emotional, to meet the many needs I had as a child. Because of the structure of my sick family, I shut down my emotional system and learned to keep my feelings buried. All feelings of love, anger, guilt, resentment, rejection, and even hatred were stifled. My emotions were frozen—I couldn't even cry. The defense systems of control and self-sufficiency took over. No meaningful communication took place, and home was not a place to relax. It was definitely not a safe place for a child.

Members of my family were very self-destructive individuals, and children raised in that kind of environment learn many unhealthy, negative behavior patterns. A basic problem arises when we take that child into adulthood with us and react with the same negative feelings and behaviors that we learned in our alcoholic family of origin.

One of the deepest and most traumatic emotions that I've had to deal with is a hard knot of shame at the core of my being. Living in this family made me very vulnerable and receptive to the psychological and physiological traumas brought on by alcoholism, and these are all shame-based. Sorting through all this shame has been very difficult, not to mention extremely painful.

In an alcoholic home, an underlying current of tension and anxiety is constantly present, and anger always hangs in the air. All time and energies are focused on the alcoholics, their problems, and their needs. Furthermore, alcoholism isolates a family from the outside world. The immediate family circle—for me, that was Mother, Father, and five older brothers— becomes a self-contained unit. Shut off from the real world, children of alcoholics experience nothing but a vicious cycle of alcohol, poverty, neglect, abuse (physical, verbal, emotional, sexual, etc.), confusion, guilt, lack of love, lack of trust, denial, isolation, and low self-esteem. But the existence of any problem is completely denied. I soon learned to cover up my own problems and thus helped enable my family members to continue in their lifestyles. Ray Boltz wrote and sings, "This house is full of people but nobody's home." These words describe my family: abandonment and rejection reigned supreme.

When I was twelve, my parents moved to the north

part of Anderson, Indiana—and next door to a Christian family. That family asked me to go to church with them, and soon the Lord saved me. His salvation, the influence of this Christian family, and my church got me through the next few years of my life. Jeremiah 1:5 says, "Before I formed you in the womb I knew you, before you were born I set you apart" (NIV). I now see that Jesus had his arms and love around me all through my childhood and growing-up years. His protection never faltered.

But I carried the dysfunction from my childhood and youth with me into adulthood until 1986 when a friend introduced me to ACOA (Adult Children of Alcoholics). At these meetings, I slowly and guardedly started to risk searching my past in an attempt to restore some sanity to my emotions and to try to find out why I reacted as I did in many situations and circumstances. This painful journey has been well worth the effort. It has been marked by much progress as well as several periods of regression.

On January 13, 1988, through Bill and Gloria Gaither's musical *In the Gardens,* the Lord showed me that my past with all its violations and abuse was in the cup Christ drank in Gethsemane. With that revelation, God's love stripped away the trauma and pain of the past. I was able to forgive my mother, father, and brothers and replace the harsh negative feelings toward them with understanding and even love. I was also able to let go of the shame I was feeling and discover that I am a lovable person. Christ offered the miracle, and I accepted it. Now, as I focus completely on God, his cleansing, healing, and restoration are bringing wholeness into my life.

My past will always be a part of me—and I praise the Lord that now I can take the energy I once used to block out feelings and past experiences and use it more productively to share my story with others. All the glory belongs to Jesus for whatever is accomplished through my life and testimony for him.

Jeffrey A. Jenness

The Fabric of Our Home

◆─────────────────────────────────◆

What a testimony Jeff Jenness is to how parents can break the pattern of the bad parenting they received! Jeff tells how his parents protected him from the pain of their past until it was appropriate to share their history and, more importantly, how his parents were able to give him so much of what they themselves hadn't received.

Jeff is currently vice president and commercial lending officer for Anderson Banking Company in Anderson, Indiana. A graduate of Anderson University, Jeff also holds a degree from the Graduate School of Banking at the University of Wisconsin, Madison.

At home in Anderson, Jeff also serves as vice-chairman of the Board of Pensions for the Church of God; as treasurer of the United Faith Housing Corporation; vice-chairman of the Anderson Symphony Orchestra; and chairman of the East Side Church of God's Coordinating Council.

Jeff and his wife, Debbie, have two children; Clarice, age five, and Austin, age two. Debbie has a degree in elementary education from Anderson University and a master's degree from Ball State. She currently teaches third grade at Forest Hills Elementary School in Noblesville, Indiana.

I'm not sure when I truly became aware of how difficult my mother's family background was, but it hasn't been all that many years. My mother grew up in a home where her parents and several siblings were alcoholics. As the only girl of six children, Mom was expected to carry heavy household responsibilities early in life. My father's growing-up years were somewhat difficult also, but in different ways. Dad grew up poor, and his opportunities were severely limited by the family's lack of financial resources. In spite of this, his family had a firm faith in God, and they openly expressed their love for one another, two important factors that shaped my dad's beliefs and ideals. I have greatly benefited from this heritage.

My respect and love for my parents grow as, more and more, I realize how amazing it is that my mother, having been so disadvantaged in her childhood, functioned at such an incredibly loving and insightful level. I see that my parents' commitment to their job of parenting shielded me from most of the pain and heartache that easily could have been passed right on to me. That is just one thing my parents did right, and there is no way to cover them all. Let me joyfully share a few things.

First of all, discipline was well defined in our house. (In fact, I wonder if Dr. James Dobson didn't receive inspiration for some of his best stuff from my parents!) The rules were black and white. We didn't have the kind of gray areas that seem to plague many families today. Our lives were not regimented, but we knew the ground rules and we enjoyed great freedom within those boundaries. Today I am attempting to apply the same consistent standards of discipline in my own family. Frequently I find myself wondering just how my folks would handle a given situation. That surely is a sign that they were doing something right!

Second, throughout my youth, faith in God and worshiping him were very important to our family. Since we were a gospel-singing family, we spent much of our time at church, and all of us were involved. At home, our conversation centered around other Christian people we admired, Scriptures and biblical concepts, and Christian music. Our family loved music—especially music that told the story of Christ's redeeming grace. Family worship took place in a variety of ways. We sang together, prayed together, and attended church together. Since family worship was such a priority in our home, faith became and continues to be a vital part of my life.

Third, my parents generously invested their time in my brother and me. But what a touch of grace! Our mother came from a dysfunctional home where love was rarely—if ever—expressed, and our father came from a financially struggling home. When they had kids of their own, though, they often passed up opportunities to do well financially so that they could totally invest themselves in our family. Much of our time together as a family was spent traveling many, many miles to sing at small churches and gatherings throughout the Midwest. Our family was influenced and enriched by the gospel music tradition that we shared and by the people we met along the way. It is a blessing of the Christian life to have contact with people who have consistently walked with the Lord through many years. Looking back, I can see the ripple effect of people committed to the Lord: They taught and encouraged my parents who, in turn, passed some treasured gifts my way. Time—quality time—was certainly a major gift they gave to me.

A fourth major aspect of the parenting I received—and no doubt the strongest thread of all—was genuine love. I am speaking of the deeply rooted love that parents have for their children that mirrors the love the heavenly Father has for his children. Some say that parental love is instinctive, but I don't believe this is true. (If parental love really is instinctive, the flow of that love can certainly be obstructed by selfishness or dysfunction as it was in my mother's home.) Being aware of my parents' backgrounds only intensifies my appreciation for the consistent love and care they gave us children. They were always there for me—all the time and in every situation—and always openly expressing love for me in so many ways.

My parents taught me. They taught my brother and me by their love for the Lord, and they demonstrated the importance of commitment. They taught me to love music and to give away my faith through singing, sharing, and having compassion for people.

My parents nurtured me. I have vivid memories of stern lectures, swift and firm correction when I was out of line, and expressions of genuine disappointment when I made poor choices. These moments were always followed quickly by hugs and reaffirming words of love, encouragement, and instruction.

My parents cheered for me. While I was growing up, I enjoyed athletics, primarily basketball—the "Hoosier Passion." Mom and Dad never missed games, and their pride in me was never dependent on my athletic performance. They truly were my greatest fans—and sometimes my only fans. It means a lot when your folks openly show approval and pleasure in what you are doing. When I was doing my best, they never said, "You should have . . ." or "Why didn't you . . . ?" This support, which has been offered for any endeavor I have undertaken, has meant more than I can express.

And my parents prayed for me. My parents offered many prayers on my behalf over the years, and I know that they pray for me and for my family today. Their earnest prayer has always been that their children would honor the Lord with their lives, and as their son, I have found great comfort in knowing they care that much. You know, come to think of it, there is a little healthy discomfort in knowing Mom and Dad communicate very well with each other and with the Lord. Heaven knows I wouldn't want to let any of them down!

I have often felt undeserving of the secure family life I enjoyed. The tremendous joy I have in sharing each day with my lovely Christian wife, Debbie, and our two beautiful children is, I think, a testimony to the things my parents did right. Although they are not perfect—and they would be the first to admit it—I am so thankful that they saw the importance of trying to manage a home the way Christ intended.

My description of my parents may not be all that unique, but I can say today without reservation that these two people and the little more than twenty years I spent with them are blessings from God that have given me a specific idea of what the Lord intended when he designed the family. The strong threads with which they wove the fabric of our home are now so evident to me: discipline, faith, time, and love . . . and the best of these has been their love. (Hey, that sounds like a paraphrase of something in Corinthians!) More than anything else, what my folks did right was to love and commit their lives to the Lord and to consistently share that love with my brother and me as we grew up. I feel that, through my parents' model and God's teaching, my assignment as husband and father has been clearly defined for me. With God's help, I will be able to do some of the same things my parents did right.

Moving to the Victory Side

$\bullet$ ———————————————————— $\bullet$

Press releases describe him as a "Christian businessman turned evangelist"; friends and coworkers say he is a teenager at heart, seemingly inexhaustible as he conducts youth rallies and maintains his radio and television outreach. I'm talking about Jack Wyrtzen, founder of Word of Life Fellowship, Inc.

When he was nineteen, Jack turned from what he calls "churchianity" to Christianity. Since then, he has been hard at work sharing the gospel of Christ with young people. Today, with Harry Bollback and George Theis, Jack directs the many Word of Life ministries, including one of the largest youth camping programs in the world. The Olympic Conference Center at Schroon Lake in New York's Adirondack Mountains attracts people from across the country and around the world. Last summer they came from thirty-nine states and thirty-one foreign countries. The latest conference center and youth camps are located in Hudson, Florida. Word of Life has camps, Bible institutes, and Bible clubs for teenagers on six continents, and the goal is to have one hundred camps throughout the world.

Jack speaks at Rotary and Kiwanis meetings as readily as he does in state and federal penitentiaries. When he appears on talk shows—Christian and secular alike—he discusses such topics as drug addiction, abortion, homosexuality, AIDS, incest, suicide, and rock music, issues very real to his target audience.

Writing here, Jack shares about his conversion from "churchianity" and the joy of sharing his faith with his parents.

I was not brought up in a Christian family. For nineteen years of my life, there was no Christianity in my family—but there was politics! In fact, I used to wonder why my parents didn't take over the White House! They would argue and fight over politics and how the country should be run. Also, although we were rather poor, my parents brought me up to be very bigoted. When I was converted, though, one of our first gospel teams was made up of a converted Jew, a converted Italian Catholic, a black fellow, and me. I guess it's the old-time religion that makes you love everybody!

My earliest remembrance of my mother is with a cigarette in one hand, a cocktail in the other, and a deck of cards in front of her. Her religion was mainly the Republican Club. Likewise, my father. They didn't go to church regularly, and if they did go on occasion, it was to very liberal churches.

I look back to when I was three or four years old in the Unitarian church where they had me stand up and sing, "Jesus loves me—this I know for the Bible tells me so." Then we moved to another town, and I went to the Methodist church and stayed around there until I got into a fist fight with one of the kids in my Sunday school class. Then I quit being a Methodist and joined the Presbyterian church because I thought they had a little more class. I stayed there until a Boy Scout troop was organized in the Baptist church, and for no other reason except to become a Boy Scout, I became a Baptist.

This Baptist church was a very liberal one. I can still remember the elderly preacher giving a half-hour discourse on why he didn't believe in hell. When the old preacher died, they brought in a young fellow just out of Bible school to serve as interim pastor, and he was on fire for God. He came to my house and preached the gospel to me as a young teenager, but I ordered him out of the house. (Nice kid, wasn't I?) I stayed around the Baptist church until I found they had better looking girls at the Reformed church, so I got myself reformed in a hurry! I stayed around there quite a while and married a girl from there. Her father, Dr. Sydney Smith, was rather well-to-do. I think he paid most of the church bills. He believed in evolution and didn't believe in the Bible, but I guess he thought going to the church and paying its bills was good business.

One day Dr. Smith's wife tuned in to Percy Crawford's "Young People's Church of the Air" broadcasts. This program revived feelings from her childhood when she had first heard the gospel. At the time, Percy Crawford was opening Pinebrook Bible Conference, and Mrs. Smith just about dragged her daughter to the conference. That's where Marge was converted. A few months before that, I had been converted through the influence of a fellow who was with me in the U.S. Army Band in the National Guard, but I had been afraid to tell Marge for fear that she would break our engagement. When she was converted, she wrote and told me all about it, and my heart leaped for joy. I said, "Well, now both of us can live for God."

The following October, we went to a reunion at Pinebrook, and we both dedicated our lives to the Lord. I guess that was the beginning of Word of Life. I continued to lead my dance band for a few months until the Lord made me so miserable that I had to give all of that up and go out and serve only Jesus Christ.

For nine years after I was saved, I worked in the insurance business. Some other fellows and I got a brass trio together and went to rescue missions and street meetings. I also remember feeling so inadequate as the Sunday school teacher of twelve black girls from inner-city Philadelphia who knew the Bible so much better than I. From there, we went to New York City where we led street meetings and ministered in jails and continued serving in rescue missions. We worked in the insurance business during the day and preached almost every noon hour, night, and weekend. We got a group of fellows and girls together and started studying the Bible every Monday night, sometimes for three or four hours. Now, fifty years later, here we are with fifteen Bible Institutes around the world and thirty-five camps spread over all six continents.

One day I had the privilege of leading my mother to the Lord, and I baptized her in Schroon Lake. My father later came to know the Lord as well. In fact, he died in a rocking chair while reading his New Testament, and Mother died in our living room while waiting for someone to take her to church. Both of them are buried in the little cemetery at Schroon Lake, New York, and when the Rapture takes place, they will both be caught up to meet the Lord in the clouds! What a great Wyrtzen family reunion we will have in heaven. Praise the Lord.

David B. Wyrtzen

Growing Up the Son of an Evangelist

D avid Wyrtzen defines his life purpose as "to be used by the Holy Spirit to generate Christlikeness in others through a balanced ministry, stressing both the proclamation of the gospel and a clear, powerful exposition of God's truth in the Scriptures"—and he seems to be doing just that!

A graduate of Dallas Theological Seminary with a master's degree and a doctorate in theology, David is currently pastor of Midlothian Bible Church in Midlothian, Texas. The church grew out of two Bible studies led by David and Ed Murray, now a member of Campus Crusade's European staff. When the Lord called Ed to Europe, he called David to assume the pastoral responsibilities in Midlothian. The church has grown from a Bible study of eight couples in 1973 to more than five hundred people and has sponsored two sister churches in neighboring Waxahachie and Mansfield.

David is also proclaiming God's truth through his writings, the recently published books Raising Worldly Wise but Innocent Kids *and* Love without Shame: Sexuality in Biblical Perspective. *His articles have appeared in* Moody, Kindred Spirit, *and* Bibliotheca Sacra.

David, the father of four children, writes here about what it was like to be one of evangelist Jack Wyrtzen's five children. He shares some of the right things his parents did to share their faith with him, his brothers, and his sisters.

Mass rallies in Madison Square Garden and Yankee Stadium, a weekly nationwide Saturday night broadcast called "The Word of Life Hour," and summers in the Adirondacks at Word of Life camps—two brothers, two sisters, and I grew up in this very public world of a well-known evangelist.

For me, as an evangelist's kid, Saturday morning meant peeking into Dad's study and hoping he would finish scribbling all over his broadcast script as he made corrections for his radio program that night. (Mutual Network required every line of the program to be written out.) I desperately wanted my dad to finish and be on the sidelines with the other parents when I quarterbacked our midget league football team at 10:00 A.M.

At 4:30 on Saturday afternoon, Dad and Mom loaded us into the car, drove underneath the Hudson River through the Lincoln Tunnel from New Jersey to Manhattan, and parked in front of the Gospel Tabernacle in the heart of Times Square. Weekly, hundreds of young people packed the old church for Dad's live broadcast and three hours of evangelistic revival. I can still feel the intense tingling in my legs, demanding my body to move, as Dad continued to preach for what I thought was an eternity.

Sunday often took us to churches in New England or Pennsylvania, and I remember sleeping cramped in the back window of our car as we rushed home to get back in time for school Monday morning. Dad's day off was Monday, but he hit the road again Tuesday through Friday. This schedule was tough on Mom as she took on both parenting roles during the week. The summers at camp gave us all a break from the pace and intensity of the evangelistic circuit. One August, however, it was my body that came close to breaking.

A summer cold turned into pneumonia, and my lungs struggled to gather enough air. I ended up in bed for the rest of the month. By September, the infection had cleared, and I breathed freely again. I entered fifth grade physically sound but emotionally frightened. When Dad and Mom left for the airport to tour the Soviet Union, my fears multiplied. I could picture them captured and imprisoned in a concentration camp because of the Bibles they were seeking to take in to believers. This was 1959, the cold war raged, and the air raid drills at school did little to quiet my dread.

These are a few scenes from my childhood. Dad was absorbed in his life's calling, and Mom struggled to raise five kids. Our home life was dysfunctional, and it misfired at times, but this is not another contemporary testimony of resentment and bitterness due to parental failure and neglect. Mom is now home with our Lord while my dad, close to eighty, continues to proclaim the gospel. Ron, my youngest brother, powerfully represents Christ in the business marketplace. My older sister, Betsy, skillfully trains children in the basics as a teacher in a Christian school. Don, my oldest brother, writes and arranges music that is sung by God's family throughout the world, and Mary Ann, the firstborn, serves as a missionary in the Word of Life Seminary in Brazil.

You have heard stories of preachers' kids who turned out bad and strayed from the faith of their fathers. This is a different story—a story of preserving grace, not of rebellion. In spite of the intense pressures and problems, Dad and Mom raised five kids who joined them in their love for Christ and their passion to bring Christ's love into the lives of others. Here are some things my parents did right—realities God used to give a spiritual dimension to life in our family.

Reality

To say that Jesus Christ must be "real" in your daily life is trite, but for the Wyrtzen household it was a given. My parents believed in Jesus' very real presence in our personal lives, a presence that would provide the confidence of eternal salvation and also the support and strength for the struggles of this life.

Both Dad and Mom received Jesus Christ late in their teens. Neither of them had been raised in an evangelical home, and the good news that Jesus died to forgive them and then rose from death to free them was the discovery of a priceless and transforming treasure.

Early in her teens, Mom missed an entire year of high school lying in bed with Saint Vitus's dance.

Terrified, she believed death would soon drag her away, so she called for her minister, confident he could give her answers. She poured out her secret fears and asked, "What are my hopes for heaven?" He responded, "Margaret, you're a good girl! There is no need to be afraid. God loves good girls like you. Your hopes for heaven are as good as mine."

Mom was young but not naive about her goodness. This soothing religious tranquilizer did nothing at all to dull her fears. She knew she was not prepared for eternity. There had to be some way to quiet a guilty conscience. Mom recovered and returned to high school a year behind her classmates. The forgiveness question, however, was not settled until after she graduated.

My grandmother tricked twenty-year-old Margaret into attending Pinebrook Bible Conference. When Mom discovered they were not going to spend the week at a swank hotel, she was furious. She resented the fact that her mother, the wife of a prominent physician, was remembering some of her early spiritual training and trying to push her headstrong little debutante of a daughter in the same direction. On the condition that they would leave first thing in the morning for a posh retreat, Mom agreed to stay for one night.

Percy Crawford's biblical message that night made clear the connection between sin and Christ's death. My mom knew that she had finally discovered the Man who could give her forgiveness and freedom from her guilt, and she thanked Jesus Christ for dying in her place. Scared to death that her salvation would mean the end of her engagement, she wrote a letter to her fiancé and explained her decision. She had no idea that he had made this same commitment almost a year before when one of his army reserve buddies had witnessed to him.

From the moment of this disclosure to one another, my mom and dad lived with the gospel at the center of their life together. They shared their discovery with friends, and a band of young people began to proclaim Christ on the streets of Long Island, in jails, and anywhere else they could get someone to listen. A young singer named George Beverly Shea joined their team; Mom played the piano, and Dad played the trombone. With their gang of new converts, they took turns giving their testimonies and preaching. By 1949 when I came on the scene, the commitment of this group to proclaiming the gospel had generated not only Word of Life, but also Youth for Christ. Because my parents completely gave themselves to the gospel, I can't remember a time when I did not know John 3:16.

When at five I made a decision to respond personally to the gospel, I joined my older brother and sisters who had already made this decision. My younger brother, Ron, joined us in the faith one night when he wanted to make sure that, if the Rapture occurred, he wouldn't be left alone in the house. Ron's decision answered my parents' nightly prayers that each of their children would be born into God's family.

Ron and I slept in a finished attic directly above Dad and Mom's room. Dad had no idea his little boys upstairs could hear his strong Wyrtzen voice. He prayed often for each of us kids, and I am thankful I got to overhear my parents praying rather than fighting. There was no pretense. Because they consistently prayed in the privacy of their bedroom, I never doubted the genuineness of the faith they openly proclaimed to a worldwide audience.

Jesus was far more than their ticket into heaven. They depended on him for everything from Mom's asthma attacks to Word of Life's need for thousands of dollars to keep the work going. We were taught to believe Jesus was present and that he would meet our daily needs.

I remember one Christmas when Word of Life was first beginning its snow-camp ministry. A heat wave had pushed the thermometer far above thirty-two degrees Fahrenheit and turned the Adirondacks into Mudville instead of a winter wonderland. A Japanese student who was celebrating the holiday with us was amazed when, at dinner, one of us kids prayed for Jesus to give us snow. I'll never forget the wonder in his eyes when Dad had to turn on the wipers to clear off his windshield as we drove up the thruway toward Albany. By the next morning, the mud was frozen and covered with white. The snow campers would have no problem skiing and tubing in the two feet of freshly fallen snow.

I also remember times when it appeared Jesus had failed us. One winter a snow and windstorm knocked a $150,000 auditorium to the ground at Word of Life Inn. Standing in the rubble, Dad bowed his head and prayed. He prayed when snow was a blessing and gave thanks, but he still prayed when the snow seemed to be a calamity.

As a child, whenever I walked into Dad and Mom's

room, my eyes faced a beautiful wall mounting framed above their bed that quoted Luke 24:15: "Jesus himself drew near and went with them" (RSV). Mom and Dad's conviction of the reality of the presence of Christ accompanying us in our daily lives was one of the right things they gave to us as kids.

Involvement

Evangelism was not Dad's job—it was his life. And he motivated us to join him in proclaiming the gospel from the time we were toddling. Mary Ann and Betsy sang, and Don played the piano. When I learned to play the trumpet, Dad made audiences suffer through my early rendition of "Shall We Gather at the River." We kids could be called on to give a word of testimony at any time in his meetings, so even the youngest stayed ready to give an answer for the hope that was in him.

At thirteen, I found it difficult to enter into adolescent rebellion. I already had the responsibility of counseling children at Word of Life Ranch. When I was sixteen, Dad gave me the opportunity to become one of the program directors, and when I was nineteen and a crisis happened in the life of one of the camp directors, he had enough confidence in me to let me, under the eye of a mature friend, oversee the ministry side of the Ranch. This encouragement to assume responsibility in the Lord's work and Dad's confidence that we could do the job were important factors in keeping us from turning away from the faith. We had firsthand exposure to the power of God to change lives, not only through our parents' ministry but also through our own. My parents involved us in the ministry, but they also tenderly gave themselves to each of us children.

When the doctor gave Dad and Mom the diagnosis that their little boy had pneumonia, Mom packed her things and moved into the hospital by my bed until I recovered. She was there in the night when I fought to breathe. In my sophomore year of college when I needed to talk to her about a dating relationship that was maturing toward marriage, she was still there for me. Although she had barely recovered from a nervous breakdown, she drove nine hours alone to spend a fall weekend with me.

On most Saturday mornings, Dad did finish correcting his radio scripts in time, and he missed very few of my midget league football games. In the spring of my eighth-grade year, he was there when I captained our junior high baseball team to the city championship game. He remained proud of me when we lost.

When my best friend on the team needed a place to live because of serious problems in his family, Dad and Mom opened their home and made another bed. The gruesome story of how my friend's father had killed his real mother did not deter them from inviting him in. The epistle of James says believers are to look after orphans in trouble (1:27), and my parents simply obeyed.

Normalcy

The life of a media evangelist is not normal, but my parents made sure there were moments of normalcy for our family. Monday after school was fun time with

Dad. We enjoyed eating out as a family and going swimming in the indoor pool at the St. George Hotel in New York City with its waterfall and high dives.

Not all Sunday afternoons were spent traveling to meetings with Dad. I also remember kids around the dining-room table playing games with Mom. She played Old Maid when we were little and Sorry!, Clue, and Monopoly as we grew older. She read Agatha Christie mysteries and puzzled with us over the plot of a good television mystery. She bought me coonskin hats when Davy Crockett was the craze and took me for chocolate cokes after school in the afternoon.

Mom's love of mysteries, chocolate cokes, and table games helped balance my dad's fervent focus on his work. She helped all of us know that Jesus could be part of hilarious laughter around the table at Thanksgiving; part of the embarrassment when Snorky, our Irish setter, used a wealthy lady's leg as a tree during a formal reception in our living room; and part of the teasing when Dad had to confess in the midst of his laughter that he actually did not get the joke we had told.

The reality of Jesus Christ, the opportunity to get involved in serving him together as a family, and the enjoyment of his presence in the normal times of life—these were the right things God graciously used to help my parents pass their faith on to the next generation.

Caught Rather Than Taught

Thanks to the ministry of his well-known father, Jack, Don Wyrtzen got an early start in music, radio, and television. Since then, Don has become recognized as one of the leading musicians in Christian music, and he has lectured on church music in many Christian universities and seminaries in America.

Don has arranged and composed more than two hundred anthems and sacred songs, including such favorites as "Yesterday, Today, and Tomorrow," "Love Was When," "Worthy Is the Lamb," and "Finally Home." In 1981, he received a Dove Award for "The Love Story," and to date more than 2 million of his musicals and cantatas (including "An Old-Fashioned Christmas," "I Love America," and "Liberty") have been sold.

Don has also arranged and orchestrated for such major artists as Sandi Patti, Larnelle Harris, Steve Green, Carman, Glad, Michael Card, Steven Curtis Chapman, and Christine Wyrtzen.

A graduate of Moody Bible Institute, The King's College, and Dallas Theological Seminary, Don is also the author of *the devotional* A Musician Looks at the Psalms, *which received the Gold Medallion Award from the Evangelical Christian Publishers Association in 1989.*

Here, Don writes about how God's grace can and does generously overcome the human limitations of parents, a fact that can encourage all of us.

◆━━━━━━━━━━━━━━━━━━━━━━━━━━━━━━◆

The Wyrtzen family is an intriguing family, as I'm sure all families are. I am the oldest son, born in the summer of '42. I have two brothers and two sisters. My dad, Jack Wyrtzen, will be seventy-eight years old this year; my mother, Marge Wyrtzen, died on the first day of 1984 (she would have been seventy-nine this year). Mary Ann is five years older than I, and I have a younger sister, Betsy, and two younger brothers, David and Ron.

My dad married a woman named Joan in the spring of 1986, and Dad and Joan are now serving as founder-directors of Word of Life International in Schroon Lake, New York. Mary Ann and her husband are in Brazil, where she and her family train Brazilians in the Word of God and biblical studies. My sister Betsy lives in Schroon Lake and teaches at Mountainside Bible Academy. David, a pastor in Midlothian, Texas, has his doctorate in theology and this year published his first two books, one on Proverbs and one on Christian sexuality. My other brother, Ron, is assistant pastor of a church in Cincinnati, Ohio; his wife, Christine, is a well-known Christian recording artist and songwriter.

Our family is very energetic, and each person is uniquely gifted. Mary Ann is a lot like my dad, with a lot of drive and enthusiasm. She and her family have been excellent missionaries.

My younger sister, Betsy, has not had an easy life. As a single parent, she has raised two children, managed to finish college, and even earned a master's degree in education. She is especially insightful and compassionate. In fact, she has been greatly used by the Lord as a "wounded healer," channeling the pain of her own life into a ministry of helping other hurting people.

David, the scholar in the family, is highly esteemed as the gifted pastor, not only to the Midlothian Bible Church in Texas, but also to our family. He has come to be a "pastor" for us all, even my dad, the patriarch.

Ron is much like Dad with his sales ability and a positive outlook on life. Ron understands how things work, so over the years he has been involved in various kinds of maintenance work and sales.

As brothers and sisters, each with our own families, we try to stay in contact through the mail and by visiting each other's homes. This is not easy since Mary Ann lives in Brazil, Betsy in Schroon Lake, Ron in Cincinnati, David in Midlothian (not far from Dallas), and I in Nashville, Tennessee. But we often see each other at Word of Life conferences when we visit the folks in Schroon Lake or when we happen to be together at one of the Word of Life conference centers around the world.

Without a doubt, the key figures in our family have

been Mom and Dad, so let me focus on them in particular.

What was Mom like? My mom was a character, almost like a character in a novel—unbelievable. She grew up in Long Island, New York. Her mother burned to death when she was an infant and soon afterward her father died of tuberculosis. She was passed around from relative to relative until she was about six years old, when she was adopted by a wealthy older physician and his wife. With this shaky start, Mom struggled all her life with physical and emotional problems. I recall that she was hospitalized twenty times for various serious physical problems, but she also suffered from emotional problems. In a lot of ways, she was a weak, fragile person, yet I firmly believe that God uses people who are weak, people who are wounded, people who are hurt. Finally, Mom was a woman of spiritual integrity.

I have a kaleidoscope of memories of Mom. My dad's headquarters for Word of Life International was on Nassau Street in downtown New York. Once, when I was three or four years old, we were all leaving his fifth-floor office. The elevator was very crowded, but we all got on except Mom. The doors shut, leaving her behind. I felt terrified and abandoned. When Mom died almost forty years later, that incident and the same feelings came back to me.

Although there were times when she resented Dad's work because of the demands made on him, she worked very hard to be supportive of him, going along to Word of Life rallies, helping in his radio and television ministries, hosting with him evangelistic boat rides up the Hudson River in New York, and helping at the various camps in the Adirondack Mountains of New York State.

Often Dad was gone during the week, traveling as an evangelist. So it was Mom who conducted family devotions at the dinner table. In fact, we learned everything from eschatology to the facts of life at the dinner table. But this wasn't the only place I learned about the facts of life. I vividly remember the day in second grade when my friend Johnny and I climbed a tall tree near our school yard. There Johnny related to me in graphic detail everything his very progressive parents had told him about sex, which was much more than I had ever been curious enough to ask. "You don't know my parents," I remember blurting out in embarrassment. "They're Christians! They would never do anything like that!"

Ironically, that afternoon in school, I misbehaved and was sent to sit in the hall outside the classroom. What timing! That was the very day Mother came to school for something and saw me being punished. That night when I got home, Mother said, "And what were you doing today?" Of course, she was talking about my sitting in the hall, but I immediately thought about the talk I'd had in the pine tree. My stomach turned over in awe and fear—I was sure Mother must be able to read my mind! She must know everything!

Fortunately, my parents tried to teach us a Christian view of sex. Mother was big on telling the truth, too, and I remember her making a real federal case out of a situation if she thought someone was lying.

But throughout my childhood and youth, Mother

was emotionally fragile. She struggled with her sense of self-worth and personhood. Even though she battled psychological problems, she still encouraged me as a musician, taught us right from wrong, and instilled in us respect for the Scriptures.

For me, the last weekend we had with her symbolized her life. She and Dad had come to our home in Grand Rapids to celebrate Christmas, and somehow she seemed warmer, freer, and more serene than I ever remembered. We went out to eat together at Charlie's Crab, a lovely seafood restaurant, and she insisted Dad pay the bill for us all. What a delightful time we had!

Mother had brought with her a lovely but fragile glass angel for the top of our tree, hand-carrying it on the plane all the way from New York. After she carefully handed it to me in the airport, I placed the delicate angel in the trunk and then went back for the rest of the luggage. Somehow, in the hurry and pressure of the holiday airport rush, I forgot all about the precious angel when I returned with the rest of the bags. As I put them in the trunk, I crushed it into a million pieces. I was sick about it. Little did I know that, only four days later, Mother would be with real angels. And at this celebration, by God's wondrous grace, she would be whole, complete, and confident, standing at last in the presence of the King of kings and Lord of lords.

Dad, in sharp contrast to my fragile mother, was and is a source of great strength, conviction, enthusiasm, and integrity. He has a positive outlook and a real type-A, entrepreneurial, executive-type personality.

But while I was growing up, this wasn't always a positive for me. One time when I was quite small, we were on a speedboat ride to Word of Life Island. I kept sticking my big toe in the gear that controlled forward and reverse. When we came into the dock, my toe was caught in the gear box. Dad was so absorbed in his thoughts that he didn't notice, and when he thrust the boat in reverse to keep us from hitting the pier, my toe was smashed. I remember screaming and yelling in a panic.

I also remember attending my Dad's Saturday night rally in New York City when I was somewhat older. In those days, in the late forties and early fifties, Times Square was much safer than it is now, and I can remember roaming the streets as a junior-high kid. In fact, one time a Jewish friend named Jimmy and I decided that we would ride the subways. Instead of buying a fifteen-cent token to get on the subway, we went underneath the turnstiles. Later that night in the car, Jimmy and I were bragging to my dad how we had ridden all over New York City without paying for our subway tokens. Becoming very serious, Dad explained to us that that was cheating. He had me write a letter to the New York City Port of Authority, apologize to them, and tape some change to a card to pay what I owed. That memory sticks out in my mind. Dad felt that being honest in little things was exceedingly important, and he wasn't going to let an opportunity to teach me this slip by. I have been grateful for his tough lesson since.

I also remember an unpleasant incident from my junior-high-school days. I took a rowboat out on

Schroon Lake. When I saw some friends of mine in another boat, I yelled to them, "Wait up!" but some people on the island thought I was yelling for help. So, in short order, there were speedboats and jeeps from the island, and all the emergency equipment they had at their disposal coming to rescue me. Dad was quite indignant; he thought I was just trying to get attention for myself.

Much later, when I was a student in college before going to Dallas Theological Seminary, I put my dad in a tough position by questioning the standards of conduct at Word of Life. I felt that many rules didn't really have biblical support. Dad was director of Word of Life, but he was also my father, and it must have been tough trying to fill both roles. He sat in on the meetings between some of us students and the leaders of Word of Life, during which we discussed theological and ethical issues and how they related to the ministry. I believe that my becoming an articulator of the faith began in some of those skirmishes as I cast my lot with true theologians who were trained in the original languages of the Scriptures and who ardently pursued the original intent of the Lord's Word.

In contrast to my mother's highly emotional temperament, my dad was very even tempered. The closest I ever remember seeing my dad come to losing his temper was once when, as a joke, some kitchen help at Word of Life filled some galvanized metal trays with broken crockery. They staged a chase scene through the dining room and dropped the tray in front of Dad's table. The pieces of dinnerware went spinning in a million directions, and Dad nearly lost it because he thought they had wasted God's money!

Even though Dad was incredibly busy with Word of Life (doing a radio program on Saturday, traveling Tuesday through Friday, and ministering on Sunday), he did his best to take Mondays off and save them for us. Sometimes he would take Mom to dinner—just the two of them—but most often he would ask us, "What would you kids like to do?" We would choose things like going swimming at the pool at the St. George Hotel in Brooklyn in the middle of the winter, having a spaghetti dinner in New York, attending Firestone concerts of light opera and Broadway musicals at the large old Center Theater in New York, walking the boardwalk at the Seaside Hotel, or going to Asbury Park. Dad also took each of us canoeing on Schroon Lake where we did a lot of talking, and he often took one of us on a trip with him alone. I remember flying from New Jersey to Chicago with him for some meetings and, in the dead of winter, flying to balmy Florida away from the snow and sleet of New York City.

Dad also took a chance on me by using my musical abilities in his early meetings. In fact, I remember when I was still playing the accordion as a little kid and was trying to play at the Little White Church on the Wildwood on Long Island. After I finished my solo, the weight of the accordion caused me to sit down with quite a thud. In later years, I graduated to playing piano and organ on his radio program. I can remember occasionally making mistakes on national radio. But what a great experience it was. Then I went to

Moody Bible Institute where we did live radio. What a marvelous experience that was for my work in the music industry today.

In some ways one could consider ours a dysfunctional family, but instead I prefer to see God's grace working in our midst. I believe that one of the ways to look at life is to look at it as a story. The Lord is not only writing his story of redemption in history, but in the lives of thousands of individuals as well, and all good stories have tension. Just as it takes dissonance to create harmony, so also in life it takes tension to create drama. But in all of life, I have seen God's grace working. I really believe that despite the fact that my parents were very human and had a lot of frailties and flaws, they did many things right.

First, they lived what they believed. They were consistent. Sometimes I didn't agree with them and sometimes I thought they were narrow and legalistic, but they consistently lived what they believed. Second, my parents were serious about evangelism. I believe that we are all called to win souls to Christ, but Dad seems to have a spiritual gift of evangelism. Third, they maintained very strong theological values. They were committed to the Bible and to a daily quiet time, which they observed come hell or high water. And whether I was observing Dad in the pulpit or Mom teaching us at family devotions, they were very committed to strong theological concepts and values. Fourth, they were involved with life. My parents held rallies, started camps, and led conferences; they were always involved with people, and there was a lot of excitement in our lives. Fifth, they stayed in close personal touch with us all. Dad still regularly calls my kids, who are college students at Wheaton, and writes them notes. He calls me once a week so we can both share what we've been up to in our lives. When Dad is gone, I am going to really miss those calls. In fact, that's one of the things that I really miss about Mom. Since she is with the Lord, I don't have the benefit of her phone calls to straighten me out and talk to me about life. Sixth, heaven is very real to Dad. Bible knowledge and theology are not abstractions but very concrete and very real in his life.

Through the years, I have been greatly influenced by the writings of Francis Schaeffer. I love the grace, excellence, and wit of Malcolm Muggeridge. I also like the brilliance and sensitivity of the writings of Frederick Buechner. But the man who has impacted me more than any of these men—more than anyone else on earth—is my own dad. I think it is because despite the imperfections and pressures of his life, he lived out biblical values over the long haul. I am convinced that values are caught rather than taught, and they are caught through observing a consistent example over a long period of time. Dad has been my mentor and model for more than fifty years now, and I will be forever grateful to him.

Epilogue

◆━━━━━━━━━━━━━━━━━━━━━━━━━━━━━◆

When I was young, I thought of parenting as a segment of life that lasts eighteen to twenty years. It was a span with dimensions. It began when a baby was born, expanded into preschool care, evolved into the growing years that swelled into adolescence, and finally tapered off when the child left for college or got married. But even while I was thinking that way, we were still needing my parents and Bill's parents to help us learn how to parent our baby. And we needed them for emotional support, encouragement, and advice as we made choices about our work and our lives together.

Now that we have been parents for twenty-seven years, we know that parenting never stops. Even when children are responsible and self-supporting, parents keep on caring and children keep on needing to be cared about.

Parenting has been and still is the most glorious and most painful, most joyful and most troubling, most demanding and most rewarding of all life's commitments.

There were days when I was sure there had never been a home as wonderful as ours. And there were days when I nearly collapsed with exhaustion and wanted to quit because I felt like such a failure. There were days I wanted to run *away—off somewhere—and resign parenting. There were other times when I was overwhelmed with the ecstasy of watching our children become.*

There were nights I had to kneel beside my children's beds to ask them to forgive me for being unfair or overly harsh and to pray for me to be a better parent. There were other nights when Bill and I would wake the children to carry them, wrapped in blankets, outside to see the shooting stars or the Milky Way or to hear the summer symphony of crickets and cicadas.

The stories about home life in this book vary widely. Privileged—poor, educated—simple, rural—urban, stable—mobile: these pieces reflect them all. Some families were affectionate and articulate; some were quiet and reserved. Some parents were professionals; others were common laborers. Some lived in lovely big houses; others spent their days in simple dwellings.

Yet, out of this diversity, these families, for the most part, shared a few things in common. Over and over these people said, "My parents loved each other and stuck it out through hard times." Most of these children somehow grew up feeling that their parents thought they were special and felt encouraged to pursue their dreams.

Many of these writers mentioned that as children they never felt as if they were a burden to their parents, but that—even when things were difficult—the family was "all in this together." Encouragement, discipline, and a sense of belonging seem to be important ingredients in the building of human beings. Oh yes! And a sense of humor!

Over and over these pieces make it clear that home is a place for instilling values: honesty, dependability, forgiveness, truthfulness, faithfulness, integrity, and creativity. Parental consistency in modeling seems to be important in making these qualities a part of a child's life.

Whether mentioned, implied, or longed for, a shared faith in God and a belief in the power of prayer surfaced time and time again as the glue that holds families together and brings children through the years of question, rebellion, and doubt.

How often in my own life did my parents pray me through the obstacles that could have stymied my development! And it has been prayer that gave Bill and me the hope and confidence that God would see our children through.

In my experience it has often been the kids themselves who lifted and encouraged me as a parent. A letter Benjy gave me for my birthday when he was sixteen kept me from "throwing in the towel" on some of my dreams. Suzanne insisting, when she was fourteen, that Bill and I continue singing even though it was hard for them to have us gone a lot, kept me from quitting a ministry God has been able to use. And this poem from Amy when she was away at college, let me know that maybe, just maybe, we had done something right.

Minus One

I think of you, sitting by the fire,
Coffee mug beside you,
Letter spread out on your lap.
The dogs lie quietly at your feet,
Stretched out in private dreams.
I smell hot apple cider,
And vegetable soup simmering on the stove.
The clock is ticking on the mantle,
And the world is silent on the November
*   afternoon;*
The gray mist outside is held at bay
By our warm walls—
And I am not there to see you.
But I know—
And when I close my eyes,
And feel you missing me, as I miss you,
Home is not so very far away.
—Amy Gaither, age 18

Other Living Books Best-sellers

400 CREATIVE WAYS TO SAY I LOVE YOU by Alice Chapin. Perhaps the flame of love has almost died in your marriage, or you have a good marriage that just needs a little spark. Here is a book of creative, practical ideas for the woman who wants to show the man in her life that she cares. 07-0919-5

COME BEFORE WINTER AND SHARE MY HOPE by Chuck Swindoll. A collection of brief vignettes offering hope and the assurance that adversity and despair are temporary setbacks we can overcome! 07-0477-0

FOR WOMEN ONLY by Evelyn R. and J. Allan Petersen. This balanced, entertaining, and diversified treatment covers all the aspects of womanhood. 07-0897-0

HINDS' FEET ON HIGH PLACES by Hannah Hurnard. A classic allegory of a journey toward faith that has sold more than a million copies! 07-1429-6 *Also on Tyndale Living Audio 15-7426-4*

JOHN, SON OF THUNDER by Ellen Gunderson Traylor. In this saga of adventure, romance, and discovery, travel with John—the disciple whom Jesus loved—down desert paths, through the courts of the Holy City, and to the foot of the cross as he leaves his luxury as a privileged son of Israel for the bitter hardship of his exile on Patmos. 07-1903-4

THE SECRET OF LOVING by Josh McDowell. McDowell explores the values and qualities that will help both the single and married reader to be the right person for someone else. He offers a fresh perspective for evaluating and improving the reader's love life. 07-5845-5

THE STRONG-WILLED CHILD by Dr. James Dobson. With practical solutions and humorous anecdotes, Dobson shows how to discipline an assertive child without breaking his spirit. Parents will learn to overcome feelings of defeat or frustration by setting boundaries and taking action. 07-5924-9 *Also on Tyndale Living Audio 15-7431-0*

WHY YOU ACT THE WAY YOU DO by Tim LaHaye. Discover how your temperament affects your work, emotions, spiritual life, and relationships, and learn how to make improvements. 07-8212-7